The Clerk of Works in the Construction Industry

The Clerk of Works
in the Construction Industry

JOHN E. JOHNSTON

Crosby Lockwood Staples   London

Granada Publishing Limited
First published in Great Britain 1975 by Crosby Lockwood Staples
Frogmore St Albans Herts and 3 Upper James Street London W1R 4BP

ISBN 0 258 96954 7

Printed in Great Britain by
Northumberland Press Limited
Gateshead

Foreword

by **Sir Frederick Snow**, CBE, CEng, FICE, FIMechE, FIStructE, MSocCE (France), FASCE, MConsE, Hon.M. Concrete Society, Hon.FICW, Hon. FIAAS, Hon.FGS, Hon. FFB, Hon.FSE

In the past I have frequently stated that workers in the building and civil engineering industry are 'the salt of the earth', provided they are properly led by people who know their job.

It follows, therefore, that the Clerk of Works, as senior practical partner co-ordinating all the disciplines, must be proficient in his own particular craft and must have a wide and varied experience in order to assess the practicability and economics of the planning of a project and to ensure a high standard of workmanship. He must also have a wide and varied experience of the quality of materials and a vast insight of human nature. Such knowledge and wisdom can only be acquired over many years.

The Clerk of Works in the Construction Industry is written by my good friend and colleague over very many years, Mr J. E. Johnston, who is a past President of the Institute of Clerks of Works (1971/72), and who was trained as a craftsman; in it will be found much relevant and helpful advice, together with descriptions and specifications, which is of real value to the practising Clerk of Works who is already a member of the Institute. The book will also be of inestimable value to the young man studying for entry into the profession, who proposes to take the Institute's examinations.

Undoubtedly, if a client wishes to ensure value for money on any project, a certified Clerk of Works is the finest insurance; in addition to his technical training and qualities of character, before he can use the letters MICW he has had to satisfy the examiners on the adequacy of his training, technical ability and experience. The Institute, in addition to seeking mature members to qualify through examination, also encourages young men to study to become full members while in the course of their training, and to this end examinations are open to them.

Many of our large organisations employ trainee students who are potential Clerks of Works and this book should certainly have a place in their libraries. In addition, in view of the widespread lack of knowledge of the role of a Clerk of Works, this volume should be especially welcome to our friends and colleagues overseas.

Frederick S. Snow

Contents

Preface

It has been apparent to me for many years that the guidelines for those who might aspire to a career as a Clerk of Works should be much more clearly defined, and the uncertainties of the first appointment reduced to a minimum through access to a recognised source of information. I remember my own difficulties in obtaining suitable information on the subject. Since there was no definitive work to which I could refer, I had to make use of the relevant parts of a variety of technical books. The person who works strictly 'by the book' is often a hindrance rather than an asset, and I found I had to adapt the information I acquired so that it was of practical use on the site. Such experience prompted me to write this book, with the intention of bringing useful information within easy grasp of the young Clerk of Works. At the same time, I hope that both the mature Clerk of Works and those responsible for other aspects of supervision on the site will find much to assist them in their day-to-day duties.

The historical facts given in the first part of the book may give encouragement to those wishing to retain the title of 'Clerk of Works', in spite of the frequent suggestions that a more 'modern' title be adopted. In Part Two I have endeavoured to embrace all those duties and responsibilities considered to belong to the Clerk of Works, together with information on regulations and documents with which he should be familiar. Constructional operations are covered in Part Three, together with materials and their use in construction, while Part Four relates to building services. The Clerk of Works is expected to have an extensive knowledge of materials and methods of construction. There is, however, a limit to the contents of a single volume, and I have attempted to cover only those subjects which appear to be generally necessary.

I am grateful to the following for permission to reproduce specific items in this book: Runcorn Development Corporation for all the contract forms and several photographs; Sir Alfred McAlpine & Son Ltd for the bar chart on page 142; Crudens Ltd for the line of balance programme on page 146; and the Unit Construction Company Ltd for the contractor's daywork sheet in the Appendix. My thanks are also due to the British Standards Institution, 2 Park Street, London W1A 2BS, for permission to use extracts from CP 301: 1971 *Building drainage*.

Compiling a book of this nature cannot be undertaken without creating some disturbance to those around us. Here I must acknowledge the patience and encouragement of my wife and family, particularly when notes and papers tended to accumulate in almost every room, and the disconcerting and erratic note of the typewriter could be heard at very odd hours of day and night.

My thanks are also due to Mr A. P. Macnamara for advice during the very early stages of the book, and to Mr Peter Riley, Architect, Mr Alan Bell, Structural Engineer, and Mr George Bird, Services Engineer, for reading sections of the draft and offering advice. I would also like to thank Mrs Jean Williams for her help in typing the final draft, and Mr Brian Williams for his assistance with the photographs.

To those others, too numerous to mention, who have assisted in an indirect way through their influence and advice at various stages of my own career, I take this opportunity to record my appreciation. Finally, let me express my thanks to Mr Douglas Fox and Miss Bridget Buckley of Crosby Lockwood Staples for their co-operation and assistance in preparing this book for publication.

J.E.J.
Helsby, Cheshire
September 1974

Part One

CHAPTER ONE

Origin of the Title

The Title

The title Clerk of Works has been in existence since the medieval period, when a clerk was recognised as a man of learning associated with Holy Orders. The use of the title 'Clerk' still retains significance in the legal profession to indicate various important offices such as Clerk of the Court, Clerk of the Council, Town Clerk, etc.

Medieval clerks were not always ordained priests, but acted in a lay capacity on behalf of the Church, those nominated as Clerk of Works being responsible for the construction and upkeep of buildings. Because of the similarity of their duties, the title was later conferred upon those who did not hold Holy Orders but who were commissioned to supervise the erection and repairs to the Royal buildings.

Early Records

Documents from the time of Edward IV (1461-83) concerning the King's Household speak of ... 'Clerke of Workes, called by the noble Edward Clerke dez oeuvres du Roy' ... who would be ... 'appoynted by the soveraynes of housholde to take wages and cloathinge with the housholde, it mought cause hym to be more attendaunt for necessary byldynges in offices in this house; and so he may take lyvery as a Squier of housholde ...'

There is an earlier reference dating from 1222 when the wardrobe in the Royal Chamber in the Tower of London was being repaired and ten shillings was paid for the robe or livery of the Clerk of Works. The first Clerk of Works named in the lists of payments from old documents is Nicholas de Tykhull (1316), who is described as 'the late Clerke of the Workes to the Palace at Westminster' and awarded £14 for timber used in connection with the coronation of Edward II. During the next fifty years no less than ten names are listed as Clerks of Works to the Tower of London and the Palace of Westminster, and in many instances they are promoted to this office from a position described as 'Supervisor'.

Ralph de la More was Clerk of Works at Windsor Castle in 1327 and William de Wykeham was later granted this office, in the first instance to assist Sir John Brocas in the construction of the Round Tower in 1351. Wykeham's successors at Windsor Castle were William de Mulso in 1361 and Adam de Hertyndon in 1366.

Further records for 1370 include Robert de Sybthorp, Clerk of Works at Shene, Eltham, and Rutherhithe, Henry de Mansfield at Childerlangley, John Edward at the Castle at Ledes, Richard Berard at Olyham, and Richard de Blore at Quenesborough Castle.

Two Clerks of Works at the Tower of London who held Holy Orders were William de Weston (1347) and William de Sleford (1361). Eustace Marshall, who also held Holy Orders, was appointed Clerk of Works in 1550 for St Fridiswide, Oxford, by Cardinal Wolsey. A name more familiar to most people will be that of Geoffrey Chaucer, poet, soldier, diplomat, and author of *The Canterbury Tales*, who was Clerk of the King's Works in 1389 '... for the Palace of Westminster, the Tower of London, the Castle of Berkhamstead, together with the King's Manors at Eltham, Kenington, Clarendon, Shene, Byfleet, Langley, and Feckenham'. With such responsibility it was not surprising that Chaucer was given authority to appoint a Deputy Clerk of Works, but in any case he did not retain the appointment long, for in June 1391 he was replaced at Windsor by John Gedney.

Two other recorded appointments of interest are William Lynde, Clerk of Works at Eton College in 1440, and his successor John Canterbury, who later in 1451 began work on King's College Chapel, Cambridge.

Powers of the Clerk of Works

Many of those appointed to the office of Clerk of Works at this time were associated with someone enjoying the royal favour, and it seems more than likely this accounted for Chaucer's obtaining the appointment.

However, Chaucer had some qualifications, since he was a widely travelled man, and indeed many of those who held the office of Clerk of Works were men who had travelled on the Continent and in the East, gaining experience in many matters, including building techniques. Combined with the skills of the master craftsmen of the period this experience contributed to the erection of many of the structures we admire so much today.

The powers of the Clerk of Works at this time were practically unlimited in respect of acquiring men and materials. His commission empowered him to seek out carpenters, masons, and other workmen in any part of town or country, and compel them to work in the service of the king. No man could claim exemption from such service unless he was able to prove that he was already employed on some church or priory.

The men were obliged to move about the country on foot, carrying the tools of their trade with them, and gathering their resources as best they could on the way. Materials for building had to be obtained locally, and woe betide any man objecting to the Clerk of Works removing timber or stone from his estates, at a price set by the Clerk of Works. Indeed, many objectors found themselves cast into the common prison, there to languish and reflect upon their folly.

Until late in the fifteenth century there is no evidence to indicate that the Clerk of Works had much experience of building procedure, and it seems safe to assume that he placed a great deal of reliance upon the master mason and the master carpenter. William de Wykeham made great efforts to secure the services of William de Wynford as his master mason at Windsor and later at Winchester, Wynford being an experienced man who had previously worked on Wells Cathedral. Wykeham's choice for master carpenter was Hugh Herland, later responsible for the hammerbeam roof of Westminster Hall in the 1390s.

Duties and Fees Paid to the Clerk of Works

In the early sixteenth century changes were occurring in the duties of those who were responsible for buildings, and in 1555 Richard Woodward is named as 'Clearke of the Honor and Castle of Windsor'; in 1575, however, Humphry Michell is again named as 'Clerk of the Works at Windsor', though he resigned his office because of opposition in carrying out his duties, and delays in receiving money to meet the accounts. Because of this disagreement he was made 'Superintendent of Works' and Henry Hawthorne was appointed 'Surveyor of Works', both men receiving a fee of two shillings each day.

By the beginning of the seventeenth century the roles were changing further and approaching the pattern we are familiar with today. A household list for Prince Henry in 1610 lists the Clerk of Works as Edward Carter, the Paymaster and Overseer as a Mr Smith, and the Surveyor of Works as Inigo Jones.

The pattern is further confirmed with the appointment of Lawrence Spencer as Clerk of Works under Sir Christopher Wren for the restoration of St Paul's Cathedral. John Tillotson succeeded Spencer in 1685 and in 1710 Henry Wood became Clerk of Works. Other offices were held by Edward Woodruff, who was surveyor and also assistant to Wren, and John Oliver as assistant surveyor.

The master mason and contractor was Thomas Strong, and the chief carpenter, who had the honour of laying the second stone of St Paul's after Wren himself had laid the first, was named Longland.

While it is not possible to obtain details of the precise duties of the medieval Clerk of Works, records do exist from the time of the restoration of St Paul's Cathedral which enable us to compare the Clerk of Works' duties at that period with those of today. 'He constantly attends the service of the work to take care that carpenters, labourers, etc, who work by the day, be employed in such business as the Surveyor has directed to be done; takes an account together with the assistant Surveyor what stores are brought into the work, receives and pays all money for the workmanship and materials according to a list of debts directed by Mr Surveyor; keeps and makes up all accounts, is chargeable with all the stores, and inspects the delivery thereof to the workmen; and is also Clerk to the Commissioners and enters all orders and contracts, etc.'

In addition to his salary the medieval Clerk of Works was receiving free board and lodgings while he was resident in the household.

A list of payments drawn up during the reign of Edward IV places the Clerk of Works at the head of the list with a fee of two shillings each day, and since he was also paid for Sundays, this amounted to £36.10.0d. per annum. He received travelling expenses of four shillings per day plus twenty pence for the hire of boats, and staff consisting of one clerk at sixpence per day.

Although the Clerk of Works' fees for this period seem commensurate with his duties, the amount did not alter much over the years, until the appointment of Lawrence Spencer to St Paul's Cathedral, where his salary as Clerk of Works was listed at £100 per annum.

It is interesting to compare this with the salaries paid at Greenwich Hospital, which was begun in 1661 and took one hundred years to complete. The office surveyor, a post once held by Sir Christopher Wren, was listed as receiving £200 per annum, and the Clerk of Works just over £90 per annum, paid at a daily rate of five shillings.

Changes of Title

In considering the recorded history of the Clerk of Works it is apparent, with one or two notable exceptions, that the title was restricted to those in the king's service, apart from its use within the Church. Although the duties shown for Lawrence Spencer and his successors have some similarities with the duties of today's Clerks of Works, the differences are much greater, and it is evident that the titles of surveyor and even architect became more commonly used for this post.

The officer attached to the Corporation of the City of London was still known as the Clerk of Works up to 1843, when J. B. Bunning was appointed 'Architect'. It is also worthy of note that there were still strong differences of opinion in correspondence to building journals in 1860 as to whether the Clerk of Works should be a technically trained person or recruited from the building crafts.

It is reasonable to assume that many of the men carrying out the duties of Clerk of Works in those days went on to become architects, some of them like Nicholas Hawksmore making a name for themselves in this profession. Of course there were others, such as George Gordon Hoskins, Fellow of the Royal Institute of British Architects, who compiled a handbook for Clerks of Works in 1876 and in his preface to the first edition speaks of himself '... as one who has held the office of Clerk of Works for several years'. Other names under which it has been suggested that the Clerk of Works may have operated are Overseer of Works or Master of Works.

The title Master of Works is still well known in Scotland today and is associated with the public office of engineer and surveyor, although a number of posts are advertised under the title of Master of Works where the duties are similar to those of a Clerk of Works.

Records suggest, however, that the Master of Works held a more senior role in the field of building in bygone days than the Clerk of Works. It is possible that the Master of Works may have been the master mason, the architect, or the 'deviser of byldynges' referred to in household lists in which the Clerk of Works is also mentioned.

A list of payments to officers during the erection of Caernarvon Castle, which began in 1284, quotes the 'Clerke of Workes' receiving eighteen pence per day, and the 'Maister of the Workes' two shillings and twopence per day.

CHAPTER TWO

The Victorian Clerk of Works

The Title

With the reorganisation of the Board of Works in 1832 the title of Clerk of Works appears to have been discarded, although presumably the duties would still require the attention of someone else under another title. Cathedral authorities continued the use of the title and regarded the Clerks of Works as important figures in the preservation of the buildings for which they were responsible.

At the time the Board of Works decided to amend their nomenclature the Clerk of Works continued to find a demand for his services on the country estates of the great landowners, or with public authorities on building poorhouses, hospitals, museums and other public buildings.

Development groups building offices and housing in the cities chose to engage Clerks of Works upon their construction schemes, either through the advice of the architect or for other reasons.

Duties

In his book referred to in the previous chapter Mr G. G. Hoskins, who was apparently practising as a Clerk of Works in the middle of the nineteenth century, outlines the duties of the Clerk of Works to the architect 'to whom he is responsible for the perfect performance and execution of the various works under his care and supervision, in accordance with the drawings and specification, and such written or verbal instructions as he may from time to time receive from the architect during the progress of the work ... make a note of work not included in a contract which may become hidden during the progress of the works, such as any extra digging, brickwork or stonework to foundations ... As regards additions and deductions, or any deviation from the contract, it should be the custom of the Clerk of Works in the case of any work intentionally omitted or altered to make marginal note to that effect on the specification, to be considered when settling with the contractor ... In the case of daywork or extras, an arrangement should be made with the contractor at the time of ordering such work to be done, for him to furnish a fortnightly return of such work, which will afford a better opportunity for checking it.

'If a complaint be necessary, an alteration required, or particulars to be furnished in connection with the work of the sub-contractor, a letter bearing on the subject, and sent to the sole contractor, should be sufficient to meet the case ...'

Training

It is evident that Clerks of Works of this era were engaged upon duties similar to those of the Clerk of Works today, but doubts were still being voiced in 1880, just as they were twenty years previously, regarding the background training for the Clerk of Works.

Many men acting as Clerks of Works had received training in the architect's office, and were accustomed to take up residence on the site, and perhaps the view of the later period, expressed by John Leaning, Fellow of the Surveyors' Institute, in his book *The Supervision of Building Work and the Duties of a Clerk of Works*, helps to prove a point: 'One of the disadvantages of the employment of this type of Clerk of Works is his possible interference with detail, of which he knows sometimes more than his employer, the architect, and he is consequently tempted to deal with matters which are not his province.'

Apart from those who were trained within the architect's office, Clerks of Works achieved their position from the site management structure of the master builder. Their career began with an apprenticeship varying from five to seven years in a craft or trade before they could be considered qualified to serve as a journeyman. In some instances they were obliged to work one or even two years as an 'improver' before they obtained recognition as a journeyman. By ability and conscientious work it was possible to achieve promotion to trade-foreman, but beyond this point, to building manager, a higher standard of education and a more technical background were essential.

For those who hoped to become a Clerk of Works, technical subjects had to be studied further, and this must have called for a great deal of determination after working a ten-hour day, often under extreme conditions. For those who were successful in being appointed Clerk of Works the desire to learn still more was strong, and the opportunity far less than it is today.

Appointments

Architects were obviously quick to spot building managers or foremen with proven ability on contracts proceeding under their authority, so that later when they were in need of a Clerk of Works for a new building or a restoration job, they would invite that man to take up the appointment under their direction, and they would advise the client accordingly. This system was beneficial to the architect, who was reasonably sure of obtaining a man sufficiently experienced in building to protect both his and the client's interests on the site. The arrangement was more than suitable to the Clerk of Works; apart from improving his salary and his status, it removed many of the problems of site management which he was otherwise responsible for as part of the contractor's staff.

The scale of payments averaged four to five guineas a week, but this varied according to the region in which the Clerk of Works was engaged. In 1860 attempts were made through the trade press to create an association which would represent Clerks of Works, but at that time it was felt this should include general foremen, since Clerks of Works sometimes acted as foremen and vice versa. It was not until 1882, however, encouraged by many prominent architects, including John Oldroyd Scott, besides the growing numbers of Clerks of Works, that an association was formed.

The aims of the new association were broadly to improve the knowledge and experience of members, as well as to provide architects with an available source of qualified men. The efforts of those men responsible for the founding of the association were rewarded with success, as the number of members has grown from 140 in 1884 to approximately 5,000 in 1972, and the association has become the present Institute of Clerks of Works.

Some Prominent Victorians

The men largely responsible for organising the association in the first instance were engaged as Clerks of Works on numerous contracts throughout the city of London, including James Brady on the Royal Courts of Justice in the Strand, James Redden on the Workhouse and Infirmary in Chelsea, J. W. Birtchwell on the new Town Hall in Westminster, and E. W. Nightingale on the new Prince's Theatre.

Thomas Potter, who was well known for his work on a number of country mansions, was also one of the founder members, but he went on to help found the Estate Clerks of Works Association. G. R. Webster, who did some fine work with J. Oldroyd Scott, was the first secretary of the association, but he had to resign when he moved to Coventry, where he supervised the restoration of St Michael's Church, the blitzed ruin of which was later included in part of the modern cathedral designed by Sir Basil Spence. The role of secretary was later taken over by Fred Dashwood, who held the office for twenty-nine years.

Not all the members were able to continue working in London, and among those who travelled to other parts of the country were J. S. Peed, appointed Clerk of Works to the estate of the Earl of Lonsdale at Whitehaven Castle, Cumberland; A. Cruickshank, appointed to St Mary's Abbey, Worcester; J. Higgs, appointed to Jesus College, Cambridge; E. C. Morgan, appointed to the Municipal Building, Glasgow; and S. J. Girling, sent to Ipswich for the rebuilding of the railway station.

CHAPTER THREE

The Modern Clerk of Works

The Title

Changes have occurred in the duties of the Clerk of Works since those issued when Lawrence Spencer was first appointed to St Paul's Cathedral, and the changes affecting the title since require the present role of the Clerk of Works to be closely defined. In its 'Particulars of Membership' the Institute of Clerks of Works defines it as follows:

> A Clerk of Works shall mean a person (not being employed by a Builder or Contractor) whose duty it is to superintend the construction of building or other works for the purpose of ensuring a proper use of labour and materials and shall include Resident Engineers, Superintendents of Works, Inspectors of Works, Works Managers, Masters of Works, and persons employed in a similar capacity.

Increase in Numbers

Unfortunately there are no accurate records available for the numbers of Clerks of Works in various sectors of the industry, but a sample survey taken recently suggests a total figure of 20,000 in Great Britain. Contracts have grown in size and become much more complex since World War II ended in 1945, and together with a general expansion of the construction industry this has increased the demand for Clerks of Works.

Before the War and in the years immediately following, it was mainly architects who required the services of the Clerk of Works, but this has now altered slightly, as both civil engineers and mechanical services engineers are equally interested in engaging qualified Clerks of Works. Equally there is a growing awareness that uneconomic maintenance costs are a result of poor building standards and the demand for quality-control becomes more insistent. The number of positions for qualified Clerks of Works now offered at reasonably high salaries may be an indication of this, and could establish more firmly the value of a qualified Clerk of Works in the present climate of the construction industry.

Sectors of Employment

The largest single employers of Clerks of Works are undoubtedly the Government departments and nationalised industries. The recently created Department of the Environment has centralised many of the posts, but there are departments that still employ their own staff. The Health and Social Security Department, through regional hospital boards, employs a large number of Clerks of Works under the title of Group Building Supervisors to deal with maintenance and minor works, but as Chief Clerks of Works, etc., on new construction.

British Railways, the National Coal Board, the Central Electricity Generating Board, etc, also have their quota of Clerks of Works.

Local Government caters for the next largest group, to supervise the construction of schools and housing, as well as public buildings. The Greater London Council is the largest employer of Clerks of Works among local authorities, together with county authorities such as Lancashire. Most local authorities employ Clerks of Works, even down to the present District Councils.

The revision of local government boundaries which became effective in April 1974 has brought about changes in staff requirements. Staff numbers appear to have increased and areas of responsibility have widened. This has resulted in the upgrading of some positions, including that of Clerk of Works. Larger authorities have also found it of advantage to appoint a Chief Clerk of Works to their staff, while greater emphasis is laid on training and career structure.

Many Clerks of Works employed by local government authorities are engaged as temporary staff, which causes concern to some persons for their future. This system is necessary to the authority in order that the costs can be charged directly to the contract upon which the Clerks are employed, for if they were on a permanent basis, the charge would fall upon the rates for the area. The numbers engaged upon the permanent staff of an authority are laid down in the establishment it is granted and this establishment is financed by local rates and government grants.

Paradoxically the temporary employment of these Clerks of Works is probably no less permanent than that of others, as they generally move direct from one contract to another without a break in their employment, and enjoy most, if not all, of the benefits received by the permanent staff.

New Towns have always provided good opportunities for Clerks of Works, but the extent to which they are involved depends upon the brief to which the Development Corporations are committed. Besides being involved in urban renewal some existing towns have undergone a facelift by the creation of new town centres, which have provided opportunities for Clerks of Works in their developments. The demand for office accommodation in towns and cities has also been a source of employment for Clerks of Works, although in some instances there have been package-deal contracts where the Clerk of Works was not involved.

The demand for university buildings has been tremendous in recent years and has resulted in similar requirements for Clerks of Works, both in new construction and subsequent maintenance supervision. Civil engineering projects such as motorway construction, with its attendant bridge-building, power stations, factory construction, and similar large-scale development have provided further opportunities for Clerks of Works to contribute their skills.

Clerks of Works are also engaged by private architectural practices, and, though appointed for specific contracts in the first instances, regular engagements inevitably continue where the arrangements are satisfactory to both parties. Many practices employ Clerks of Works on a permanent basis, delegating varying degrees of responsibility to them, and in some cases they act almost in the role of an architect's agent.

Mechanical Services

The increased complexity of services installed in modern structures calls for a greater intensity of supervision and inspection, especially as these activities invariably coincide with a critical period in the erection of the structural elements. Where the extent of the services installation requires such supervision, it is becoming increasingly recognised that an additional Clerk of Works, qualified in mechanical services, should be engaged.

The importance of the installation will decide the background training of the Services Clerk of Works, either electrical or mechanical. Whether he will operate as an assistant to the main Clerk of Works or as a member of the consultant's staff will be decided by contract conditions. Where the contract is predominantly mechanical services, of course, it might be that the Services Clerk of Works would play the major role, with the construction Clerk of Works assisting him.

Private Housing

Since the introduction of the National House Building Council, a system of inspection of private house-building has been established, though it is still limited at present. Many of those who have been engaged to carry out this inspection have been employed previously as Clerks of Works on other contracts, and as their role is similar, they continue to regard themselves as Clerks of Works in their new field of operations.

Estate Clerks of Works

The Estate Clerk of Works has a great deal in common with his medieval counterpart, being closely attached to the estate and obtaining most of his construction materials from his own resources. Apart from the need to meet problems common to modern construction methods, the Estate Clerk of Works requires a very specialised knowledge of agricultural requirements. Surveys, estimates, drawings, building supervision – these are all part of the daily routine of the Estate Clerk of Works.

Sometimes he operates as a freelance consultant, but more often he is a responsible member of the staff administering a large country estate. He enjoys a special place in the rural community, and for those with a true appreciation of country life, the role of Estate Clerk of Works offers many rewards and opportunities. Many men in general construction work turn to this form of engagement and apparently find it to their liking.

Maintenance and Minor Works

There are equally as many Clerks of Works engaged in the maintenance section of the industry as in the new construction sector, and while the duties of the Clerk of Works on new construction can be reasonably defined, the duties of those in the maintenance sector can be very difficult to assess. Their duties however call for more than a knowledge of building construction, for they require a good working knowledge of outdated as well as modern materials.

Many Clerks of Works on maintenance work are called upon to prepare specifications, dilapidation schedules, preliminary sketches and estimates, and they may be required to prepare surveys and reports for committees. They are also expected in some instances to control a direct labour force, and be involved with the purchase of materials for the work carried out by the section.

Clerks of Works working for hospital boards are generally referred to as Hospital Building Supervisors, and work in conjunction with the Engineer, who is invariably a mechanical engineer with a complex arrangement of services to maintain.

Industrial and commercial organisations may refer to their maintenance supervisor by several names other than Clerk of Works – Resident Engineer, Building Manager, Master of Works – but he is often the Clerk of Works of the original building who decided to stay with the firm and still thinks of himself as holding that position.

Local government authorities employ a large number of Clerks of Works on maintenance and minor works, especially in housing and education, where the work can be of a repetitive nature.

Cathedrals and Universities

Clerks of Works are still engaged on such buildings as St Paul's Cathedral and Lincoln Cathedral, as well as the Houses of Parliament and other public buildings, including many of the older universities. Theirs is maintenance work of a kind which commands a certain prestige. Most of them have a great affection for such ancient buildings, and steep themselves in the traditions surrounding them. Their association with ancient construction techniques gives them a better understanding of the skills of the past, skills they are expected to maintain in remedial work to the structure. They have to control a suitable labour force, and the ability of the Clerk of Works can often be reflected in the skills of the team he gathers round him. Besides buying his own materials, he often reclaims much that can be re-used, and the value of reclaimed materials must always be kept in mind where these buildings have to be maintained.

In many instances the Clerk of Works is also responsible for storage of much that is of value about the building, besides carrying out decorations and furnishings where rooms, etc, are restored. He can also be involved in any pageantry which the building he is engaged upon is concerned in, and such organisation can occupy a fair proportion of time on some of the very important buildings.

The Clerk of Works Overseas

It is not clear to what extent the role of Clerk of Works exists on the Continent, although there are many examples of British designers appointing a Clerk of Works when operating in Europe.

In the Scandinavian countries and Germany the person operating as Clerk of Works follows the same methods of training as in this country, i.e., years of craft training coupled with technical education. Not enough facts are known at present, but it is sufficient to say there are those carrying out a similar task in the European construction industry, whether the title is similar or not.

In most countries which have been affected by British influence in the past, the practice of engaging a Clerk of Works still continues, especially in the African countries, where the demand is increasing. Australia, too, has its own Clerk of Works organisation; and in New Zealand it is an offence to practice as a Clerk of Works without registration, which can only be achieved by passing the appropriate examinations in the same way that architects must do in this country.

At least one organisation of Clerks of Works exists in the United States, in California, but whether the duties are the same is not known.

Plenty of opportunity exists for a Clerk of Works who is interested in working overseas, and many of these positions are very remunerative, although there are obvious pitfalls to be avoided and advice should be taken from the Institute, which has members already operating abroad.

Generally, the work offered demands great initiative and ability, owing to the problem of communication, for the design office can be hundreds or even thousands of miles distant. For those with the necessary qualifications, however, coupled with the right temperament for the climate, the rewards can be very great indeed. These positions are invariably advertised through trade journals, or the national press, by the Governments concerned or by Crown Agents.

Members of the Department of the Environment in the course of their careers are normally expected to complete a tour of duty overseas, and while some are content to complete their tour and return home, others spend many years working on different projects and find it to their taste.

Where a touch of adventure, travel, and unusual contracts are considered to be an additional zest to one's way of life, the Forces provide excellent opportunities and facilities for training as a Clerk of Works. Indeed, many experienced Clerks of Works engaged upon major civil contracts today obtained their training as Military Clerks of Works, and are enjoying the benefit of such training in their present roles.

Part Two

CHAPTER FOUR

Appointment of Clerks of Works

It is obviously in the interests of both client and architect that the Clerk of Works appointed is a reliable and qualified person, so both parties should be represented when the appointment is made.

Clerks of Works employed in Government departments or with local authorities are generally engaged as technical officers, but many Clerks of Works operate on a freelance basis, taking engagements for the duration of contract only. In such circumstances, where the Clerk of Works is engaged and paid direct by the client, it is important to appreciate that he will still operate under the direction of the architect or engineer. Where the Clerk of Works is appointed and paid direct by the architect, his salary will be included as an additional charge to the client when the architect submits his fees.

Personal Contracts

A form of contract has been produced by the Institute of Clerks of Works covering the terms of appointment of a Clerk of Works, and this is used where a private architect or client engages the Clerk of Works for the duration of contract only.

Inspector for the Employer

Under the JCT Standard Form of Contract it is important to understand that the Clerk of Works is the inspector on behalf of the employer, and not an agent of the architect, although under Clause 10 he is empowered to 'give directions on any matter in which the Architect is empowered to give instructions'. This authority can only be delegated to the Clerk of Works by the Architect, who must confirm any such instruction within two working days. The reference to the Clerk of Works being an inspector on behalf of the employer has not changed since the Standard Form of Contract was drawn up in 1909. The authority for him to issue directions was included in the same clause when the 1963 edition of the Standard Form was issued.

Qualities Required

In suggesting the qualities required it would be misleading to imply that Clerks of Works differ from any other profession, as it is essential for all of them to have integrity, but Clerks of Works have isolated roles on site and can be subjected to many pressures.

They must always behave in such a way as to earn respect for their office from those with whom they work, whether it be the architect and his staff, or the contractor and his representatives. The Clerk of Works must command authority at all times, asserting that authority in a fair and just manner; he should be courteous to both men and management alike, remembering it is easy to take advantage of a position of authority and easier still to fall into a slovenly habit of expressing that authority.

The Clerk of Works should be capable of dealing tactfully with site problems as they occur, and while referring the matter to the architect where this is necessary, it is important that he interprets the situation correctly beforehand.

He must never take things for granted nor make assumptions in matters concerning the contract; he must check the facts as far as possible, and act accordingly. It is part of his responsibility to be looking ahead for possible problems in the execution of the contract to avoid any delays or expense to the client.

Good records of site activities are expected from the Clerk of Works, and though he is not regarded as a skilled draughtsman, he must have the ability to produce clear sketches which will illustrate details of site agreements that may otherwise not be recorded. Such details may prove to be invaluable to both the architect and the quantity surveyor at a later stage in the contract. Reference is occasionally made in letters and articles of the trade press for the need to provide quality-control officers, co-ordinators, a progress chaser, a link-man, and several other titles, yet for at least one and a half centuries these have been the functions of the Clerk of Works.

Training

A Clerk of Works is still recruited from the site management sector of the contractor, having reached that position in a slightly less arduous manner than his Victorian counterpart, and with the added advantage of one day each week for technical training. Unfortunately, under the present arrangements, once they are appointed as a Clerk of Works and leave the contractor's organisation, the opportunity for them to continue their technical training becomes less, and often ceases altogether.

The role of Clerk of Works calls for an appreciation of technical matters and an intimate knowledge of construction methods. Besides this he requires an insight into human relationships that will enable him to obtain results the medieval Clerk of Works achieved by more direct methods.

Qualifications

The recognised qualification for a Clerk of Works is the Diploma issued by the Institute of Clerks of Works to candidates who have completed the Final Examination, Parts 1 and 2.

The ICW Examinations cater for those wishing to qualify as Clerks of Works in building, civil engineering, or mechanical engineering, separate papers being set for each section. The examinations are held annually in different centres throughout the United Kingdom as well as in other parts of the world.

Courses Available

Courses are available in colleges throughout the United Kingdom as well as overseas, and require three years' part-time day and evening study; entry to the courses requires certain minimum qualifications, which vary from time to time. Special courses are arranged by the Institute for further training in organisation and management as they affect the Clerk of Works.

Future Training

Developments within the industry are likely to affect existing methods of training manpower, and this is bound to react upon the present system of recruiting management. Revised methods for training Clerks of Works are also inevitable, and careful consideration will be necessary to ensure that the person carrying out this role fully understands the practical application of materials and construction techniques. Clerks of Works must be trained from a much earlier age than at present, and be provided with a positive career structure in quality control. No matter what erection procedures may develop in the future, the student Clerk of Works must be allowed to develop his appreciation of site problems by actual site training rather than academic exercises. At the same time, if full advantage is to be gained from having a Clerk of Works on site, he must be given the opportunity to increase his technical knowledge in the same way as other professions. Good quality control is in the interests of all sides of the industry, as it should produce a higher performance at the same costs, eventually producing better construction and fair profits to both manufacturers and contractors. The Clerk of Works is least affected by the pressures of costs and man-management, which suggests he is most likely to be impartial in his judgement of quality, and this should be in the interests of both the manufacturing and construction industries. The main parties to the contract could find it advantageous to show greater interest in the training of Clerks of Works; the advantages to the architectural profession hardly require explanation, but the advantages to the contractor are constantly overlooked.

Under the present system of recruiting, Clerks of Works are products of the contractor's organisations, and so their ability to interpret situations on the site have been influenced by their training with contractors. This seems an excellent reason why contractors should support and encourage the training of Clerks of Works. It is true that there are already training courses available for supervisory roles with established organisations, but this only partly meets the requirements of a Clerk of Works. While the Clerk of Works can never be considered as a replacement for the contractor's supervision on the site, the actual interpretation of workmanship, materials and site operations can rest with him in many instances. This requires him to be always up-to-date with the progress of the work on all sections of the contract if delays are to be avoided; otherwise work which does not conform with the specification at some stage or other in the contract is more likely to be questioned, and that creates problems for all concerned.

A competent Clerk of Works is more than essential in the interests of the client, and where this affects a public body, there are training facilities provided in a number of sectors, though all do not have the same opportunity to take advantage of these. The Clerk of Works himself must be aware of the need to keep abreast of developments and take full advantage of any training facilities available, bearing in mind the importance of understanding the particular role of others.

Authority of Clerk of Works

Until such times as he hands over the completed works to the architect the site legally belongs to the contractor, and the Clerk of Works requires authority to perform his duties upon the site. Clause 10 in the Standard Form of Contract provides that authority, and the other forms of contract contain a similar implication.

Although it is necessary to have authority in the contract for the Clerk of Works to operate on the site, if he is unable to implement that authority without continually referring to clauses in a contract, the situation could become intolerable for contractor, architect and Clerk of Works. Like many other forms of contract, a building contract requires goodwill on the part of all concerned, and without that there can be very little hope of a successful conclusion. It is well to establish the requirements in practical terms at the outset of the building contract, thus avoiding any misunderstanding later when issues may be much more confused.

Duties

The variety of roles carried out by the Clerk of Works as shown in previous pages establishes a difficulty in defining his duties precisely. By considering the terms of the contract he is employed under, however, it becomes much clearer what those duties are, and while they still cannot be set down in detail, they can be defined within certain parameters.

Clerks of Works engaged in new construction projects are likely to be affected by the JCT Standard Form of Contract, the ICE Conditions of Contract, and the government contract form GC/Works/1 – all referred to at length in further pages.

Role within the Contract

The Clerk of Works is now mentioned by name in the government form GC/Works/1 where previously reference was made to 'The representative of the Superintending Officer'.

The ICE Conditions of Contract refer to the 'Engineer's Representative' but goes on to define this as 'the Resident Engineer, assistant of the Engineer, or any Clerk of Works appointed from time to time by the Employer or the Engineer'.

The JCT Standard Form of Contract, however, is quite specific in naming the Clerk of Works, and in Clause 10 defines his duties and authority within the contract, as follows:

The Employer shall be able to appoint a Clerk of Works whose duty shall be to act solely as inspector on behalf of the Employer under the direction of the Architect/Supervising Officer and the Contractor shall afford every reasonable facility for the performance of that duty. If any directions are given to the Contractor or his foreman upon the Works by the Clerk of Works the same shall be of no effect unless given in regard to a matter in respect of which the Architect/Supervising Officer is empowered by these conditions to issue instructions and unless confirmed in writing by the Architect/Supervising Officer within two working days of their being given. If any such directions are so given and confirmed then as from the date of confirmation they shall be deemed to be Architect's/Supervising Officer's instructions.

Positive or Negative Role

Both the GC/Works/1 Form and the ICE Conditions allow the Superintending Officer or the Engineer to invest the Clerk of Works with powers which give him a positive role in the Works, whereas the Standard Form restricts his role to that of inspector. If the Clerk of Works is to work strictly to the wording in the Standard Form, his role would appear to be entirely negative, which is far from being the case. The wording has been necessary to overcome any misunderstanding of the authority of the Clerk of Works to issue instructions that might vary the contract, which of course he cannot do.

Responsibility for the Contract

The architect is responsible for the contract under the JCT Standard Form of Contract and has no authority to pass any of that responsibility to the Clerk of Works, yet the Clerk of Works has still a responsibility to the client, to ensure that materials and workmanship are in accordance with the contract. He must retain the power to reject any workmanship, materials or activities which do not conform with the contract, unless he has written instructions from the architect to vary that part of the work.

Architect and Clerk of Works

It is most important in the interests of the contract as well as of the client that there is mutual respect between the architect and the Clerk of Works, besides a clear understanding where each other's responsibility lies. Where the Clerk of Works is operating with a qualified architect, such problems should be unlikely to arise, but this is not always the case in quite a number of instances. Where the Clerk of Works finds himself in a situation in which there is a conflict with the Contract Documents for which he may bear some responsibility later, he should put the facts in writing to the architect with a copy to the senior architect responsible for the project. The Clerk of Works may not always appreciate the role of the architect and the difficulties which affect him, but by having sufficient knowledge of the relevant clauses within the contract the Clerk of Works should be able to assist by accurately recording conditions and operations which may affect the work subsequently, besides reporting items of importance at the appropriate time rather than when matters have reached a head.

Unless this rapport can be established from the outset of the contract, the contractor's site management will recognise the difficulty and have doubts concerning the authority of the Clerk of Works. Demands may then be made upon the architect himself which he may find physically impossible to fulfil, and this can result in the inevitable uncertainties, delays, misunderstandings, claims and counter-claims which often arise from these situations, causing expense and dissatisfaction to all those concerned.

Architect's Supervision

The architect can only give a limited amount of supervision to the construction of the work, yet he is bound to ensure that the work is carried out to the correct terms of the contract. Where he considers the amount of supervision he can give to the contract is insufficient, under his terms of engagement with the client he is entitled to ask that a Clerk of Works be engaged to provide the additional supervision under his direction. During his on-site inspections made in accordance with Clause 1.33 of his Conditions of Engagement, the architect 'shall endeavour to guard the Client against defects and deficiencies in the work of the Contractor, but shall not be required to make exhaustive or continuous inspections to check the quality or the quantity of the work'. Clause 1.61 goes on to state: 'Where frequent or constant inspection is required, a Clerk or Clerks of Works should be employed. He should be nominated or approved by the architect and be under the architect's direction and control. He may be appointed and paid by the client or employed by the architect.'

Liability of Clerk of Works

There is little evidence of the Clerk of Works being successfully sued, although cases have been submitted to the courts. Present contractual rulings, however, have produced some unexpected results, and perhaps the Clerk of Works would be well advised to consider his position in regard to the law.

Common Law

Anyone who offers a service to others and claims an expert's knowledge in that service has a responsibility to those who accept that offer. In agreeing to provide that service a contract is made when the service is performed on the terms stated. It is possible for the Clerk of Works to find himself sued either by the client as his employer, or by the architect where he is being held responsible for a matter which should clearly have been reported to him by the Clerk of Works.

Additional Liability

There is some anxiety among certain members of the architectural profession concerning the responsibility of the Clerk of Works, as the architect's duties under his conditions of engagement with the client only call for periodic supervision. The Clerk of Works' presence upon the site presupposes wider limits of supervision, which the architect has acknowledged, and they therefore could increase his responsibility to the client.

This situation has already been ruled on in court, and increases the possibility of the Clerk of Works becoming involved in litigation.

In many organisations professional indemnity policies are taken up, but the cost of obtaining cover over recent years has been so prohibitive that many people are reconsidering the position, which in itself may increase the possibility of the Clerk of Works being involved in legal action.

CHAPTER SIX

Pre-Contract Role

Early Appointment

To gain full advantage of the Clerk of Works, he should be appointed several weeks before the contract is due to start, and the meantime should be spent in the architect's office studying the project, as well as gaining an understanding of the office procedures. This can be of enormous benefit in avoiding the misunderstandings which arise from time to time in communications between site and office during the first few months of the contract.

The architect would have an opportunity to explain thoroughly the complete project, using all available drawings to create the image he is attempting to achieve. This will enable the Clerk of Works to have a better understanding of the work, helping him to interpret any problems which may arise later. The Clerk of Works should then be given sufficient time to study the drawings before arranging a further discussion, when any matters he does not understand can be either explained or amended.

Many architects tend to overlook the fact that a scheme may not be so easily interpreted from its drawings by a newcomer as it may by one who has grown with it from the beginning. Revisions to drawings in the design stage sometimes create errors in details which can be overlooked, and these errors may be picked up by a fresh mind approaching the scheme.

Agreement of Standards

The architect can also take advantage of the situation to give the Clerk of Works guidance on the standards of quality he hopes to achieve, and visiting previous projects carried out by the office will avoid any misunderstandings in such matters when work is proceeding on the new contract. Standards of quality can so easily become a matter for convenience these days, with excuses ranging from pressures due to completion dates to lack of ability on the part of the contractor.

Contract Briefing

When tenders have been evaluated, a meeting is usually arranged with the successful contractor; these are known as pre-contract meetings or contract briefing meetings. The purpose is to hand over several sets of drawings, copies of bills, specifications and schedules to the contractor; to introduce the principals involved on both sides; to discuss general procedures in administrating the contract; and to arrange an inspection of site before the contractor takes possession. The Clerk of Works should be introduced to the contractor at this meeting, as well as to the other professional men concerned, and the opportunity should be taken to establish the Clerk of Works as a responsible member of the team, besides being the client's quality-control on the site. (See Fig. 1 for bases of contract organisation.)

This can be best achieved by allowing the Clerk of Works to state in the meeting procedures for carrying out dayworks on site, presenting sheets for signature, measurement of work to be covered up, submission of samples of materials, and requirements in connection with labour returns.

Choice of Clerk of Works

If the architect has any misgivings in allowing the Clerk of Works to deal with these matters, he should briefly run through the whole procedure with him before the meeting. By establishing the authority of the Clerk of Works at this stage the architect will improve the possibility of achieving contract completion to his own satisfaction. If he does not find this confidence in the Clerk of Works, he has chosen unwisely and should not expect satisfactory results at the end of the contract. He is also acknowledging the fact that he must give more attention to supervision of the contract himself to safeguard both his and the client's interests.

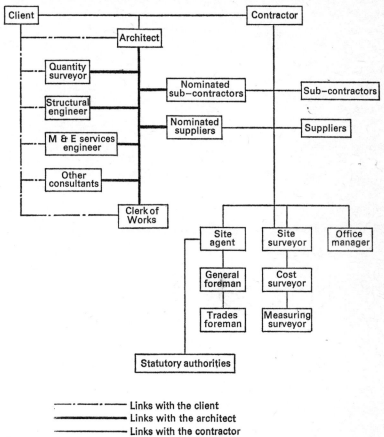

Fig. 1.

Assuming the Clerk of Works has been given the opportunity to study the project before it has reached this stage, he will be better qualified to advise on such matters as siting of compounds and site offices when these are submitted by the contractor for approval. He will also be in a position to comment on the programme when the contractor submits this for consideration, and given the opportunity, he may be able to contribute in the selection of nominated sub-contractors and suppliers, as he may already have experience of these in the past.

Where the architect decides for his own reasons to leave the appointment of the Clerk of Works until the final moment, apart from restricting his own choice, he will also find a demand upon his own time which might easily have been avoided. When the work commences on the site, both Clerk of Works and site agent may well be discovering the problems simultaneously, and such problems may be costing the client further outlay. At any rate it is certain it will be unlikely to help progress on site, and may cause errors which might otherwise have been avoided.

The Client

In the contract the client is generally referred to as 'the employer' and can quite easily be either an individual or a group of persons in the form of a public authority or a large industrial concern. It is the client who produces the capital to finance the project, but apart from his involvement with the architect, he plays no part in the actual construction operations.

The Construction Team

To perform his duties within the contract it is important for the Clerk of Works to be fully conversant with the functions and the responsibilities of all other members of the construction industry. Unless he understands the basic responsibilities of each of these roles, he may inadvertently make decisions outside the scope of his responsibility, or create situations unfavourable to the client, whom he represents on the site.

The Architect

He is appointed by the client to act as his agent in all respects in procuring the erection of the development to the 'brief' supplied by the client.

The 'brief' is a statement of the client's requirements, and includes the performance he expects the project to provide him with, at the price he is willing to pay. The architect has to produce a preliminary sketch design based upon the brief given to him, and from this he is able to discuss the client's requirements with him in much greater detail. Having finalised the brief, the architect can prepare his final design, from which he can then produce an estimate. When this is finally settled with the client, the architect can begin his working drawings and prepare for tendering procedure.

The Quantity Surveyor

He is appointed by the client on the recommendation of the architect, and on a large development will provide costing information during the design period, and prepare a cost plan on the final scheme, based upon his knowledge of current prices. If the cost plan is acceptable to the client, and he gives the architect permission to proceed with the project, the quantity surveyor will prepare a specification based upon information provided by the architect, and a detailed list of materials and operations required to carry out the work – the Bill of Quantities. The quantity surveyor will also evaluate the tenders when they are received and advise the architect before the most suitable tender is accepted.

The Structural Engineer

He is appointed by the client on the recommendation of the architect, and will design the foundations and structural elements of the project, which include floors, stairs, roof, and any bridges or ramps. Besides providing structural drawings, the structural engineer will provide reinforcement and bending schedules, and will also give a limited amount of supervision to the structural work in progress.

Mechanical and Electrical Services Engineer

The appointment is made by the client on the recommendation of the architect for the provision of all drawings and specification details in connection with the services within the contract. On a large development the services engineers will provide details for power and lighting installations, sprinkler systems, fire alarms, communications, heating and plumbing services, drainage and waste disposal, etc. Contract supervision will depend upon the extent of the work, but a limited amount of supervision must be given.

Consultants

They will be appointed by the client on the advice of the architect, and will invariably be specialists in designing specific services: for example, on a large abattoir the architect may consider it necessary to call in consultants either to advise or to design the whole of the cold storage requirements. Both the structural and mechanical services engineers are also consultants in the same way.

The Contractor

Using the contract drawings, specifications and contract bills supplied to him by the architect, the contractor prices all the items in the bills and produces a total figure which he submits as his tender price to carry out the work. In his tender figure the contractor is agreeing to use his expertise to construct the whole of the development as outlined in the contract drawings, specifications and bills of quantities wi hin the period specified as the contract period.

Sub-Contractors and Suppliers

Those described as 'nominated' are selected by the architect but enter into a contract with the main contractor, who adds a percentage to the sub-contractor's price to meet his overheads, etc. Those who are described as 'specified' are also selected by the architect, but in this case it is left to the contractor to obtain a price which is favourable also to him. All remaining sub-contractors or suppliers within the contract are appointed direct by the main contractor, but they must be approved by the architect, and bound fully under the conditions of contract.

The Building Surveyor

All buildings and structures must comply with statutory regulations, and those concerned with density, floor space, etc, are covered by Town Planning Regulations. Plans must be submitted to the planning authority before any work can proceed.

All matters concerning structural strength, fire regulations, weatherproofing, etc, are covered by the Building Regulations and are the responsibility of the local government building surveyor. He is also concerned with drainage, soil and waste disposal, etc, and either he or his inspector will visit the site to ensure that these regulations are being carried out.

Notification must be submitted to the building surveyor when work begins on the site, or when foundations or drainage work are in progress.

Statutory Authorities

The Fire Officer will carry out an inspection of the building before it can be occupied, to ensure that requirements laid down when the drawings were submitted for approval have been carried out. On a public building he will be concerned with such matters as fire-points and hose reels, smoke doors, fire exits, etc, and tests will be required to the dry-riser.

The Highways Inspector will maintain an interest in any works which obstruct the highway or interfere with road or pedestrian traffic. He will also be concerned with any damage to the highway caused by transfer of heavy plant or machinery, as well as opening up the road for sewer or service connections. Statutory notices must be sent to the authority before proceeding with such operations.

The Water Board Inspector will probably be one of the first to visit the site, to survey the provision of a water supply for the contractor. He will also call at regular intervals to ensure there is no attempt to ignore the regulations, which may waste water. He will be particularly concerned with the water installation and fittings, especially with ball-valves and overflows.

The Electricity Board Inspector is concerned with anything in the installation which may lead to fire risk or electric shock. He will take note of any infringement of the Electricity Regulations, which refer to installations, electrical equipment, testing and maintenance of supplies.

The Gas Board Inspector is also concerned with the installation of gas pipes within the structure, including anything which may produce a hazard to the occupants.

Statutory Service Authorities must be satisfied with the installation within the building before they will be prepared to provide mains services.

Communication Services. An inspector from the Post Office will visit the contract in connection with normal supply of telephone services, but on larger contracts, where special rooms are necessary to house the equipment, the inspector will be more closely involved to ensure the provision of ducts, etc, as well as other requirements within the rooms.

The Clerk of Works would be well advised to maintain contact with all these people concerned with inspection, not only to ensure there are no errors likely to affect the client's interests, but because of the useful advice he is likely to acquire for the future.

The Site Agent

The first contact the Clerk of Works is likely to make on site will be the contractor's agent, and while personality problems may arise from time to time, the Clerk of Works must attempt to avoid all friction. The site agent has a very responsible position, as well as many difficult problems demanding his attention, so perhaps occasionally he should be forgiven for displaying signs of irritation. If the Clerk of Works treats him with the respect his position demands, the agent will be likely to reciprocate. So many Clerks of Works forget, or perhaps have never experienced, the problems of labour management, and fail to take into account the numerous responsibilities of the site agent apart from the supervision of the structure.

The Clerk of Works should always be in a position to understand the contract difficulties affecting the site agent; otherwise he will be unable to judge fairly. Sympathy for the site agent's position may arise because the Clerk of Works understands the problem himself, but the client has not engaged him to be sympathetic. However, this does not prevent him from being understanding and professional in his dealings with the site agent.

Certain Clerks of Works may perhaps over-emphasise the problems of the site agent and the contractor by getting too closely involved with the situation. This is unwise and can prevent the Clerk of Works from giving a lead to the contractor, who will find no advantage in having a fellow-worrier. Keeping ahead of the erection progress should help the Clerk of Works to see many pitfalls, and by tactfully advising the site agent, he will succeed in establishing his position in the contract to the advantage of all concerned.

Where sour relations do exist between the Clerk of Works and the site agent, this cannot always be dismissed as a fault on one side only. A tactful Clerk of Works can often handle a difficult agent and perhaps vice versa.

The Clerk of Works should avoid passing personal views regarding the contractor's performance on the site, and should confine his remarks to the quality demanded by the contract drawings and bills. He should make it a rule to deal direct with the site agent only, thereby avoiding mistakes which can arise through chance remarks to trades-foremen.

It is easy to overlook the amount of time spent throughout one's life just working, and unpleasant relationships do not help. In dealing with others throughout the contract a good maxim for the Clerk of Works to follow is BE FIRM: BE FAIR: AND BE FRIENDLY.

CHAPTER SEVEN

Forms and Documents

Quite a number of terms and forms used for contract procedures are not fully appreciated by all practising Clerks of Works apart from those taking up their first appointment. The interpretation placed upon architect's instructions and variation orders is often only partly correct, while the confusion which exists over site instructions can lead to poor site relations with the contractor and expense to the client.

Contract Documents

These are referred to at the beginning of the bills of quantities and consists of a form of contract, signed by the client and the contractor, the contract drawings as produced by the architect, and the contract bills prepared by the quantity surveyor from the drawings.

The Form of Contract depends upon the type of client and the type of contract. Government contracts will come under the conditions stated in Form GC/Works/1, civil engineering work carried out by local government and private clients will be under ICE Conditions of Contract, and building works under the JCT Form of Contract. These contracts are discussed more fully in Chapter 8, and although the Clerk of Works will not always have the opportunity to see the signed contract, there is no reason why he should not be supplied with a plain copy to assist him in his duties.

The Contract Drawings are those upon which the contractor has based his tender to carry out the works as shown at an agreed price and in a given period of time. These drawings are stamped and initialled by both parties when the contract is signed, to confirm they are the drawings referred to in remaining documents.

The Contract Bills are the detailed operations and quantities of materials measured from the contract drawings by the quantity surveyor, and fully priced by the contractor in arriving at his tender figure.

A specification and various schedules relating to the works will be included with the bills of quantities, and the contractor will be obliged to comply with the contents of these documents also. Sometimes the bills are divided into two or more volumes, depending upon the extent of the contract; and sometimes no quantities are issued, only a specification and schedules, but this will be clearly stated in the other contract documents.

The Clerk of Works will be supplied with an unpriced copy of the bills and copies of the specification and schedules.

Architect's Instructions*

These must be given in writing and refer to matters which the architect is empowered to issue under the contract.

The contractor must comply with the instruction within a specified period or the employer (client) will be entitled to have the work carried out by others, and charge all costs involved against the contractor. In other words, where the contractor fails to correct any work rejected by the architect, and still refuses or ignores a further warning, the architect may call in another contractor to do the work. While this sounds feasible in print, it would obviously create a number of problems in practice, unless it was a major item deserving such direct action.

Architect's instructions are issued where defective work requires correction during the progress of the contract, or where it is necessary for work to be opened up for inspection by the architect, or for the removal of defective materials from the site.

Variation Orders

The architect will issue these on the same form as is used for an architect's instruction, but the wording is arranged to allow part of it to be struck out;

---

* Where the engineer or a superintending officer is in control of the contract, this should be read accordingly.

a variation order implies an alteration or modification to the design set out in the contract drawings, or the quality or quantity as given in the contract bills. Variation orders can affect the contract sum not only because of the actual work involved but because interruptions can be caused to the contract by indirect means. This could apply where plant is in use on the site but, because of the variation order, may have to stand idle for short intervals, or when labour may have to be redirected to other parts of the site.

Delays to the contract which are outside the control of the contractor may warrant an extension of time to the contract period, and this permission would be issued by the architect as a variation order. It is important to appreciate that any extension to the contract is likely to affect the cost through overheads, generally described as the preliminaries.

Site Instructions

Under the contract the Clerk of Works is entitled to issue instructions to the contractor so long as these do not vary the contract. There is some dispute whether they are correctly referred to as 'instructions' or 'directions', but the practical effect on the site is just the same. The Clerk of Works should be able to issue a site instruction which draws attention to discrepancies between the drawings or the bills, for tests to the works, opening up works for inspection, removal of faulty work or materials, and disposal of antiquities. Wherever possible, and in any case where a variation to the works may result, the Clerk of Works should contact the architect before issuing the site instruction. A copy of the instruction should be forwarded to the architect as soon as possible to enable him to confirm the instruction with an official architect's instruction in the time required by the contract.

Dayworks

This method provides one way of reimbursing the contractor for work carried out under variation orders, and requires the time and materials used in carrying out that portion of the works to be recorded by the contractor and confirmed by the Clerk of Works.

The Clerk of Works in signing Dayworks *does not approve them* but merely confirms that the information is correct. In any case the quantity surveyor may possibly find the item can be measured under rates already given in the bills.

It is important that the Clerk of Works should be informed if any work to be put in hand is likely to be submitted for his confirmation, in order that he may keep records of its progress. The sheets should also be presented to him for signature in the week following that in which the work was carried out.

Valuations

The contractor is entitled to be paid for all approved work carried out, together with the value of materials delivered to the site, less an agreed percentage. The work and materials are measured and listed by the quantity surveyor at regular intervals during the contract and valued in accordance with the rates given in the bills.

All sub-contractors work as well as materials from suppliers is included in the valuation prepared by the quantity surveyor, which is submitted to the architect.

The contractor's surveyor is entitled to be present when the valuation is made, and in practice it is often carried out jointly between the surveyors.

Interim Payments

When the architect receives the valuation issued by the quantity surveyor he issues a certificate to the client authorising payment to the contractor of the valuation, less a retention sum, passing a copy of the certificate at the same time to the contractor. The intervals at which the interim payments are to be made are given in the contract documents, and generally this occurs once each month. Each payment is a useful guide to the progress of the works, providing it is considered together with the other factors.

Retention Fund

The architect will deduct 10 per cent from the valuation compiled by the quantity surveyor before issuing his certificate to the client for payment to the contractor. This 10 per cent of the monthly valuation will continue to be deducted until 5 per cent of the total contract sum is being withheld. The sum held is referred to as the retention fund and will be retained until practical completion of the contract, when $2\frac{1}{2}$ per cent will be released.

Prime Cost Sums

These may be referred to also as PC items and are sums of money included in the bills to cover the cost of goods which the architect wishes to specify, and the contractor must add to this sum any other costs, including his profit for fixing, etc. He will also be obliged to produce vouchers or invoices for the goods showing actual prices, less discount received.

Provisional Sums

This is a sum in the contract bills to enable the architect to provide for such items as sub-contract or specialist work at a stage after the contract has been signed with the contractor. When he is pricing these items in the bills, the contractor must add for any profit and attendance he considers necessary.

Practical Completion Certificate

Once the contract has been completed to the satisfaction of the architect, he will issue the practical completion certificate to the client, who will then pay all money due to the contractor under the contract sum, with the exception of $2\frac{1}{2}$ per cent of the contract which will be held as the retention fund.

Various definitions are suggested as to what constitutes practical completion, but it has been generally established that it means precisely what it says, that the works have been completed for all practical purposes, even though they may not be totally complete.

All the items which have not been provided by the contractor and are shown in the contract bills, together with all defective items of materials and workmanship, should be completely listed before the practical completion certificate is issued.

Liquidated Damages

This must not be confused with penalty clauses, etc, which could be contested by the contractor if the rates were too high, so that the employer would be obliged to prove his loss.

Liquidated damages refer to an agreed nominal sum to be paid to the employer by the contractor for each week, or month, during which the contract may overrun the agreed completion date.

Agreeing the rate beforehand overcomes any claim by the employer that he has lost more financially because of further situations, or claims by the contractor that the Employer failed to make use of the works for a time after they were available. The amounts are quite specifically entered into the contract documents, and the contractor will not be obliged to pay any liquidated damages for such periods beyond the completion date for which he is granted an extension of time under the contract.

Defects Liability Period

The defects liability period begins immediately the practical completion certificate is issued by the architect, and while in most cases it is for a period of six months, this can be varied under the contract (it is advisable that a winter should be included). During the liability period the contractor is held responsible for all defects arising from materials and workmanship not being in accordance with the contract. The architect can issue instructions for such defective work or materials to be corrected immediately wherever they may be causing a nuisance to the client.

Schedule of Defects

At the end of the defects liability period the architect must produce a schedule of defects to be issued to the contractor within fourteen days after the date ending the liability period. The contractor is obliged to complete the items listed in the schedule within a reasonable period of its issue.

Final Completion Certificate

When all defects shown on the schedule have been corrected to the satisfaction of the architect, he will issue a final certificate to the client confirming that the works have been completed in accordance with the contract documents. This should mean the release of the $2\frac{1}{2}$ per cent retention fund held by the client, but in fact it means the quantity surveyor can proceed with the final account. This will involve payments to the contractor for work carried out as dayworks, variations, etc, and can often amount to a considerable sum, taking several months to work out.

Forms of Contract

JCT Standard Form of Contract

Although the contract form is correctly termed the JCT Standard Form of Contract, it is still common to hear it referred to as the RIBA Form of Contract. There are four versions available to meet different requirements:

(a) Used by local government authorities where quantities form part of the contract.
(b) The same as (a) but no quantities are supplied, although a specification and schedules may be provided.
(c) Used by private architects and employers where quantities form part of the contract.
(d) The same as (c) but no quantities are supplied, although a specification and schedules may be provided.

While there is sufficient guidance within the contract bills for the Clerk of Works to administer his responsibilities under the contract, it is advisable for him to possess a copy of the contract conditions, and the following pages will help him to understand the various clauses until he becomes more familiar with them.

Under each one of the versions shown the contract is for a lump sum payment to the contractor for completing the works laid down in the documents. The sum can be varied as well as the works according to the rights of each of the parties involved, i.e. either the client or the contractor.

The wording is not very precise in the contract regarding the quality of either workmanship or materials used in the contract. The specification generally refers to the various codes of practice and the British Standard Specification, which in themselves are rather indefinite.

Where there are no quantities provided, this will be stated within the contract, and reference will be made to any specification or schedules supplied.

Contracts are sometimes drawn 'under seal', which binds both parties to claims at common law for twelve years from the date upon which a difference is registered. Contracts which are not 'under seal' reduce the period under which a claim may be made to six years from the date upon which the difference is declared.

Clause 1: Contractor's Obligations

The contractor is obliged to carry out the works as shown in the contract drawings and bills, etc, to the reasonable satisfaction of the architect. This means that the Clerk of Works must always draw attention to any work which does not conform with this clause, although the architect may quite rightly decide the standard is in accordance with the intent of the specification.

Any discrepancies between the drawings or the bills should be brought to the attention of the architect, as well as any other matters which are likely to be contrary to current regulations. Although the Clerk of Works will collaborate with the contractor or his agent as much as possible, he should be careful in discussing any discrepancies with them before he has brought these to the attention of the architect. The architect will instruct the Clerk of Works what action has to be taken, and if necessary will issue an architect's instruction to cover the discrepancy.

Clause 2: Architect's Instructions

The architect has powers to issue instructions to the contractor for a number of reasons, and he can instruct the Clerk of Works to issue site instructions on these matters.

Clerk of Works' site instructions must be confirmed by an architect's instruction within two working days, which could include a Saturday or even a Sunday if the contractor is regularly working on these days. The Clerk of Works should make a note when architect's instructions are issued, and record any action taken by the contractor, as well as any effect such instructions may have upon the progress of the works. Such instructions might easily result in arbitration at a future date, so the Clerk of Works must make the necessary entries in the site diary at the time.

Clause 3: Contract Documents

The various documents included in the contract are listed under this clause, and have been referred to on previous pages of this book. No one has the right to alter the terms of the contract other than the client and the contractor, who may do so by mutual agreement.

Clause 4: Statutory Obligations

While it is the contractor's responsibility to deal with all statutory bodies such as local authorities, water boards, electricity boards, etc, it is also in the interests of the client to ensure that no errors are likely to affect the satisfactory completion of the contract. The Clerk of Works should keep himself informed upon all these matters, and should take advantage of any offer by the contractor for him to 'sit in' on any meetings taking place with statutory bodies.

Clause 5: Levels and Setting Out

It is easy to dismiss this as the responsibility of the contractor, but the presence of the Clerk of Works upon the site demands that he should check all levels and setting out at the appropriate time. It is obviously much more practical to check the setting out, etc, in conjunction with the contractor or his agent at the time it is carried out. Checking the setting out does not relieve the contractor of any of his responsibilities in the matter at any stage of the contract, but it does help to avoid any delay which may occur at a later stage and which may not be in the interests of the client.

Clause 6: Materials, Goods and Workmanship

The materials and workmanship are generally covered by implication as 'being the best of their kind' or to good general practice, etc, but this is very difficult to define; therefore, samples of materials and agreed standards of workmanship should be laid down at the outset of the work.

The Clerk of Works must maintain a close watch to ensure there is no variation from the specified materials, and where this does occur without instructions from the architect, he should notify the quantity surveyor as well as the architect. It must be remembered that the contractor has no cause to concern himself with the suitability of the materials specified by the architect, and for this reason the Clerk of Works must pay close attention to the performance of specified materials, bringing the architect's attention to any which may be doubtful. The contractor can be instructed by the architect to remove materials or workmen from the site under this clause if he considers it to be in the interests of the contract.

Clause 7: Royalties and Patent Rights

This clause is intended to protect the client from any claims which may arise because of the contractor using materials or methods likely to be the subject of copyright or patent. This could apply in the case of system building where the patent is held by one particular firm, which agrees to its system being used in a modified form by the contractor.

Clause 8: Foreman in Charge

The contract clearly states that the contractor must keep a 'competent' foreman on the site at all times to receive instructions from the architect, and any instructions given to the foreman in charge are regarded as having been given to the contractor himself. It might help to improve the supervision and control if the contractor was compelled to name his foreman in charge in the contract. Equally from the contractor's point of view it might clarify the position to some extent if the Clerk of Works was also named in the contract. At least it would establish two very important roles directly concerned with the construction on the site.

Clause 9: Access to the Site

The contractor must give reasonable access for inspection of the work on site, as well as at any workshop, factory, etc, where goods are manufactured specifically for the contract. This would not apply in the case of standard or proprietary goods which are specified. Access to the works implies provision of scaffolding, ladders, lighting, etc, to enable the Clerk of Works to perform his duties under the contract. Obviously the demands must be reasonable and due notice given where necessary to allow the contractor to provide the facilities for access.

Clause 10: Clerk of Works

This is probably the most controversial clause so far as the Clerk of Works is concerned, but it clearly outlines his responsibilities.

Just as with any other clause, the interpretation tends to be varied according to the person who is making the assessment, but again like each one of the remaining clauses it is subject to legal argument, and judicial decisions are not always so clear cut. The Clerk of Works should bear in mind that he is an inspector on behalf of the client, and while he may be under the direction of the architect, he cannot be absolved from his responsibilities to the employer. It is often said he is unable to give instructions on the site, yet he is expected to do so in the majority of instances. Legally no one can give an instruction under the contract other than the architect, not even the consultants, who might sometimes be engaged upon the major portion of the works; yet they cannot always wait for the architect to issue an instruction if they are to avoid delays or errors to the construction on site. To cover such emergencies the Clerk of Works is invariably asked to issue a site instruction, but to be effective this must be confirmed by the architect within two working days. It is obviously to avoid any variation to the design or cost of the contract that such restrictions are necessary.

Clause 11: Variations, Provisional and Prime Costs

Variations are a continuous source of difficulty on most contracts, as they affect not only the costs but also the completion date of the contract. A variation can also affect a number of other items apart from that referred to in the architect's instruction, and there might also be a dispute with the contractor whether it constitutes a variation. All instructions should be carefully noted by the Clerk of Works, with the effects such instructions may have upon other aspects of the works.

Provisional Sums are included within the contract sum to cover the cost of work that could not adequately be assessed at the time the contract was drawn up. This could involve the Clerk of Works in keeping separate records for work carried out by specialists.

Prime Costs are sums included within the contract sum for supplies which could not be selected at the time the contract was drawn up.

Contingency Sum is an amount within the contract to cover items which could not reasonably have been foreseen when the bills were produced. It is the architect's responsibility to control the expenditure of any of these items and he will issue instructions accordingly.

Dayworks. In some cases variations to the contract can be measured against a schedule of rates included with the contractor's tender figure, but other works can be difficult to measure and the contractor may wish to record the actual time and materials involved. He will claim this as daywork and the record sheets must be presented to the Clerk of Works for his signature confirming the accuracy of the claim. The contractor should notify the Clerk of Works before beginning any work he considers should be classified as daywork, and must present the sheets for signature in the week following the one in which the works were actually carried out.

Records should be kept by the Clerk of Works, noting the relevant details involved in the work and entering these in the site diary to be checked against the daywork sheets presented later by the contractor.

If the sheets are presented in accordance with the contract and the items recorded are correct, the Clerk of Works has no authority to refuse to sign them because he considers they are not qualified as daywork. He should make any observations he may have on the copy to be forwarded to the quantity surveyor, who will take note of such details when completing the final account.

Clause 12: Contract Bills

Any errors noted by the Clerk of Works in the bills should be brought to the attention of the architect immediately.

A contract which includes a bill of quantities should be reasonably easy for the Clerk of Works to follow, but where no bills are provided, it becomes very important to pay close attention to the detail drawings. Unless stated to the contrary, the bills will be drawn up in accordance with the procedure laid down in either the *Standard Method of Measurement for Building Works* or the *Code for the Measurement of Building Works in Small Dwellings*. The contract bills refer not only to the quantity of work involved but also to the quality so far as it can be ascertained, and the Clerk of Works should study the bills very carefully throughout the contract.

Clause 13: Contract Sum

This is the total sum for which the contractor has agreed to carry out all the works in accordance with the contract drawings and bills. The sum is subject to variation for a number of reasons: for example, it may be increased for additional works to the contract, or for any delays to the contract which are outside the contractor's liability; or it may be reduced where certain items are omitted from the works, although they may have the effect of increasing the unit price quoted by the contractor in his schedule of prices. The Clerk of Works must be particularly aware of any avoidable delays, bringing such matters to the attention of the architect and the quantity surveyor.

Clause 14: Materials and Goods Unfixed or Off Site

Materials delivered to site are included in the valuation each month, and therefore are the property of the client. The Clerk of Works must ensure that such materials are not removed from the site without the express permission of the architect, and are adequately protected at all times. Materials which have been approved and included in the valuations but retained in a factory or workshop off site should be inspected periodically by the Clerk of Works.

Clause 15: Practical Completion and Defects Liability

This can be a confusing and frustrating situation, as opinions differ on practical completion, and it is important to remember that when the architect issues the certificates of practical completion, it establishes the period for defects liability and the period for final measurement of the contract.

It also expresses the satisfaction of the architect with the work carried out, insofar as he can be expected to see the works, and it also ends the contractor's liability for damage to the works but not for latent defects.

The certificate entitles the contractor to terminate his insurance for the works, and to receive half the retention sum, leaving $2\frac{1}{2}$ per cent of the contract sum to cover his liabilities to the end of the defects liability period.

Defects which occur during that period are notified to the contractor on an architect's instruction. These defects must be attended to within a reasonable period or the employer will have the right to have the work carried out by others and charge all costs involved to the contractor.

It should be noted that frost damage occurring *after* practical completion of the contract is not the liability of the contractor.

Clause 16: Sectional Completion

This situation often arises where the client needs possession of part of the works before the whole of the contract is completed. An example of this can occur where the beginning of term on a school contract requires classrooms, gymnasia, or laboratories to be equipped while the remainder of the contract is proceeding. It is important to ensure that all outstanding or defective work is recorded and brought to the attention of the client as well as the contractor to avoid disputes at a later date.

Clause 17: Sub-Letting the Works

The contractor is not entitled to sub-let the whole of the works without the written consent of the employer, or part of the works without the written consent of the architect. This is to prevent the contractor from passing his responsibilities over to others, and to make certain that sub-letting will only be carried out under the terms of the contract.

Clause 17a is used by local government authorities to bind the contractor to observe all regulations concerning rates of pay and conditions in the area, and to keep proper records of wages paid and time worked on the site, etc, by his workmen. The contractor must also ensure that all sub-contractors conform to the same conditions, either on site or in workshops producing components for the contract.

Clause 18: Injury to Persons and Property

This establishes the liability of the contractor to indemnify the client against any claims under statute or common law for injury to persons or to property. It is important to note that the clause states 'unless due to any act or neglect of the Employer or for any person for whom the Employer is responsible'. The employer is responsible for the Clerk of Works so that any action or decision he may make might well involve the employer in a claim. This might easily cause the employer to take some action against the Clerk of Works, although it is most unlikely. It does emphasise, however, the importance of the Clerk of Works carrying out his duties with due care throughout the contract.

Clause 19: Insurances against Injury to Persons and Property

The previous clause was to ensure that the employer was indemnified against any claims, while this clause ensures that the contractor and all sub-contractors are equally indemnified against claims which may arise through carrying out the works.

Clause 20: Insurance of the Works against Fire

The works must be adequately insured against fire during the whole of the construction period, as the client has already paid for the project through monthly valuations (with the exception of the retention sum). The client's legal adviser will normally investigate all insurances taken out by the contractor under the terms of the contract, to ensure they are in order.

There are two further sections to this clause, 20(b) and 20(c), under which the employer takes out the necessary insurances himself.

The first is an alternative to the contractor taking out the insurance, and in this case it might seem that the contractor is not bound to take the same amount of care as he would if he were the insurer. In such instances the Clerk of Works must pay particular attention to any conditions likely to create a fire hazard, and he should report this immediately to the architect.

Clause 20(c) applies where the contract is for alterations to an existing building which is already occupied by the client and will require suitable insurances in the name of the client.

Clause 21: Possession and Completion

This clause authorises the contractor to take possession of the site in order to carry out the works and to return it to the client when the works are completed. Quite often there is some pressure from the architect or the client for the contractor to take possession and start the work to meet the conditions of a grant or subsidy payable to the client, and the contractor may not always be prepared to accept the site in the conditions existing.

Any delay with the date for possession of the site will naturally affect the date for completion of the contract, and while this will be of importance to the client, it might also give the contractor the right to claim for loss and expense through not being able to proceed with the contract as he planned.

An inspection of site should be arranged when the contractor takes possession, and all relevant facts which may interfere with his progress should then be noted.

Clause 22: Damages for Non-completion

The employer has the right to deduct damages for non-completion of the contract after all claims for variations and delays have been considered by the architect. In certain instances the damages will be for an agreed rate, while in others they will be assessed damages.

Clause 23: Extension of Time

Architect's instructions, inclement weather, fire breaking out on the contract site, riots, and many other instances may be put forward as reasons for an extension of time by the contractor. This particular clause is frequently a reason for reference to the Clerk of Works' site diary, and too much emphasis cannot be placed upon the importance of this being kept up to date. Quite often the Clerk of Works' diary is the only detailed record of site incidents, and it is equally important that it is legible and unambiguous. It is almost impossible to determine what grounds are likely to be invoked as a claim under this clause, making it difficult to decide which matters are important when making entries in the diary.

The site diary should provide a fair and accurate record of the work and progress on the site, and should not be a Clerk of Works' biased view of the contractor's progress and endeavour. It must be remembered that a contract is an agreement between two parties who desire neither to gain nor lose more than their just entitlement under the contract, and that is how the Clerk of Works should interpret the situation when entering up his records. He must be scrupulously fair in his assessment if his records are to be of value at a later stage.

Claims which may be made under this clause might be for delays in providing information, or even for interference by the Clerk of Works in the progress of the work, so close attention to records is important.

Clause 24: Disturbance of Regular Progress of the Works

The contractor can claim additional payment for any delays to progress caused through lack of information, drawings, levels, or instructions from the architect or those representing him on the site.

Claims must be made in writing within a reasonable period after delay to the progress becomes apparent, and if the architect agrees with the claim, the amount will be added to the contract sum and included in interim payments.

Claims can be included under this clause where work has been opened up for inspection upon instructions from the architect and is found to be in accordance with the contract specification. Testing of materials, etc, will also qualify for additional payment if carried out under instructions and is proved to comply with the conditions of the contract.

Delays caused by tradesmen employed under clause 29 will also qualify for additional payment if this affects the progress of the contract.

Delays caused through discrepancies between the contract bills and the contract drawings can also be a reason for claims, and postponement of any part of the works by the architect.

Interference with the work by the Clerk of Works could well be a claim for delay by the contractor and the Clerk of Works would do well to remember that all directions must be issued in the prescribed manner

Clause 25: Determination by the Employer

The employer can determine the contract for an act of corruption on the part of the contractor, failing to proceed with the works in a manner stated by the contract, or for bankruptcy. Unfortunately the latter situation might easily occur almost overnight without the employer being aware of it. Where it seems likely that the employer will determine the contract, the Clerk of Works should draw up an accurate record of the works at that time, including any items liable to cause loss or damage to the client.

Clause 26: Determination by the Contractor

The contractor has the right to determine the contract under certain conditions and is entitled to recover loss of profit as well as any damages under the contract.

He can determine the contract for non-payment of a certificate, interference or obstruction by the employer in the payment of certificates, and delay in proceeding with the works due to matters that are not the concern of the contractor. Such delays could occur following a serious fire on the site, or even repeated strike action. The Clerk of Works cannot influence the situation but his records may prove important in the claims which follow.

Clause 27: Nominated Sub-contractors

The contractor is responsible for all work carried out by nominated sub-contractors just as though he was carrying out the work himself. Defects in materials and in workmanship carried out by the sub-contractor remain the liability of the main contractor.

If there is an element of design included in the contract with the nominated sub-contractor, the contractor may refuse to accept any liability for this by claiming that design is the function of the architect. Delays caused by the nominated sub-contractor may form the basis of a claim for an extension of contract by the contractor; this might be either delay in proceeding with the work or even failing to provide information which could delay other trades.

Clause 28: Nominated Suppliers

Nominated suppliers are often dealt with in the same way as nominated sub-contractors, i.e. through provisional sums or prime costs items expended on the instructions of the architect. The contractor is allowed to add 2½ per cent on the price allowed for the nominated sub-contractor and 5 per cent on the nominated supplier's price, but he has no responsibility for the quality of the goods ordered; he is only responsible for ordering, receiving and providing storage, and in some instances he is not even responsible for fixing the goods. The Clerk of Works must maintain close supervision over nominated supplies, both on their quality and deliveries, and also when they are included into the works.

The contractor may claim delays because of problems in fitting nominated goods and the Clerk of Works should keep a close check on such possibilities.

Clause 29: Artists and Tradesmen

Under certain circumstances the employer will wish to call in specialists to carry out certain parts of the works, but they will not be classed either as sub-contractors or nominated sub-contractors. Because of this the contractor bears no responsibility for them other than to allow them free access to the site to proceed with their work.

The Clerk of Works may be obliged to maintain records of the work and progress of such specialists throughout their stay upon the contract.

Clause 30: Certificates and Payments

All payments to the contractor are made under this clause, and the Clerk of Works will only be affected where the valuation involves unsatisfactory workmanship or materials which do not conform to the specification. Any matters likely to affect the valuation should always be brought to the attention of the quantity surveyor as soon as possible, to enable him to make the necessary adjustment to his certificate.

The Clerk of Works can assist the quantity surveyor by making sure that sufficient records are available at the end of the contract, perhaps when he himself will no longer be available to answer queries concerning the contract.

Clause 31: Fluctuations

Contracts may be based on a 'fixed price', but where fluctuations are permitted within the contract, the Clerk of Works may be required to check labour on site and certify the work-sheets of the contractor each week or month. Sometimes the quantity surveyor will agree these payments on a pro-rata basis, which avoids a lot of paperwork and achieves the same result.

Clause 32: Outbreak of Hostilities

Clause 33: War Damage

Both these clauses are included to regulate the situation should an emergency occur, as it might bring about the termination of the contract to the disadvantage of both parties.

Clause 34: Antiquities

The likelihood of this clause becoming operative are greater in some parts of the country than in others, and the Clerk of Works must be alert to the discovery of matters of architectural or archaeological interest within the contract boundaries. Many instances have occurred where items which are listed under 'treasure-trove' have been discovered and not disclosed at the time, leading to further investigations at a later stage interfering with the progress of the works.

Clause 35: Arbitration

Either contractor or client has the right to agree to refer any dispute which may arise between them to an arbitrator. The powers of the arbitrator are wide, allowing him to review all decisions made by the architect where they concern the point in dispute.

As all information is reviewed, the site diary may play an important part in providing information of the situation on the site at the relevant period. As stated previously, therefore, an accurate and unbiased record is important.

ICE Conditions of Contract

The ICE Conditions of Contract were first issued in December 1945 after agreement between the Institution of Civil Engineers and the Federation of Civil Engineering Contractors. In January 1950 the conditions were revised by the two parties in conjunction with the Association of Consulting Engineers, and a third edition was issued in March 1951. The fourth edition was issued in 1955, and additional clauses in 1969 (Clause 69

Metrication), 1970 (Clause 70 Tax Fluctuations), and 1971 (Clause 71 Value Added Tax). The conditions have again been revised and in June 1973 the fifth edition was issued.

The whole document consists of the conditions of contract numbering seventy-two clauses; a form of tender, including an appendix stating the period of the contract, period of maintenance, liquidated damages, insurances and several similar aspects; a form of agreement to be signed by the employer and the contractor; and a form of bond to be signed by the contractor and his sureties, presumably a bank or insurance company.

Clause 1: Definitions

All persons are defined in the contract according to their role, and terms and expressions used in the contract are equally defined. The Clerk of Works who has been engaged on other forms of contract should note the differences outlined in para (d) of this clause, which states: 'Engineer's Representative means a person being the resident engineer or assistant of the Engineer or Clerk of Works appointed from time to time by the Employer or the Engineer and notified in writing to the Contractor by the Engineer to perform the functions set forth in Clause 2(1).' This implies that the Clerk of Works is clearly the representative of the engineer and not of the employer.

Clause 2: Engineer's Representative

Where the Clerk of Works is fulfilling this role, his duties are clearly defined, 'to watch and supervise the construction completion and maintenance of the Works'.

This clause has been extended in the revised edition to enable the engineer, or his representative, to appoint others to assist him, but he must notify the contractor of the names and function of these assistants. These assistants have no power to issue instructions to the contractor other than those which affect their duties regarding materials or workmanship in accordance with the specification and drawings, for instance on a large contract where inspectors of works may be employed. The engineer can extend the powers of his representative on site by informing the contractor in writing, but these powers will not concern delays, extra costs, or extension of time, etc.

It would be advisable for the Clerk of Works to be clearly aware of his role upon the site when he is appointed.

Clause 3: Assignment

Clause 4: Sub-letting

The contractor cannot assign the contract or any part of it unless he receives written consent from the employer. Such a possibility might arise where the contractor was unable to undertake the contract because of the financial involvement, and it might be in the interests of the employer to allow a large organisation to underwrite the contract, while allowing the contractor to carry out the works.

All sub-contractors selected by the contractor must be approved by the engineer, and details of their past activities are invariably noted before approval is given.

The contractor will remain liable for all work carried out by the sub-contractors and will be obliged to correct any faulty workmanship or materials at his own expense, should anything occur to determine the continuity of the sub-contractor on the site.

It is interesting to note that the contractor has no need to obtain approval from the engineer for 'piece-work' labour on the site. A careful record should be maintained in the site diary of all sub-contractors on site, not only for discussion at site meetings but for information when subsequent contracts are being considered.

Clause 5: Interpretation of Documents

Clause 6: Supply of Documents

Clause 7: Drawings and Instructions

5. The documents forming the contract are to be taken as being mutually explanatory of each other, and where any ambiguity or discrepancies occur, these will be explained and adjusted by the engineer with an instruction in writing to the contractor. The documents under the contract are as follows:

> The Form of Agreement
> The Form of Tender
> The Contract Drawings
> The Conditions of Contract
> The Contract Specification
> The Priced Bill of Quantities.

6. The contract drawings will remain in the custody of the engineer, together with the specification and the bill of quantities, but once the tender has been accepted, the contractor will be supplied with two copies of the drawings, specification and bills of quantities. He will also be able to receive further copies at his own expense should it be necessary, but at the end of the contract all drawings and specifications must be returned to the engineer.

In practice, the contractor is generally supplied with additional sets of drawings as he requires these for negotiations with sub-contractors and suppliers, and for use within his own organisation.

7. The engineer is empowered to issue additional drawings where he considers this necessary for the purpose of the contract, and he can also issue further instructions to the contractor in respect of the works; the contractor must comply with these drawings and instructions. The contractor must give adequate notice to the engineer of any drawings he considers to be necessary to assist him in carrying out work which is not properly explained in the drawings in his possession. The Clerk of Works should note in good time, wherever possible, any instances where he considers additional drawings may be required, in order that the engineer will have time to prepare these. Any ambiguities or discrepancies in the drawings or large-scale details may be submitted as a basis for additional payments by the contractor at a later stage, and by studying the drawings at the correct phase in the contract the Clerk of Works may help to avoid this situation.

One copy of the drawings and specification must be retained on the site by the contractor and must be available for inspection and use of the engineer's representative at all reasonable times.

Clause 8: Contractor's Responsibilities

Clause 9: Contract Agreement

Clause 10: Sureties

8. Subject to any provisions within the contract, it is the responsibility of the contractor to construct and maintain the works, providing all necessary labour and materials. He must supply all plant and equipment required for the construction of the works, and carry out any temporary works necessary to complete the main works. He must take full responsibility for the stability and safety of all site operations and methods of construction

but not for any temporary or permanent works designed by the engineer.

9. The contract agreement is prepared by the employer, and when a tender has been accepted from the contractor for the work concerned, he is invited by the employer to complete the agreement. In practice this is often a formality in the sense that a contract has already been made by the employer inviting the contractor to tender, and an official tender having been submitted to the contractor. Many contracts are not signed by the parties concerned until well into the contract period.

10. The contractor is obliged to provide two sureties, or to obtain the guarantee of a bank or insurance company to be jointly bound with the contractor in a sum not exceeding 10 per cent of the tender for the completion of the works according to the contract. The arrangements for this bond can sometimes take a little time, which has a delaying effect upon the completion of the documents, as already stated. Unless the contract is amended accordingly, the contractor must pay all expenses incurred in the provision of the sureties to the contract.

When the sureties have been offered by the contractor, they must be approved by the employer, whose legal adviser will no doubt wish to examine all the relevant documents concerned in the arrangements.

Clause 11: Inspection of Site

The contractor must visit the site and assure himself of the conditions and nature of the ground and surroundings, availability of access, and all the plant and materials he considers will be necessary to carry out the works. In certain instances he will be provided by the employer with additional information to assist him, but this will not imply any warranty, as the contractor will be advised to check such information for accuracy before using it in his estimate.

Borehole information is usually available to the contractor, as the employer will have authorised the engineer to carry out a site investigation to plan the works in the first instance.

The contractor must satisfy himself that the tender he submits is sufficient to cover the works and conditions outlined in the contract, and that the prices shown against the items in the bills of quantities, as well as in the schedules of rates and prices, are all sufficient to cover his obligations within the contract. This must include any work required during the maintenance period as well as during construction.

Clause 12: Adverse Physical Conditions and Obstructions

(1) When the contract has begun and physical conditions are such that it might reasonably be judged the contractor was unable to foresee them, he may submit a claim to the engineer, based on the schedule of rates and prices, for additional labour and the use of further plant on site. The claim must be submitted in writing, outlining the problem and specifying the additional work and plant involved, together with all consequential delays.

The Clerk of Works will have noted all relevant details of the situation and should forward a report to the Engineer as soon as possible to assist him when considering the contractor's claim.

(2) Upon receiving notice from the contractor the engineer may ask for an estimate of the cost involved, with the measures the contractor is taking or proposing to take. Alternatively he may give approval to the proposals with or without modifications, or give instructions how the matter is to be dealt with. A further choice the engineer can make is to suspend that part of the work under Clause 40 or issue a variation under Clause 51.

(3) If the engineer decides that the contractor could not reasonably have foreseen the existing situation, or at least could not be expected to have foreseen the whole of the problem, he can award an extension of time to offset any delays the contractor may have suffered thereby.

(4) If the engineer decides that the contractor should have foreseen the position, he will inform the contractor in writing as soon as he makes the decision.

Where the engineer has allowed the contractor to proceed either in whole or in part with the work, the contractor must provide the Clerk of Works with the labour strength involved in such work, and lists of any materials which are used.

The Clerk of Works must keep an accurate record of such works, since he may be called upon to certify the labour and materials involved when the contractor submits his claim-sheets. The Clerk of Works will not be authorising payment, merely confirming the accuracy of the information. It is advisable to check all vouchers in connection with materials, as these are difficult to check otherwise.

Clause 13: Work to be to Satisfaction of Engineer

Not only must the contractor carry out the construction of the work in accordance with the drawings and specifications, this work must be to the satisfaction of the engineer.

Where the Clerk of Works is the engineer's representative, it follows that the work must be carried out to his satisfaction, but this must not be unreasonable. The contract clearly states that the contractor must comply with all instructions and directions given to him, but so far as the Clerk of Works is concerned this must be upon matters on which he is authorised to give instructions. He must not vary the work given on the drawings and specifications so that the employer has to meet additional payments.

Instructions must not be given which remove the contractor's liability within the contract, and the Clerk of Works must take care when issuing instructions or directions that may be wrongly interpreted. Instructions should always be given in writing and a copy passed to the engineer at the same time.

Clause 14: Programme to be Provided

Within twenty-one days of the acceptance of his tender the contractor must submit his programme to the engineer showing the order and the methods he proposes to use to execute the works shown on the drawings. Where the engineer considers the work is not proceeding to the programme, he will be entitled to ask the contractor to produce a revised programme with such modifications to the original programme as to complete the work within the contract period, or within any period of extension granted under the contract.

Where the engineer considers it necessary, he may oblige the contractor to produce detailed information of his proposed methods for carrying out either temporary or permanent sections of the works. The engineer will be obliged to inform the contractor in writing whether he considers the proposals are acceptable or not, and in the latter instance the contractor must make the required alterations to satisfy him.

Approval by the engineer of the proposals will not relieve the contractor of his responsibilities under the contract.

The Clerk of Works should note the periods set aside for each operation in the programme as well as the sequence proposed, and where this does not appear to be in the best interests of the contract he should draw this fact to the attention of the engineer. When the contract is in progress the Clerk of Works must keep the programme marked up each day, so that an accurate record is available to the engineer. Where the progress is falling behind, this should be reported to the engineer on the weekly progress reports.

Clause 15: Contractor's Superintendence

The contractor must provide all the necessary supervision during the progress of the works, and the supervisors must be persons with adequate knowledge of the operations to be carried out. They must understand the techniques required to avoid hazards and prevent accidents occurring during the progress of the works.

A responsible agent must be retained on site during the progress of the work, and must remain so long as the engineer considers this to be necessary. The agent must be in complete charge of the works and will receive all instructions and directions on behalf of the contractor from the engineer or his representative.

Clause 16: Removal of Contractor's Employees

The contractor must employ workmen who are skilled and experienced in the work they are to perform, and where the engineer considers any of the men are not capable, he is entitled to instruct the contractor to remove them from the site.

Men who are guilty of misconduct, incompetence or negligence should be removed from the site.

The Clerk of Works should take care not to demand the removal of any workman from the site; he should tactfully refer the matter to the engineer for him to deal with. Where the Clerk of Works considers the agent to be incompetent, again he should refer the facts to the engineer.

It must always be remembered that a man can only be removed from the site when it is proved he is negligent, incompetent, etc, and care must be taken with accusations which may be difficult to substantiate, for such a person might easily take legal action for wrongful dismissal.

Clause 17: Setting Out

The contractor is responsible for establishing all levels and setting out the works in accordance with the information supplied to him; in addition he must supply all instruments and equipment for the setting out of the works as well as supplying all necessary labour. The contractor is obliged to do the setting out, but he is also obliged to provide the equipment and labour to assist the engineer or his representative to check the work as it proceeds.

Any errors arising during the course of the works that may be attributable to the setting out or establishing levels must be corrected by the contractor entirely at his own expense.

The Clerk of Works should check the setting out and levels before the work progresses too far, although it must not be overlooked that the responsibility is entirely that of the contractor, and his agent. Where errors of this nature do arise the contractor may well claim the responsibility is not entirely his, due to incorrect data having been supplied by the engineer or his representative. Such a possibility is very real, and the Clerk of Works should ensure that any directions or instructions concerning levels or setting out are given in writing after being thoroughly checked.

The Clerk of Works should check that all benchmarks and sight-rails are correctly established and marked so as to be easily identified; they must also be protected and maintained as long as necessary throughout the contract, for they may be required for confirmation of the setting out. The Clerk of Works should determine which of the benchmarks should be retained, and make constant checks during the construction.

Clause 18: Boreholes and Exploratory Excavation

Where it becomes necessary to take further boreholes or to carry out exploratory excavation, the contractor should be given instructions in writing. If no provision has been made in the bills for such work, the engineer will issue this as a variation order, but in either case the Clerk of Works should keep a record of such activities. The type of machine used for boring and the labour and hours worked should be noted, and the information available from other boreholes used as a comparison while the work is proceeding.

Clause 19: Safety and Security

The contractor is obliged to provide adequate safety precautions on the site and the works must be kept in such state as will avoid any danger to all persons entitled to be on the site. He must also provide adequate fencing, warning signs, lighting, etc, to ensure protection of the works, and where the safety of the public is affected he must take all the necessary precautions.

If the employer engages any labour to carry out works upon the site, he will be obliged to take the same precautions for that part of the works as applies to the contractor. Where sub-contractors are engaged by the employer, he must instruct them to comply with these same precautions.

Clause 20: Care of the Works

The contractor is responsible for the care of the works right from the date the work begins, and will remain so until 14 days after the engineer has issued a certificate of completion. If certificates are issued for part-completion of the works, then the contractor will cease to be responsible for that part of the works from 14 days after the engineer issues the certificate. Where there is still work outstanding during the period of maintenance, the contractor will remain responsible for this up to the time it is completed.

The contractor is responsible for the whole of the works in respect of any damage or loss, and will be forced to make it good at his own expense. This clause makes allowance for any damage or loss which may arise through war or similar occurrence, or to any fault in the design of the work other than that for which the contractor may be responsible. Any loss or damage caused through the employer occupying the works will be made good by the contractor if the engineer issues an instruction to this effect, and the cost will be met by the employer.

Clause 21: Insurance of the Works, etc

Clause 22: Damage to Persons & Property

Clause 23: Insurance Against Damage to Persons, etc

Clause 24: Accident or Injury to Workmen

Clause 25: Contractor's Failure to Insure

The insurances taken out by the contractor must include one in the joint names of the employer and the contractor for any loss or damage to the works during the period of construction. The policy must cover any damage arising as a result of the contractor's responsibility during the period of maintenance, as well as all the plant brought on the site. The policy must cover full value of the work as it stands from time to time.

The contractor must also indemnify the Employer, under the policies, against any claims in respect of injury to persons or property arising from the construction of the works.

The contractor is not expected to insure against matters which are the sole responsibility of the employer, such as wayleaves and rights concerning light, air, etc, or any injury or damage to persons or property as a result of negligence on the part of other contractors or the employer and his agents.

The contractor must insure in the joint names of the employer and the contractor against any injury, loss, or damage to persons or to property caused through the execution of the works, and the insurance must be taken out immediately the contract begins. The amount payable must be at least the amount shown as the tender sum, and the company insuring the works must be approved by the employer. The receipts for the premiums must also be produced so that the employer can assure himself these are in order.

The contractor is responsible for insuring against accidents or injury to his workmen as well as those of the sub-contractors. He must also indemnify the employer against such claims.

There is no reason for the contractor to take out insurances specifically on behalf of the sub-contractors, but adequate insurance must be taken by the sub-contractors themselves and the policies checked. The Clerk of Works should clear his own position with regard to insurance cover:

(a) Is he covered by the employer or the contractor?
(b) Is he covered in the event of liability for neglect, etc, which may result in an accident to persons or property?

It is usual for the employer or his legal adviser to see all insurance policy premium receipts before the contract is signed, at the same time as the bond is produced.

Subsequent premium receipts must be produced as they arise so that the employer may be assured they are in order, and where the contractor is neglectful in paying such premiums, the employer is entitled to pay these himself and deduct any such sums from monies due to the contractor.

Clause 26: Notices and Payment of Fees

The contractor must give all notices and pay any fees due under statutory regulations, Act of Parliament, byelaws, etc, in order that he can proceed with the works. Where the engineer confirms the payment of these dues, the amounts will become repayable through the contract. Where the contractor is complying with the drawings or an instruction from the engineer, he will not be required to indemnify the employer, but the engineer will issue a variation to correct this situation.

Clause 27: Public Utilities Street Works Act 1950

The employer will notify the contractor whether any of the works are emergency works or are to be carried out in controlled land or prospectively maintained highway; this information should be given before the work starts.

Where any variation is issued affecting the above, then this will be drawn to the contractor's attention at the time.

Notices under this Act will be served by the employer, and the contractor must give notice of his intention to start such work. The notice must be in writing to the employer, stating the date and the place where work is to begin at least 21 days before work can begin. If the contractor does not carry out the work within two months of giving notice then he must repeat the procedure all over again. Any delays to the contract arising from a variation issued by the engineer for works in connection with these regulations will be given consideration by the engineer for any extension of time.

In carrying out the works under this Act the Contractor will still be liable for compliance with any regulations and must indemnify the employer against any claims.

Clause 28: Patent Rights and Royalties

Many patent processes are concerned in the construction industry, as in other industries, and the contractor must indemnify the employer against any claims arising from such a source.

Clause 29: Interference with Traffic and Adjoining Property

Access in or around the site must not interfere unnecessarily with the convenience and rights of the public, and private roads, passageways, public roads and pavements must not be unduly obstructed.

Care must be taken with storage of plant and materials, as well as in carrying out the works to ensure a proper access is maintained, even by providing alternative access.

Unwarranted interference with the rights of people in adjoining properties may be regarded as a nuisance constituting a liability against the contractor. All work must be carried out without unreasonable noise or disturbance either by day or by night, and the employer must be indemnified against any claims. The Clerk of Works should maintain accurate records in respect of this clause as subsequent claims may involve the employer and the engineer in litigation.

Clause 30: Avoidance of Damage to Highways

All routes used to gain access to the site should be given consideration at the outset of the contract, and where there is likelihood of possible damage to the highway, because of site traffic, then the engineer should be informed of transport details.

This problem can be best dealt with by discussions with the highway authority early in the contract, and the Clerk of Works should maintain a record of the volume and incidence of the traffic using the relevant routes during the contract, in particular noting dates and times of peak traffic or special loads.

The contractor will be held responsible for strengthening bridges or for any road alterations which may be necessary for the movement of plant or equipment required to carry out the works, and the employer must be indemnified against any claims in respect of damage to either. Any damage occurring to bridges or roads communicating with the site through transport of materials or prefabricated items for the contract should be reported to the engineer when the contractor receives a claim from the authority concerned. Where the haulier is required to indemnify the highway authority against damage to bridges, roads, etc, by Act of Parliament, the employer cannot be held responsible.

In other instances the employer will negotiate and settle all claims as well as indemnifying the contractor against claims, unless the engineer considers there was a failure on the part of the contractor to provide reasonable means to prevent damage occurring. In such cases the amount certified by the engineer to be due to the contractor's failure shall be deducted from any monies due to the contractor.

Clause 31: Facilities for other Contractors

The contractor does not have exclusive rights to the site and must allow reasonable access to statutory authorities and contractors employed by the employer on a separate contract.

The Clerk of Works should record any problems of this nature which may arise during the contract, and so far as possible the contractor should be encouraged to hold meetings with other contractors concerned to overcome differences affecting responsibility and liability.

Where the contractor is involved in any delays or cost through complying with this clause because of circumstances which an experienced contractor could not reasonably have foreseen, the engineer will consider any such extension of time or repayment to which the contractor may be entitled.

Clause 32: Fossils, etc

Fossils, coins, articles of value or antiquity, of geological interest or architectural merit, if discovered during excavations must be reported to the Clerk of Works, who will notify the engineer.

Many valuable discoveries have been made in this way; where such findings are labelled 'treasure-trove' they become the property of the Crown and any attempt to conceal the facts may result in prosecution.

Where items of archaeological interest occur there may be delays to the contract because of the investigations which follow; such possibilities are inclined to deter certain persons from reporting such 'finds' and the Clerk of Works should be alert for such possibilities where these may be likely.

Clause 33: Clearance of Site on Completion

On completion of the work, the contractor must remove all plant, surplus materials, debris and temporary works to leave the site and the permanent construction in a satisfactory condition.

Clause 34: Rates of Wages, Hours and Conditions

Wherever conditions and wages for the region are laid down by agreement between the negotiating parties for the region, contractors must confirm that they are observing these conditions and have done so for at least three months before the submission of the tender.

Where there are no agreements, the rates and conditions must be equivalent to those generally observed by contractors in similar circumstances in the region. If conditions are less than stated, this constitutes a breach of contract affecting the contractor's right to extension of time through labour problems, besides the employer's right to claim damages. Where he is aware of circumstances contrary to this clause the Clerk of Works should record the matter and notify the engineer. It is the contractor's responsibility to ensure that all sub-contractors and suppliers are complying with this clause.

The conditions, etc, are those at present prescribed by the Civil Engineering Construction Conciliation Board for Great Britain, and must comply with the Fair Wages Resolution passed by the House of Commons on 14 October 1946.

Clause 35: Returns of Labour and Plant

The contractor is obliged to supply a daily return of labour employed on the contract, including those sub-contractors for whom he is responsible. Information should also be supplied on the type of plant in use and on site, whether operating or otherwise.

The Clerk of Works will find such information necessary to compile his reports to the engineer and must insist upon such information being provided.

Clause 36: Materials and Workmanship

All materials and workmanship must comply with the specification, and tests must be carried out where directed either at the place of manufacture or on site. The contractor must provide all facilities and labour to enable the works or materials to be tested, and samples of materials should be submitted for approval before inclusion in the work. Where tests are required through an independent source and this is not catered for in the bills, the contractor will be obliged to meet the cost where the materials do not comply with the specification; otherwise the cost will be met by the employer.

Clause 37: Access to Site

The Engineer or his representative must be allowed access to the site or any other place where work is prepared for the contract. Any authorised person nominated by the engineer must be allowed similar access, but at all times demand for access must not be unreasonable. Where manufacture is proceeding in factories or workshops, the method of manufacture should be inspected early on in production.

Clause 38: Examination of Work before Covering Up

Facilities must be provided to enable the Clerk of Works to inspect any work before it is covered over permanently, and reasonable notice should be given to enable inspections to be carried out, especially with drains, sewers and foundations. It is equally important that the Clerk of Works does not delay carrying out his inspections, or the contractor may be justified in claiming a delay to the contract. Where work has been covered up, it will be necessary for a written instruction to be issued by the engineer or his representative, and work which does not comply with the specification will be repeated at the expense of the contractor; if it does comply, the cost will be borne by the employer.

Clause 39: Removal of Improper Work and Materials

Any materials not in accordance with the specification must be removed from site upon instructions to this effect from the engineer, and faulty workmanship must be taken down and reconstructed to the satisfaction of the engineer.

Instructions must also be complied with in the time stated on the instruction, otherwise the employer may have the work carried out by other contractors with the expenses involved charged to the contractor. Failure by the Clerk of Works or the engineer to disapprove of any work or materials does not prejudice their power to disapprove such work or materials at a subsequent stage.

Clause 40: Suspension of the Work

The engineer may suspend the whole or part of the works by informing the contractor in writing to this effect, and during the suspended period the works must be protected to the satisfaction of the engineer. The contractor is entitled to be paid for any extra cost incurred through the suspension of the work unless it is provided for in the contract, or because of weather conditions, default on the part of the contractor, or for the safety of the works. The engineer will take into consideration any of these facts when assessing an extension of time to the contractor. Where the work is delayed for three months, unless the delay is provided for in the contract, the contractor may submit a written notice to the engineer for permission to proceed with the work within 28 days. If permission is not granted, the contractor may assume that the whole of the works or the part in question has been abandoned.

The Clerk of Works must give special attention to recording the situation arising each day when these circumstances have been met, owing to the difficulty in assessing the true facts at a subsequent stage in the contract.

Clause 41: Commencement of Work

Clause 42: Possession of Site

Clause 43: Time for Completion

Clause 44: Extension of Time

Clause 45: Night and Sunday Work

41. Within a reasonable period after acceptance of the tender the engineer will notify the contractor of the date for commencement of the works and the contractor will be obliged to start the work within a reasonable period

from this date and proceed with diligence to complete the work.

42. The employer must give the contractor either the whole of the site or such parts as are necessary for him to proceed in accordance with his programme once the date for commencement of the works has been issued. If the contractor is delayed because of failure to grant him possession of the site, he will be entitled to an extension of time unless the matter is provided for in the contract.

Special or temporary wayleaves for access to the site must be arranged by the contractor, who will also bear any expenses arising.

43. The whole of the works and any section shown in the appendix to be completed within a certain time shall be handed over to the employer within the stated period, which will be calculated from the date for commencement of the works. Any extension of time granted under Clause 44 will be taken into account when assessing the date for completion.

44. Extensions of time may be granted by the engineer for variations to the contract, increased quantities, exceptional adverse weather conditions, or any special circumstances which may occur. The contractor must notify the engineer within 28 days of any circumstances which have caused delay to the contract, giving full details and particulars. The engineer will give full consideration to the circumstances and assess the period of the extension, unless he does not consider that the contractor is entitled to an extension of time, in which case he will notify the contractor of this in writing and also the employer of his decision.

The engineer may review the circumstances when the certificate of final completion is due and grant an extension of time, but no extension can be reduced at this stage.

45. None of the works shall be carried out during the night or on Sunday unless this is provided for in the bills or approved by the engineer for the safety of the works, etc.

Clause 46: Rate of Progress

Where the rate of progress suggests that the contractor is unlikely to complete the works by the contract date, and there are no further reasons why an extension of time should be granted, the engineer will inform the contractor of this in writing, instructing him to take the necessary action to rectify the situation.

The contractor should inform the engineer of the action he proposes to take, and if this involves working at night or on Sundays, then the engineer must grant permission if there is no practical alternative. In such an instance, the contractor will be obliged to carry out the work without unreasonable disturbance and must indemnify the employer against any claims which may arise because of the work.

Clause 47: Liquidated Damages

If the contractor fails to complete the whole of the works, or any section of the works scheduled for completion by an agreed date in the contract, and he is not entitled to any further extensions of time for the work, then a sum of money as stated in the appendix will be deducted from any monies due to the contractor, and this will be regarded as liquidated damages. These are agreed sums payable for each day or each week in which the contract is delayed, and are not to be regarded as penalty clauses in the contract, as the sums are purely nominal and do not reflect the loss caused to the employer.

Payment of these damages does not relieve the contractor of any of his obligations under the contract.

The damages will be reduced in proportion for any part of the works certified as complete by the engineer and occupied by the employer before the actual date of completion.

Clause 48: Completion Certificate

When the contractor considers that the whole of the works have been completed in accordance with the terms of the contract, he can notify the engineer or his representative in writing, together with an undertaking to complete any outstanding work during the period of maintenance.

The engineer or his representative will confirm that the work is complete or issue instructions in writing to the contractor specifying the work he considers must be completed before the contractor will be entitled to the completion certificate. Where the contract includes completion for sections of the works, the completion certificate may be issued for that part of the work concerned under the same conditions. Unless the certificate states it, reinstatement of ground surfaces is not included.

Clause 49: Maintenance and Defects

The period of maintenance is stated in the appendix to the Form of Tender and is calculated from the date given on the certificate of completion issued by the engineer. If it becomes of relevance, the certificate of completion will be assessed as having been issued at midnight preceding the date shown on the certificate.

The contractor may be issued with a list of items to be corrected when the certificate of completion is issued, and having undertaken to complete the items, these should have been completed within a reasonable time. If these items have not been completed, they will be added to a list of all defects and remedial works which will be drawn up and issued to the contractor as soon as practicable after the end of the maintenance period, but not later than 14 days after that date.

The Clerk of Works will prepare the list for the engineer to issue with a notification for these to be corrected.

Where the work at fault is due to materials or workmanship which do not comply with the specification, or is due to the contractor's neglect or failure to comply with his obligations under the contract, the work will be carried out at his expense.

Where the work at fault is due to causes outside the liability of the contractor, it will be paid for as additional work and an instruction issued to that effect by the engineer.

The contractor must complete all defects and remedial works notified to him by the engineer during the period of maintenance, and where he fails to carry out the work after due notice, the employer is entitled to have the work carried out by other contractors and may recover the total expense incurred from any monies due to the contractor.

Clause 50: Contractor to Search

Defects or faults arising during the contract must be investigated by the contractor under the direction of the engineer, who will inform the contractor of this in writing.

If the defect or fault is one for which the contractor is liable under the contract, then he will have to bear the expenses incurred, but if he is not liable, the expense will be borne by the employer; but the contractor must still continue with the work as directed by the engineer.

Clause 51: Variations

Clause 52: Value of Variations
             Dayworks

51. The engineer is entitled to order variations to any part of the works and the contractor must carry out such variations when instructed by the engineer. The variations may change the character or quality of the work and lines or levels may be altered, but these variations will not invalidate the contract in any way, although the contractor will be entitled to payment for such work if it is not already covered in the bills of quantities.

Instructions may be given orally by the engineer or his representative, but they must be confirmed in writing later. Where instructions are given orally and have not been confirmed, the contractor may confirm the instruction in writing to the engineer, and if this is not contradicted in writing by the engineer, it will be regarded as a written instruction. Where the quantities in the work to be carried out are increased or decreased from those given in the bills, but are not the result of any variation in the works, it is not necessary to issue any instruction on the matter. The Clerk of Works has no power to vary the works without the confirmation of the engineer, nor the contractor to carry out any variations without instructions.

52. After consultation with the contractor, the engineer will determine the value of extra or additional work to the contract, or for any work omitted under his instructions, the value being assessed under the rates given in the contract documents.

Where no rates are applicable because of the nature of the work, the engineer may determine the rates in consultation with the contractor. If agreement cannot be reached, then the engineer will determine the rates and inform the contractor accordingly.

The engineer may instruct the contractor to carry out the works on a daywork basis and the contractor will be paid under the conditions set out in the daywork schedule included in the bills of quantities. Before ordering materials for the work to be carried out as daywork, the contractor must submit quotations to the engineer for his approval, and invoices and receipts must be submitted to prove the amounts paid. A list of names and occupations of all men employed on dayworks must be submitted each day to the Clerk of Works, together with a statement of the materials and plant used.

If he agrees with the statement of labour and materials, etc, the Clerk of Works will sign the duplicate copy and return it to the contractor. A priced statement of all labour, materials and plant will be submitted at the end of each month and this must be checked by the Clerk of Works or the engineer before it can be accepted. If the engineer decides that a list is impracticable, then he is entitled to authorise as daywork any such work, provided he is satisfied with the time and labour, etc, used in the work.

Where the contractor does not accept the ruling of the engineer with regard to the rates allowed, then he must notify the engineer that he intends to claim higher rates. He must then notify the engineer of this within 28 days of being informed by the engineer of his assessment.

Clause 53: Plant and Materials

Clause 54: Approval of Materials

53. Where the contractor forfeits his rights under the contract, due to bankruptcy, etc, the plant and equipment which the contractor may have on hire could legally become inaccessible to the employer if he wished to proceed with the contract through other means. To safeguard him against such circumstances this clause establishes the rights of the employer, and all plant, goods and materials owned by the contractor, or by any company in which the contractor has a controlling interest, will be considered the property of the employer while it is on the site.

54. In order that he may receive payment for goods and materials intended for use within the contract, but which are still held at a manufacturer's depot, etc, the contractor must provide the engineer with full details of every item concerned and suitably mark these items so that they can be identified by the engineer. If the engineer approves the contractor's request, the materials, etc, become the sole property of the employer, and the contractor is then responsible for delivery as and when items are required.

The contractor will still remain liable for any loss or damage to the items concerned and any additional insurance to cover this eventuality. The engineer will still have the right to reject any or all of the items where they are not in accordance with the conditions of the contract, and where materials are rejected, they will become the liability of the contractor. If the contractor becomes bankrupt, etc, he must deliver any of the items concerned to the employer, and where he fails to deliver them, the employer has the right to enter the premises of either the contractor or his subcontractors and remove the items concerned.

The contractor must ensure that the clause is inserted into any conditions he agrees with sub-contractors employed within the contract.

Clause 55: Errors in the Quantities

Clause 56: Measurement and Valuation

Clause 57: Method of Measurement

55. The quantities set out in the bills are only estimated quantities and the contractor must not assume that these amounts can be used for placing any orders for the works. He must assess any quantities regarding the works by using the drawings issued to him by the engineer, and any error in quantities will be adjusted by the engineer under Clause 52.

Any errors or wrong estimates in the description, rates and prices provided by the contractor in the contract bills will not be rectified under this clause.

56. The work in progress will be measured by the engineer or the Clerk of Works and the contractor will be given the opportunity to be present when the measurement is being made, so that his representative may be available to record such measurement.

Where the quantities are greater or less than those given in the bills, the engineer may determine whether the prices submitted by the contractor are unreasonable or not applicable, and he will notify the contractor of this.

57. Unless it is stated to the contrary in the bills of quantities, all measurement of the works shall be carried out in accordance with the procedures given in the 'Standard Method of Measurement of Civil Engineering Quantities' issued by the Institution of Civil Engineers as stated in the appendix to the Form of Tender.

Clause 58: Provisional Sums and PC Items

Clause 59A: Nominated Sub-Contractors
59B: Forfeiture of Sub-Contract
59C: Payments to Nominated Sub-Contractors

58. The contractor will only be liable for any design or specification to be included in a nominated sub-contract if this is expressly stated as such in the contract. The engineer is entitled to instruct the contractor to employ a sub-contractor nominated by him to supply any goods or services, or to carry out any of the work specified as a prime cost item. With the agreement of the contractor, the engineer can instruct him to carry out any of these

services or works on acceptance of a quotation given by the contractor.

The engineer can also order the contractor to carry out any works which are included in the contract as provisional sums, or instruct him to employ a nominated sub-contractor.

The contractor must produce all quotations, invoices, sub-contractor's documents, accounts and receipts in respect of work carried out by any nominated sub-contractor.

59A. The contractor has the right to refuse to accept any sub-contractor nominated by the engineer to whom he has reasonable objections or who declines to enter into a sub-contract except under amended conditions which could be unfavourable to the contractor. The nominated sub-contractor must be obliged to enter into conditions equal to those which the contractor has to comply with.

In these circumstances the engineer can either nominate another sub-contractor or instruct the contractor to enter into an agreement with the first nominated sub-contractor on terms specified by the engineer and agreed by the employer, or vary the work so that it can be carried out by the contractor, in which case the contractor's percentage on the item for profit and charges will be deducted from the contract.

In the event of the nominated sub-contractor being in breach of contract, the employer will not enforce any award or judgement which he obtains against the contractor, other than those which the contractor will be able to recover against the nominated sub-contractor.

59B. The contractor will include provisions in his contract with all nominated sub-contractors equal to those given in Clause 63 in respect of forfeiture of contract. Where the contractor wishes to exercise his right in respect of forfeiture with any nominated sub-contractor, he must notify the engineer in writing and obtain the employer's consent. If the engineer does not inform the contractor within 7 days of the decision, the contractor may assume that the employer has given his assent.

Where the contractor terminates his contract with a nominated sub-contractor, the engineer can proceed as described in Clause 59A – either nominate again or vary the work, etc.

Any delays or extra cost to the contract arising out of the forfeiture of the nominated sub-contractor will be considered by the engineer, but if the contractor terminates the nominated sub-contract without the consent of the employer, he will not be entitled to any charges or profit as shown in the contract.

The contractor will be obliged to take all the necessary steps to recover the employer's loss from the nominated sub-contractor.

59C. The engineer will be entitled to see all reasonable proof that sums included in previous certificates in respect of nominated sub-contractors have been paid to them before including any amounts in subsequent certificates. The employer will be able to pay nominated sub-contractors direct unless the contractor can show sufficient reason why he has withheld money and proof that he has informed the nominated sub-contractor accordingly.

Clause 60: Certificates and Payments

Clause 61: Maintenance Certificate

60. At the end of each month the contractor will submit to the engineer a statement of the estimated value of the works complete to that date, and a list of materials on site, together with goods in store for which it has been agreed to make payment, plus any amounts the contractor considers himself entitled to under the contract.

Within 28 days after the contractor has delivered his monthly statement to the engineer or his representative, the employer must pay the amount which is due in the opinion of the engineer for the value of work to the contract, and any work done or goods delivered which the engineer is dissatisfied with may be deducted from the claims of the contractor. The engineer will not debate or reduce any sum previously certified by him in other interim certificates.

Where the employer fails to make payment or the engineer to issue any certificate in accordance with these clauses, the contractor will be entitled to interest on the amount overdue.

The amounts in respect of nominated sub-contractors will be shown separately on the certificates each month.

The retention will be up to 5 per cent of the amount due to the contractor until a reserve has accumulated in the hands of the employer up to the following limits:

(a) Where the tender total does not exceed £50,000, 5 per cent will be deducted so long as this does not exceed £1,500.

(b) Where the tender total exceeds £50,000, the deduction will be 3 per cent.

Within 14 days of the engineer issuing a certificate of completion for part of the works a sum equal to $1\frac{1}{2}$ per cent of the sum due to the contractor shall be paid, and where the certificate is for the whole of the works, the amount to be paid shall be equal to half the retention sum.

When the contractor has completed outstanding works at the end of the period of maintenance, he will receive the other half of the retention sum irrespective of any claims which may be outstanding against him.

The contractor must submit his final account to the engineer within three months after the maintenance certificate has been issued, and within three months after receiving the account the engineer should issue a final certificate, provided he has been supplied with information to satisfy him the account is correct. Every certificate issued by the engineer must be sent to the employer and a copy to the contractor at the same time.

61. Within 14 days after the date upon which the period of maintenance ends the Clerk of Works will have supplied a list of defects and outstanding work to the contractor, and when this work has been satisfactorily completed, the engineer will issue the maintenance certificate to the employer, with a copy to the contractor.

The issue of the maintenance certificate does not relieve either the employer or the contractor of his obligations under the contract.

Clause 62: Urgent Repairs

Where it becomes necessary to carry out immediate repairs or remedial works during the execution of the works or the period of maintenance and the contractor is either unable or unwilling to do the work, the employer will be entitled to have the work carried out by his own or other workmen to the extent which the engineer considers necessary. If the work was necessary, and in the opinion of the engineer it was the liability of the contractor, then the employer may claim all the expenses incurred from the contractor, and if the latter fails to pay, the money may be deducted from any money due to him from the employer.

Clause 63: Forfeiture

There are a number of reasons whereby the employer may be justified in considering the contractor to have forfeited his rights within the contract, and some of these are:

He has become a bankrupt, or gone into forced liquidation, etc.

He has assigned the contract without obtaining the employer's consent.

The engineer has certified that the contractor has abandoned the contract, failed to start the works in accordance with Clause 41, suspended work for 14 days after due notice from the engineer to proceed, is persistently in breach of his obligations under the contract; and several other reasons.

The employer may issue 7 days' notice to the contractor, after which he can take possession of the works without releasing the contractor from any of his obligations under the contract. The engineer may then require the contractor to assign the benefits of all his agreements for the supply of goods, etc, as well as for the execution of any work in connection with the contract, over to the employer.

It will be necessary, as soon as possible after the employer has taken possession of the site, for the engineer to assess the value of the work completed, and the materials and goods remaining on the site.

The employer will not be obliged to pay any money due to the contractor until the period of maintenance has been completed, when all other expenses have been correctly assessed by the engineer.

In these circumstances the Clerk of Works will have foreseen the position on site and should make the necessary records of work completed, defective work and materials on site, together with all plant and equipment on site before and after the employer has taken possession.

Clause 64: Frustration

Clause 65: War Clause

These clauses are necessary to prepare for such eventualities and full details are given for the guidance of all parties who may become involved in such matters.

Clause 66: Settlement of Disputes

Any disputes or differences in connection with the contract which arise between the employer and the contractor will be settled by the engineer, who will state his decision in writing to both parties. Where the engineer fails to give a decision, or where either party does not accept the decision, both the employer and the contractor can agree to refer the matter to arbitration, which can be carried out after completion of the contract.

Where any dispute affects a certificate which should be issued by the engineer, or is applicable to adverse physical conditions on site, etc, or the retention of money to which the contractor claims he is entitled, the arbitrator may proceed whether the works have been completed or not.

Clause 67: Application to Scotland

Where the works are situated in Scotland, the contract will be interpreted in accordance with Scots law and operate as a Scottish contract.

Clause 68: Notices

Any notices to either employer or contractor must be sent by post to the last known address, whether this be his principal place of business or, in the event of either being a company, at the registered office.

Clause 69: Tax Fluctuations

The contractor shall be obliged to notify the engineer of any fluctuations which are likely to affect the contract, and shall keep such records which will enable the engineer to ascertain any increase or decrease in the contract sum. All details shall be included in any claims for payment, and where the variation is on labour or materials, the Clerk of Works may be required by the engineer to maintain detailed records of such items.

Clause 70: Value Added Tax

This is unlikely to involve the Clerk of Works any more than the previous clause, but the contractor will be required to maintain detailed records.

Clause 71: Metrication

This applies to materials, etc, which are specified or detailed in either metric or imperial dimensions, and if the contractor is being involved in additional expense and delay through these being unavailable, the engineer will give a decision as to the action the contractor must take.

Clause 72: This is left available for any special condition to be inserted into the conditions of contract

Conditions for Government Contracts – Form GC/Works/1

This form outlines the general conditions for government contracts on building and civil engineering works, and replaced Form CCC/Wks/1 from March 1974.

No reference was made to the Clerk of Works, the engineer or the quantity surveyor in the previous form but recognition is now given to these services in the revised form. Even though it can reasonably be assumed that the designation 'Superintending officer' will refer to the architect, in most instances he is still not mentioned specifically. Where the content of the works is mainly engineering it may equally be assumed that the superintending officer will be either a civil or a mechanical engineer.

Clause 1: Definitions

Reference to 'the contract' means the tender and form of acceptance together with any other documents mentioned, including conditions of contract, specification, bills of quantities, drawings and schedule of rates (if included).

References to the works, the contractor, contract sum, completion dates, accepted risks, etc, are in general similar to those in the other forms of contract.

The Clerk of Works should note Para. (4) to Clause 1 which states that 'any decision to be made by the Authority may be made by any person . . . authorised to act . . . for that purpose . . .' and goes on to say: '(Any decision) . . . may be made in such manner and on such evidence or information as he . . . may think fit'. This paragraph appears to endow the Clerk of Works with more authority to implement his role than is suggested within the JCT Form of Contract.

Clause 1 (6) goes on to confirm that notices under the contract must be in writing. Where the contractor or sub-contractor cannot be contacted, it also states, 'if sent by registered post to the last known place of abode or business', it will be deemed to have been issued on the normal date of receipt.

The abstract of particulars which names the superintending officer is similar to the articles and form of agreement given in the Standard Form and ICE Conditions.

Clause 2: Contractor to Satisfy

The contractor must follow the usual procedure to satisfy himself that the tender covers the actual conditions existing on the site, in relation to contours, subsoils, access, etc, and to the risk of damage to adjacent property, as well as ensuring the availability of labour and materials; and no claim will be admitted for his failure to do so.

Clause 3: Materials and Plant not to be Removed

Once the contract has started, all plant and materials brought on to site, whether to be incorporated into the works or not, become the property of the authority, and they have the power to reject any materials not approved.

The contractor will not be allowed to remove any materials or plant without the written permission of the superintending officer, but the authority are not responsible for any damage to plant or materials which might occur on the site.

The Clerk of Works will be expected to have some control and record of the movement of plant and materials during the contract.

Clause 4: Contract Documents

Where any difference occurs between the bills, drawings, specification or conditions, then the provisions laid down under the conditions will apply. This clause quite clearly states that figured dimensions on the drawings must be followed, and the Clerk of Works must record all discrepancies which come to his attention and pass this information direct to the SO as soon as possible if it is likely to affect the contract.

The contractor is supplied with three copies of the contract drawings, specification and unpriced bills for his use in completing the contract. One copy of any further drawing issued will be supplied to the contractor, and all drawings, specifications, etc, shall, if required, be returned to the SO on completion of the contract.

The contractor must keep one set of drawings, bills, etc, on the site throughout the contract, and these are for the use of the Clerk of Works as well as the SO if the former is not resident on the site. Where the Clerk of Works is resident, he will have his own documents and drawings.

Clause 5: Bills of Quantities

Errors arising in descriptions or quantities in the bills are not accepted as reason to terminate the contract, but if the contractor has based his tender on such quantities, then a variation can be issued by the SO to correct the situation. This does not allow the contractor to claim for errors in his price through calculations, omissions, wrong estimates, etc.

Quantities given in provisional bills or appropriate quantities will neither limit nor be used as a gauge for the amount of work to be carried out by the contractor.

Where conditions are outside normal expectancy in carrying out the work, an accurate record should be maintained by the Clerk of Works for use in the event of subsequent claims by the contractor. Such conditions could arise during excavations because of subsoil formation or excess water problems.

Clause 5A: Authority's Schedule of Rates

Where this forms part of the contract, the authority's schedule of rates shall not be used to define or limit the amount of work to be carried out under the contract.

Clause 5B: Contractor's Schedule of Rates

Where neither bills of quantities nor schedule of rates have been provided by the authority, the contractor may be required to provide a detailed schedule of rates from those used to produce the contract sum or sub-contract sum, whichever applies. Such rates will be used by the quantity surveyor in assessing the value of alterations, additions or omissions to the contract.

Clause 6: Progress of the Works

The contractor will be given a starting order in writing and will be expected to proceed from that date with the works on a regular basis, as well as by direction of the SO, so that the work is completed to the contract date for completion.

In referring to progress it is perhaps important for the Clerk of Works to ensure that he cannot be accused of 'interfering' and creating delays through his manner in dealing with the contractor.

Clause 7: SO's Instructions

This clause details the authority under which the SO issues any instructions to the contractor throughout the contract. His decision regarding instructions is considered to be final and the contractor must comply with the instructions.

The SO may issue oral or written instructions to the contractor on any of the following matters, and he must confirm oral instructions within 14 days in writing, if the contractor requests this:

(a) Vary, modify, add or omit the design, quality or quantity of the works.

(b) Amend any discrepancy arising in the bills, specification or drawings.
(c) Order the removal of any materials from site, and their replacement.
(d) Order removal and re-execution of work carried out by the contractor.
(e) Vary the method of progressing the works.
(f) Vary the hours of work, including overtime and nightwork.
(g) Suspend either the whole or part of the works.
(h) Order the dismissal of any foreman or employee below that grade.
(i) Order work to be reopened for inspection.
(j) Instruct the contractor to amend or make good defects under Clause 32.
(k) Carry out emergency work required for security reasons.
(l) Allow the use of materials obtained from excavations on site.
(m) For any reason where it may be expedient to issue instructions, directions or explanations.

Clause 8: Failure to Comply

Should the contractor fail to comply with any instructions issued by the SO, then a further instruction may be issued by him giving the contractor a specified period in which to carry out the work. If the contractor still fails to comply, the authority are entitled to carry out the work themselves or employ another contractor to do the work, and recover the costs and expenses from the main contractor.

Clause 9: Valuation of SO's Instructions

The contractor must not cause any variation in the work from the drawings, bills, etc, without written instructions from the SO, and any variation will be valued by the quantity surveyor in accordance with contract. Such variations will not invalidate the contract. Where the contractor incurs expense beyond that implied within the contract by complying with instructions received from the SO, he will be reimbursed for such expense. To be entitled to payment he should receive the instructions in writing from the SO and give notice within 14 days that he is being involved in extra expense and considers himself entitled to additional payments. For alterations, additions or omissions, payment will, of course, be made under valuations within the contract.

Where the rates cannot be assessed by the rates or prices in the bills or schedules it will be valued as daywork or at agreed rates between the contractor and the authority.

The SO will value any work carried out and covered up by the contractor without giving notice it would be covered, and the decision of the SO shall be final.

Clause 10: Valuations by Measurement

Where the contract is based upon approximate quantities, etc, the value of the work which has been carried out to the satisfaction of the SO shall then be measured and valued as stated in Clause 9.

Clause 11G: Variation of Price (Labour Tax)

This clause covers any variation in price due to the contractor receiving or paying any tax levy or contribution in respect of his work force. This does not apply to VAT, income tax or the Industrial Training Act 1964 levy, but it does include National Insurance contributions, etc.

As the number of men employed on the site could affect such matters it may be necessary for the Clerk of Works to maintain special records or to make routine checks, but he is advised to clarify the position with the quantity surveyor at an early stage in the contract.

Clause 12: Setting Out

The contractor is completely responsible for setting out the whole of the works, as well as providing all instruments necessary for this to be done.

He must also fix pegs, profiles, and templates and maintain these so long as they are considered necessary, presumably in the opinion of the SO/ Clerk of Works.

All necessary information must be supplied by the SO to enable the contractor to properly set out the works.

The Clerk of Works will note references elsewhere to his own responsibility in checking the setting out of the work, and where boundaries are affected care must be taken to ensure the information given has been correct.

Clause 13: Materials and Workmanship

Both items cover the reason for the Clerk of Works' presence on the site, and any variation from the specification or drawings must be referred to the SO.

All materials must be of the kind described in the specification or bills, and if the SO considers it necessary, the contractor must produce evidence of this fact.

Both the SO and the Clerk of Works shall have power to visit, inspect and examine any materials to be used in the works wherever they may be manufactured or produced. Presumably this refers to any factory, workshop, plant or quarry, etc. Both are also entitled to carry out the same degree of inspection throughout the works.

The SO is also entitled to have tests of any materials supplied by the contractor, who must provide the facilities for this purpose.

Where the SO considers independent testing is required, the cost will be borne by the contractor only if the materials do not conform to the specification. The report from the independent source will be regarded as final and conclusive.

The costs of concrete test cubes and other routine tests remain the responsibility of the contractor.

Where work or materials do not comply with the contract documents, they must be replaced and faulty materials removed from the site.

Clause 14: Notices and Fees

Notices concerning regulations and statutory authorities must be submitted by the contractor, who will be responsible for any fees involved. Any drawings or plans necessary in connection with such notices must also be supplied by the contractor.

Clause 15: Royalties and Patents

Licences, royalties, fees, etc, must all be included by the contractor when he submits his tender, and the authority must be indemnified against any claims in connection with royalties, etc.

Where charges arise due to an instruction given by the SO under the contract for which the contractor could not reasonably be expected to allow, then these will be regarded as recoverable expenses under the contract.

Clause 16: Appointment of RE or Clerk of Works

Authority is provided under this clause for the appointment of a resident engineer or a Clerk of Works who may exercise such powers as are granted to the SO in respect of materials and workmanship. Authority is also given for the resident engineer or the Clerk of Works to inspect the work on site or the manufacture of components either on site or in a factory or workshop. Failure to use these powers correctly by the Clerk of Works or resident engineer will in no way limit the SO from subsequently exercising these powers where necessary.

Clause 17: Protection of Works

The contractor must provide all the necessary watchmen to protect the site, works and materials throughout the contract, and he will be held responsible for protecting and lighting any portions of the work which are likely to prove a danger either to his own workmen or to any person whatever.

Clause 18: Nuisance to Others

The contractor must take all reasonable precautions to prevent his employees creating a nuisance or inconvenience to those on adjacent properties or to the public in general.

Adequate precautions must be taken to avoid any pollution to either streams or waterways during the contract.

Clause 19: Removal of Rubbish

The site must at all times be kept free from rubbish, and waste arising from the execution of the works must also be removed.

Clause 20: Excavated Materials and Antiquities

Objects of interest found in or around the site must be reported to the SO/ Clerk of Works, who will issue instructions regarding their disposal. Excavated materials suitable for use in the construction of the work shall be dealt with as directed by the SO/Clerk of Works, and if used within the contrast, will be charged at an agreed cost with the contractor.

Clause 21: Foundations

The contractor is not entitled to proceed with foundations until the excavations have been examined by the SO and approved by him.

It does not say 'or his representative', yet it seems unlikely the SO is going to visit the site to inspect every section of the foundations with a Clerk of Works resident, when that is likely to cause delay.

Clause 33 states that the agent must be in attendance on the site during all working hours, except when required to attend at the office of the SO, which suggests the latter is not resident on the site.

Clause 22: Notice Prior to Covering up Work

The contractor is expected to give reasonable notice of his intention to cover the work with earth or otherwise, and if he proceeds without the SO Clerk of Works inspecting the work, he can be instructed to open it up again. The clause does not suggest he will be paid for reopening the work, even if it is found to be correct.

It would seem the contractor must wait for authority to allow him to proceed, and any resulting delay could be claimed for under the contract. The Clerk of Works, therefore, may be considered responsible if he causes any undue delay inspecting the work.

Clause 23: Suspension for Frost, etc

Where there is risk of damage to the work from frost or inclement weather, etc, the SO is entitled to suspend the work and the contractor cannot claim any reimbursement for the delay unless he can demonstrate that he has carried out the conditions relating to such items in the specification.

These last three clauses are so mandatory that the contractor may decide to challenge the decisions by going to arbitration; therefore, the Clerk of Works should be certain to record such matters fully when they occur.

Clause 24: Dayworks

Reasonable notice must be given to the SO/Clerk of Works before the start of any work either ordered or to be claimed as daywork. Records of the labour and materials involved must be delivered to the Clerk of Works in duplicate within one week of the end of the payweek concerned. One of the copies will be certified by the SO/Clerk of Works, if agreed, and returned to the contractor, who must produce the copy at the adjustment of final accounts.

Clause 25: Fire and Other Risks

The contractor must take precautions to prevent loss or damage from any of the accepted risks (Clause 1(2)) either caused by his own staff or by representatives of the employing authority. He must comply with any instructions given in writing by the SO to achieve such precautions.

Regulations covering the storage of petrol, explosives, etc, on site must be fully effected at all times.

Clause 26: Damage to Works, Plant, etc

Plant, temporary buildings, equipment, etc, provided either by or on behalf of the contractor, will be his sole responsibility, provided they are for the construction of the works, and he must make good any loss or damage right away. He will be obliged to make good any loss or damage to the works with all speed irrespective of the cause, unless the authority determines the contract.

Where the cause is covered by the accepted risks, or due to neglect or default of the employer's staff, the cost will be met by the employer, and a variation order will be issued to cover such amount. The Clerk of Works should take note of any situation which may become the subject of a claim by the contractor in which he may himself be involved.

Clause 27: Assignment or Transfer of Contract

The contractor cannot assign or transfer any part of the contract without the written authority of the employer.

Clause 28: Completion Date/Extensions

The work must be carried out and completed to the satisfaction of the SO, and all plant, materials, etc, removed from the site upon his written instructions.

Provided the contractor informs the SO in writing immediately he becomes aware of any circumstance likely to cause delay to the contract, he will be granted reasonable extensions of time after the SO has considered the circumstances.

Considerations will be given to delays arising from modifications or additions to the works, inclement weather, default by the authority, strikes which are not due to the negligence of the contractor, risks listed under Clause 1(2), or due to circumstances beyond the control of the contractor which he could not have foreseen at the time of tender. The contractor must notify the SO of any situation arising which is likely to involve an extension of the contract; he is also obliged to use his expertise to avoid and minimise such delays.

Clause 28A: Partial Possession Before Completion

Sections of the works may be taken over by the authority and certificates of completion issued accordingly where the work has been completed to the satisfaction of the SO. Sectional completion may be specified in the abstract of particulars, but in any case, provided both parties agree, any section can be taken over on completion. The maintenance period will, of course, take effect from the issue of the certificate of completion, and retention sums will be varied accordingly.

Clause 29: Liquidated Damages

Where the contract period is overrun after taking account of all extensions granted, the contractor will be obliged to pay the employer a sum of money calculated in accordance with assessed damages detailed in the abstract of particulars. These sums are not to be considered as penalties, as in most instances they will not cover the losses incurred by the employer; they can be considered as agreed token damages.

Clause 30: Sub-contracts

Clause 31: Sub-contractors

No portion of the works can be sublet by the contractor without written authority of the SO.

The contractor may object to any sub-contractor nominated by the employer, as he will then be responsible for such sub-contractor, just in the same way as he will be responsible for any other sub-contractors or specialists whom he himself appoints, with the approval of the employer.

Any loss or damage incurred by the sub-contractor to the contract will be the responsibility of the contractor.

Clause 32: Defects After Completion

The maintenance period is stated in the abstract and is related to the completion date. Any defects in the works arising through failure or neglect on the part of the contractor must be made good by him, and failure to do so will permit the employer to carry out the work and recover the expense involved from the contractor. The contractor will not be responsible for any damage caused by frost which does not appear until after the completion date.

Clause 33: Contractor's Agent

The contractor must maintain a competent agent on site during all working hours to supervise the works and take directions from the SO or his representative.

Clause 34: Daily Returns

The agent must supply the Clerk of Works each morning with a distribution list of the labour employed on site.

Clause 35: Conforming with Regulations

The contractor must arrange for his men to conform with any regulations in force within a government establishment where work is proceeding. No claims will be accepted for loss or delay caused through the establishment being closed down for holiday periods, etc, but the SO may grant permission for additional working hours without extra costs, if this is requested in writing by the contractor.

Clause 36: Dismissal of Contractor's Staff

The SO may instruct the contractor to remove any foreman or person below that grade considered by him to be undesirable, and such person must be replaced.

The authority may instruct the contractor to remove the agent or any person above the level of foreman whom they consider undesirable on the site. Such persons who are removed must be replaced, and decisions made by the SO or the authority under this condition are final.

Clause 37: Measurements

The contractor will be required to arrange for his representative to be present to take measurements of work executed, at a time stated by the quantity surveyor. If the contractor's representative fails to be present at the time appointed, the quantity surveyor is entitled to proceed and prepare accounts based on his own measurements. The contractor must provide the quantity surveyor with all information and documents properly certified to enable the final sum to be properly calculated. The Clerk of Works may be concerned in certifying some of these documents, such as daywork sheets, labour returns, etc, therefore he must take care to ensure that such items are correct before adding his signature.

Clause 38: Prime Costs

Clause 39: Provisional Sums

Such items will be reserved for selection and nomination by the SO, who will issue an instruction to the contractor accordingly. The Clerk of Works should note that payment for fixing includes unloading and unpacking, besides returning such packings and empty crates.

Clause 40: Advances on Account

During the progress of the works the contractor will be entitled to receive monthly payments for 97 per cent of the value of work completed and 90 per cent of the value of materials and components on the site, provided this is to the satisfaction of the SO. It is more than likely that the Clerk of Works will be required to confirm the condition and amount of materials and components on the site as well as reporting that storage is in accordance with the specification.

Payments on account for suppliers and sub-contractors are also covered within this clause, but will be a matter for the quantity surveyor and the SO.

Clause 41: Payment on and after Completion

When the practical completion certificate has been issued, the contractor will be entitled to receive the final sum less one half the amount of the retention. The balance of the money will become payable upon issue of the final completion certificate by the SO, and the authority can always make payments during the maintenance period to reduce the retention amount. Because of these payments it will be important for the Clerk of Works to report on any matters which are likely to affect such payments being made.

Clause 42: Certificates

The SO will issue the certificates which entitle the contractor to payment; these will be issued at intervals during the contract as well as upon completion of the works. Valuations will be certified to the SO by the quantity surveyor but, as suggested in the previous clause, the Clerk of Works must ensure that matters concerning him are reported to the SO. In certain instances the contractor may refer a dispute over certificates to the authority.

Clause 43: Recovery of Sums due from the Contractor

Any amount recoverable from the contractor under the conditions of the contract may be deducted by the authority from money due to him under the contract. Where the final sum has already been paid, the authority is still entitled to deduct the amount due from any monies to which the contractor may be entitled from other government departments.

Clause 44: Special Powers of Determination

The authority is entitled at any time to determine the contract by giving notice to the contractor. Directions will be issued within three months of such notice being given in respect of work to be carried out, protection to completed work, removal of plant, etc, from site, making good or carrying out safety measures, termination of sub-contracts or other matters which the authority considers to be necessary.

Determination of the contract will be likely to involve the Clerk of Works in many matters, not least ensuring the protection of the works. Records will be required of the state of the works to date, plant and materials on site, and safety of incompleted work. As the circumstances vary in each case, the authority will give instructions regarding the procedure to be followed by the Clerk of Works.

Clause 45: Determination of Contract Due to Default of Contractor

Determination may arise through delays to the contract by the contractor or because of inferior workmanship. Where the contractor fails to comply with an instruction from the SO to rectify certain items within the specified period, the authority can decide to determine the contract; such matters may well involve the Clerk of Works, especially in respect of previous notice or action. Where the contractor goes into liquidation or becomes bankrupt this will be a case for determination of the contract.

Clause 46: Provisions in case of Determination of Contract

This relates to payments due from or to the contractor by the authority, provision for entering and taking possession of the site, and procedure for retaining sub-contractors and suppliers where the works are to continue. While the Clerk of Works will not be concerned in these decisions, he may be required for liaison with those operating on the site.

Clause 47: Persons and Property

The contractor must indemnify the authority for any claims, and the Clerk of Works must take steps to record any incident likely to come under this heading.

Clause 48: Damage to Public Roads

The authority will indemnify the contractor for claims in respect of damage to roads, bridges, pipes, or cables caused by extraordinary traffic of the contractor, but he will be obliged to take all reasonable steps to prevent such damage, and must comply with instructions given by the SO on such matters.

Clause 49: Emergency Powers

If the SO considers it necessary to carry out immediate remedial works to forestall any risk of accident, works failure, or security, and the contractor is unable to do the work, the SO may call in the authority's work force. If the work should have been carried out under the contract, the cost shall be recoverable from the contractor.

Clause 50: Other Works

The authority is empowered to execute other works, whether connected with the contract or not, and the contractor must give reasonable facilities for such work to be carried out.

Clause 51: Fair Wages

The contractor will be obliged to fulfil the conditions of the Fair Wages Resolution passed by the House of Commons in October 1946. This requires him to pay rates of wages and observe conditions no less favourable than those established in the region where work is proceeding.

The contractor must also ensure that sub-contractors are conforming to this clause.

Clause 52: Racial Discrimination

This complies with the Race Relations Act, 1968.

Clause 55: Corrupt Gifts and Payment of Commission

The authority can determine the contract where any gift or inducement

is offered to any of its servants with a view to receiving any favours in connection with the contract.

Clause 57: Passes

Clause 58: Photographs

Clause 59: Secrecy

The contractor is required to follow strict rules regarding persons having access to the site or works, and must follow instructions issued to him by the SO in this respect.

If passes are to be issued, this will be referred to in the abstract of particulars, and the SO may require a list of names and addresses of all those connected with the works from the contractor, as well as requiring evidence of their identity.

The contractor has no authority to take or allow photographs to be taken by others, of the site or the works, unless permission has been granted by the authority in writing.

The contractor and his employees are bound by the Official Secrets Act and such conditions must be observed both during the contract and also after completion.

Clause 60

This has been omitted.

Clause 61: Arbitration

All disputes, etc, arising between the authority and the contractor in connection with the contract shall be referred to a single arbitrator agreed by both parties.

Arbitration will not take place until after the completion of the works, abandonment of the works, or determination of the contract.

CHAPTER NINE

Selection of Materials and Components

Interpretation

The contract documents generally attempt to specify the materials and components required within the contract as clearly as possible, and because of this there is an assumption by most members of the construction team that it will produce the desired result on the site. The number of individuals involved can easily be further influenced by commercial pressures. interpretations of the specification, while the judgement of some who are involved can easily be further influenced by commercial pressures.

The spiralling costs of materials and components has caused those responsible for specifying these items to look more closely into the performance they consider sufficient to meet the requirements. In effect, this reduces the quality of the item, and makes more stringent inspection necessary.

Early Agreement

Delays are frequently caused to the contract because materials and components delivered to site do not comply with the specification. This can and should be easily avoided by submitting samples to the architect for his agreement and confirmation at an early stage in the contract.

An advantage of inspecting and even testing samples at an early stage in the contract can be twofold: in the first instance it makes those who are providing the items much more aware of the inspection procedures they must meet; and secondly, suppliers and manufacturers generally appreciate an interest in their products at this stage, as it helps them to determine exactly what is expected of them within the specification. It also provides better communication between the parties involved, helping to promote a strive to meet the demands within the specified requirements while still better understanding throughout the contract, and encouraging everyone to remaining aware of the cost implications.

The Clerk of Works should treat all materials as of equal importance, and would be well advised to insist that samples be agreed before they are used within the construction; even the smallest item overlooked may create problems through incompatibility with other materials and components.

Inspection

Inspection should naturally be provided by the manufacturers to ensure they are complying with the specification, and subsequently by the purchaser, who will be responsible for the item's function within the finished product.

The architect is entitled to expect the Clerk of Works to inspect and report on samples submitted to the site, judging the workmanship and materials on the basis of his practical experience in such matters. While this experience of traditional materials will assist the Clerk of Works to judge such items, modern techniques in the use of these materials, etc, may lead him to misread the situation unless he keeps up to date. The advent of plastics and other similar products demands that he makes himself thoroughly conversant with these materials.

There is no substitute for vigilance in carrying out any inspection procedures, though the number of mechanical aids and instruments is strictly limited, sometimes by cost alone.

It is necessary to distinguish between inspection and testing, as these are often regarded in the same light. While there is often a degree of inspection provided for construction on most sites, testing is reserved for concreting procedures. The Clerk of Works should follow a regular formula both for inspections and for testing materials, in the first instance dividing them into separate groups, i.e. materials and components.

Materials can be interpreted as items for use on site to produce components, and should be examined for their suitability to achieve that objective. Where visual inspection is insufficient to satisfy him that the materials will meet their requirements, he must take samples in accordance with the recommended practices for those materials and submit them for laboratory testing.

Modern construction techniques result in more and more components being delivered to site, and inspecting these should be considered under the following headings:

(a) Materials.
(b) Fabrication methods.
(c) Workmanship.
(d) Performance.
(e) Maintenance.

Sample components should not be specially produced to gain initial approval from the architect, but must be representative of the standards to be submitted throughout the contract. Equally it would be wrong to insist on a higher standard for the sample than is called for in the specification; perhaps it might be better to select a standard below which the manufacturer must not go, and the sample should be retained on site for comparison.

Records and Reports

The architect is responsible for ensuring that all materials and workmanship are provided in accordance with the contract terms, and cannot avoid legal responsibility for any subsequent defects by suggesting that the Clerk of Works must share responsibility in the matter. Of course, this does not apply in the case of the employer, who is entitled to expect the Clerk of Works to protect his interests in such matters.

The Clerk of Works should consider it a matter of professional competence to submit reports direct to the architect on materials delivered to site. This will enable the architect to assess whether he needs to make further inspections. A busy architect anyway will always welcome practical advice on workmanship and quality of samples delivered to site.

To offer criticism of samples at a later stage in the contract, when the architect and everyone else can see the problems, is neither helpful nor tactful, and will be avoided by the experienced Clerk of Works. He will be sure to make his comments at the appropriate stage of the contract.

A register should be maintained of all samples submitted to site, and comments should be included from time to time on subsequent deliveries throughout the contract to provide an assessment of the quality achieved by the supplier.

If samples are eventually fixed within the contract, a record of their position should also be made, as this will provide useful information after completion of the contract. Although it may seem an elementary precaution, the Clerk of Works is advised to ensure that the sample can always be identified; otherwise there may be confusion in referring to it later.

Storage

Suitable storage should be provided on the site for all samples, to provide direct and easy access for comparison with deliveries throughout the contract. A sample store should be included in the bills for a large contract, and might suitably be provided as an annexe to the contractor's main site store, where the items would be under the supervision of the storeman.

All samples must be easily identifiable. Fixing ironmongery and fittings to display boards for quick reference, and preparing sample boards of nails and screws to be used on the contract, will avoid unnecessary mistakes with these items later. A mock-up of manufactured items will overcome problems which might otherwise not become apparent until the actual fixing operations are taking place; time expended in this manner is amply rewarded by a reduction in delays and frustration of workmen through amended details.

The conditions for storage must be given careful consideration beforehand. Good ventilation must be maintained and undue moisture or excessive heat avoided to offset any possibility of distortion to samples. They must be properly stored and not left to lie around without support where necessary, or in conditions which might lead to damage.

The Clerk of Works should make a practice of inspecting the samples at intervals and entering up his comments in the records book for that purpose; any faults which become apparent should be reported to the architect, and an inspection made of any similar products included in the construction.

Subsequent Deliveries

Once samples have been submitted and approved, there should be no reason for errors to occur, but unfortunately the matter is not always treated with sufficient attention and often the first of the site deliveries become yet again a sample load.

While every delivery should be checked by making random comparisons with the sample, the first delivery is worthy of a complete inspection. Components which are liable to distortion or damage should be inspected when delivered to note the method of transportation and condition of the load.

The Clerk of Works should make arrangements with the agent to be notified of deliveries which he considers should be inspected, and apart from being diligent in attending to the inspection without unnecessary delay, the Clerk of Works should check the storage facilities provided each time. Suitable storage, even if included in the bills, can be a major problem on the site through limited space, speed of erection, careless handling, poor supervision or even an irresponsible attitude by the contractor to such matters.

The Clerk of Works must not tolerate indifferent attempts to provide adequate storage of materials once they have been delivered and approved, as they will be included in valuations drawn up by the quantity surveyor at the end of the month.

Valuations

Where the Clerk of Works finds that materials or components are not receiving adequate protection to ensure that they will be 'the best of their respective kind' when included in the construction, he should report the facts to the quantity surveyor, who will adjust the valuation accordingly.

Materials and components should not be stored on site over an undue length of time unless the storage conditions are good enough to prevent any deterioration.

At No Extra Cost

Where materials or components are delivered to site without samples having been agreed, and are found contrary to specification, the problem is often solved by the architect compromising with the specification to avoid delays, etc, and accepting the delivery, using the added proviso 'at no extra cost to the contract'. Unfortunately this can be meaningless, as it takes no account of hidden costs, which never reveal themselves until it is much too late and can be very difficult to allocate.

CHAPTER TEN

The Clerk of Works on Site

Inspections

Immediately he takes up residence on the site, the Clerk of Works will find it necessary to organise his office and inspection procedures, and it is very important for him to establish certain disciplines at this stage if he is to avoid confusing his priorities later.

The primary task of the Clerk of Works is to inspect the work as it proceeds to ensure it is carried out in accordance with the contract drawings and specification. This cannot be achieved unless he is prepared to spend a considerable portion of each day physically checking the work.

The practice of casually walking around the site once or twice during the day may help to keep the Clerk of Works up-to-date with the general progress maintained by the contractor, but it will hardly achieve the degree of supervision likely to persuade the architect of his abilities as a professional colleague.

Unfortunately there are Clerks of Works who imagine a daily walk is sufficient to fulfil their brief 'to act solely as an inspector on behalf of the employer'. They also appear quite content to note obvious errors in the construction as it proceeds, drawing the attention of the contractor to what he is probably already aware of, and passing the information to the architect whenever the contractor fails to pay heed.

The professional Clerk of Works, on the other hand, is so well versed in the elements of construction that he anticipates the problems before they arise, and by advising the contractor, or his agent, gains their respect as well as the co-operation which stems from such confidence.

Inspection procedures should be varied as much as possible, as familiarity with his routine will quickly establish the whereabouts of the Clerk of Works, leading to complacency amongst those sections most in need of good supervision.

The Clerk of Works will not take long to realise, no matter how astute he may consider himself, that it is only possible for him to be in one place at a time. From this discovery he will also learn that there are many ways of being in the right place at the right moment, for there are those anxious to draw discrepancies to his attention who are perhaps hoping to avoid too close an interest in their own efforts.

Older Clerks of Works will recall previous days when the general foreman was forever anxious to attend to every comfort of the Clerk of Works. Tea was permanently available, while on cold damp days the combustion stove in the Clerk of Works' office glowed a deep red, providing a seductive warmth which demanded an iron will to venture outside. Many similar arrangements were adopted, all for the same end; some were successful and others failed. Today the tactics are more sophisticated – so many queries are raised that there would be little time to see the progress of the works if they all were answered with the urgency they apparently require.

While carrying out his inspections, the Clerk of Works must remember he has no authority to interfere with the progress of the work in any way; he cannot advise the contractor or his men how the work should be carried out. He can object, however, to the way the work is being done, if contrary to good practice as implied in the bills, or to the Code or Practice for that particular operation.

He must not attempt to disfigure the work already carried out by the contractor by using indelible chalk or ink, unless he has previously agreed with the contractor that this means should be used to identify work which the Clerk of Works considers to be below the specified standards.

The Clerk of Works must be on guard against the possibilities which could arise should he attempt physically to damage the work carried out by the contractor, irrespective of whether it conforms to the specification or not.

While the contractor may be prepared to agree that the work is defective, he is within his rights to decide what steps he will take to correct the defect before presenting the work for further inspection. He would also be within his rights to claim reimbursement for the full amount of any damage caused by the Clerk of Works, and more than likely such a claim would be successful.

Procedure

The contract quite clearly states that the contractor must provide the Clerk of Works with every assistance to carry out his duties. In the early stages of the contract the Clerk of Works must establish the principle that he is kept informed of the sequence of operations in order that he can programme his own work. He should also make it clear to the contractor's agent that the sequence of operations is not automatically continued without giving the Clerk of Works the opportunity to inspect the work.

The Clerk of Works is not entitled to assume an operation is complete or otherwise until informed by the contractor's agent, and this is authorised in the bills and also in the building regulations. Failure on the part of the agent to co-operate may easily result in instructions having to be issued by the architect for work to be opened up again for inspection. Should such work be found contrary to the specification or bills the contractor will be called upon to pay for opening up the work besides paying for correcting the work carried out, and this can prove expensive. Of course, if the work is found to be correct, then the client will pay the costs of opening up the work.

Irrespective of who has to pay, however, such situations can only cause delays as well as friction between the persons involved and are detrimental in many ways to the contract. Every effort should be made early in the contract to prevent this situation arising, and an experienced Clerk of Works should be able to convince the agent of the wisdom of the correct procedure.

The contractor is equally entitled to expect the Clerk of Works to carry out his inspection without unreasonable delays, and this should also be noted early in the contract.

Delays

Claims for extensions to the contract through delays must be high on the list of matters for discussion during the progress of the work and later in trying to settle the final account.

Any delay to the contract caused through the action of the Clerk of Works, unless there is good reason for such action, will become the subject of a claim by the contractor, and may warrant the architect granting an extension of time with all the relevant expenses involved. By adopting a reasonable attitude in the performance of his duties, the Clerk of Works will avoid any danger arising under this possibility. He must take care to see that any instructions or directions given to the contractor are perfectly clear. Unless acting on instructions from the architect, the Clerk of Works will only issue instructions relating to workmanship or materials not complying with the contract, and it is wise to note in the site diary all verbal as well as written instructions.

Wherever the Clerk of Works sees opportunity of avoiding delays, whether caused through matters concerning the architect or activities of the contractor, he must take action to bring this to the attention of the architect, or to the agent if he is concerned. While it could be suggested that it is not correct for the Clerk of Works to involve himself on the contractor's behalf in such matters, and the architect may not welcome the suggestion he is causing a delay, it is still true that the Clerk of Works is the employee of the client and must have a responsibility to see that the client's interests are watched.

There have been many instances of delays to contracts at first seeming attributable to the contractor's shortcomings, and then later, under litigation, seen to be only partly his fault.

It is the job of the professional Clerk of Works to interest himself in all matters concerning the contract that are likely to lead to a successful completion of the project for the client. After all, the Clerk of Works has the advantage generally of being permanently resident on the site, without responsibility for design, finance or labour to distract him from his main concern – to record quality and progress. There are, of course, those who are not resident on the site and rely on periodic visits of inspection, and their responsibility is the same as the architect's, supervision being related to time available.

Checking Drawings

Because of the possibility of errors, the Clerk of Works should spend as much time as he can systematically studying the drawings immediately he receives them. Begin by checking detailed dimensions and cross-checking them against overall dimensions. Detail drawings must be checked against the plans and elevations of the section concerned. Floor plans should be checked at various levels with the roof plans to ensure all openings coincide, especially where service drawings are affected. Piling layouts, setting-out drawings and foundation plans must be carefully cross-checked for dimensional errors and overall dimensions noted where they are likely to affect site boundaries.

When he is studying the drawings, the Clerk of Works should make all figures and calculations on the drawing concerned, as this may prove valuable later in assessing how and why certain decisions were given. They will also prove useful if someone other than the Clerk of Works is called upon to refer to the drawings.

Any errors or items which provide insufficient information should be referred to the architect at once, and site dimensions should be supplied where they may help to provide the architect with current information. Where the information on one drawing conflicts with that on another, the rule is to accept the information on the larger scale drawing as correct, but the matter should also be reported to the architect.

Any effort he puts into understanding the drawings will make the Clerk of Works' task easier as the work proceeds, as well as extending his ability and knowledge on future contracts, perhaps without his fully realising the fact.

Amended Drawings

Where a drawing is amended, the Clerk of Works should remove the previous drawing from the files immediately, as site errors are often caused through the wrong drawing being used. Amended drawings should be rolled up, labelled and stored in racks, although an alternate is to fix the drawings between two laths with thumb screws and suspend them on two brackets fitted to the wall of the office. This system enables quick reference to be made to amended drawings when a particular point may be in question some time after the amendment was issued.

Theoretically, of course, once a drawing has been amended it should be destroyed, but in practice this is not a wise policy, as even the architect may have amended the negative without retaining previous details for reference later.

Amendments are often made through verbal as well as through written instructions and are not always transferred to the drawings.

If the drawings were destroyed the calculations and notes which it is recommended the Clerk of Works should make when studying the drawings would be lost, and such information could be valuable to the quantity surveyor at the end of the contract when producing the final account.

Amendments affect so many aspects of the work that the architect may occasionally consider it impossible to check through all drawings, and the standard form of contract advises the contractor to report any discrepancies between drawings and contract bills.

The Clerk of Works should amend his copies of the drawings where any variations are effected on the site, which is most likely to occur when drainage is in progress. By recording the drainage 'as laid' the Clerk of Works will be able to forward a copy to the architect on completion.

Relations with Site Staff

The modern tendency in organisations to use christian names as a means of improving communications may be successful in some instances but not in others, and the danger to the Clerk of Works from over-familiarity on a construction site cannot be underestimated. Some persons have a natural ability to indulge in familiarity with their subordinates and still maintain control, but this is a gift with which everyone is not endowed. Until he has established himself, the Clerk of Works would be advised to be friendly but never familiar if he hopes to maintain his responsibility within his control. It is worth remembering how much easier relaxing and granting a concession in the interests of the contract is than attempting to apply pressure to obtain what is right within the contract.

The Clerk of Works holds rather an invidious position on the site in some respects, as he can quite easily be regarded as a brake on the progress of the work by the contractor and his agent, a critic of their competence and skills by the operatives, and a necessary but difficult member of his team by the architect.

Realising the narrow path he treads in the early days of the contract, the Clerk of Works must gain the confidence of the agent. First he must make it clear that he is there to see the work carried out to the contract bills and specification, second that he is there to assist in the progress of the works, and third, and most important, that his word can be relied upon.

The Clerk of Works' standing with the operatives will depend upon his decisions and demeanour; although he may be human, he cannot afford to be wrong. Before making any decisions affecting the work he must check all his facts thoroughly, and, having made his decision, he must ensure it is endorsed by the architect and carried out by the contractor. Only in this way can he hope to have sufficient influence to make his presence on the site effective, and if he cannot, he should seek other employment. Practices or attitudes which are likely to produce standards lower than those required under the contract must be controlled from the beginning, and when the Clerk of Works notes them, he must resist the temptation to discuss them with the operatives involved.

Only by adapting himself to the procedures laid down under the contract can he expect others to practise the same rule; he must, therefore, refer all matters concerning the work direct to the agent. Occasionally it may become obvious that the fault on site lies with the agent, who may be inept in handling the difficult situations which all too frequently occur on construction sites. An experienced Clerk of Works may see this long before it becomes apparent to the contractor, but even in such cases the Clerk of Works must continue to co-operate and notify the agent of any irregularities which take place. At the same time it is advisable tactfully to draw the attention of the architect to such matters, as this may have a bearing upon the successful completion of the project.

The experienced Clerk of Works will always recognise the experienced contractor's agent, even though his methods may be completely different from those generally adopted, and a tactful approach may be necessary in the early stages before a proper understanding is established.

The Clerk of Works must understand that the contractor has no responsibility to carry out work which is not included in the contract, unless he has received written instructions to do so from the architect.

Where the relationship on site is good, problems relating to instructions are likely to be much fewer than where the relationship is poor.

Inspection Records

The frequency with which incidents occur on any normal construction site during the working day are sufficient to tax the memory of most people unless they are properly recorded at the time. While many of these incidents may turn out to be relatively unimportant, a fair percentage will be the cause of further discussion and possibly even the subject of future claims under the contract. There is only one safe way to record such events and that is to make written note of them at the time they occur, and for this the Clerk of Works will require notebook and pencil.

The date should be entered at the top of the page when making the first entry of the day, and each item of the day's events noted briefly. It is a good idea to form a column at the side of the page to enable the action taken in respect of the entry also to be recorded. Notebooks should be numbered and retained throughout the contract to refresh the memory when necessary.

The habit of using the notebook regularly will soon be acquired, and the Clerk of Works will be able to enter up his site diary at the end of each day without the danger of overlooking what may have been a small incident at the time but very important later.

On large contracts the difficulty of continuously making written notes, however brief, can be most time-consuming. The problem can be overcome quite easily by using one of the small tape-recorders, available today at very reasonable prices, which can be slipped into the pocket with the same ease as a notebook.

This method of recording information obviously requires a little practice, but once the novelty of the situation has been overcome, and the mind adjusted to transferring orally rather than visually, it will be found to be both quick and efficient. A great deal more information can be gathered in this way for transferring into the site diary at the end of the day than by using a notebook.

Recording the Weather

The importance of keeping accurate records on site of weather conditions is increasing because the contractor is becoming more aware of his right to claim under Clause 23(b) for delays due to the weather. The general practice of recording daily temperatures is often inadequate for decision-making, as the record is generally related to readings on a maximum-minimum thermometer taken in the early morning. Most sites rely upon such instruments for recording temperatures when concreting is taking place, and several thermometers may need to be distributed around the site. Apart from the dangers of interference with the readings, there is the added problem of the thermometers disappearing altogether.

Records and information can be obtained from the local weather centres, but experience proves that the weather can vary extensively over a relatively small area, making such records rather inconclusive.

A thermo-hydrograph on the site will record both temperatures and humidity readings on a chart, which is changed daily, for the whole day and night. This is a robust and reliable instrument operating on a clockwork motor enclosed within a drum, and the recordings, made in coloured inks on graph paper, give clear indications of the readings.

Rainfall can be recorded in a rain gauge which traps the rain in a cylinder; this moisture can be poured into a measuring glass and the total rainfall during the period recorded. Unfortunately this method gives no indication of the sudden shower or cloudburst, nor does it indicate whether the rain fell during the working day or outside work hours.

A much better type of rain gauge is the syphon rainfall recorder, which also traps the amount of rainfall but whose chart, fixed to a revolving drum and operated by a clockwork motor, records the amount of rainfall as it occurs. Cloudburst or light showers are all equally recorded, providing charts which are available for discussion at a later stage in the contract.

Progress on construction sites can also be seriously affected by high winds, and on high-rise construction the degree of wind pressure can be critical, especially where certain types of tower cranes are used. In these cases the use of anemometers will provide suitable records for discussion regarding any delays through winds. Cup anemometers with generators are recommended. They should be placed on a suitably high point, either on a mast or fixed high up the building. The signal can be passed to an indicator or a recording chart up to 915 m distant, and the chart is available to provide readings in either knots or miles per hour. Charts can be changed at any interval to suit requirements up to one month.

This instrument requires only minimum maintenance, which can quite easily be carried out by the Clerk of Works himself.

The cost of such instruments can be set against the information they provide and the fact that claims can be met on a more realistic basis than by the usual methods of recording the weather conditions on most sites.

Photographic Records

A Clerk of Works who is also an amateur photographer can rightly claim to be adding yet another asset to his list of accomplishments. He has the means of producing an accurate visual record of the progress of work throughout the contract. If such a record is to be of full value, it is essential that selected vantage points are established from which the progress photographs will be taken. The vantage points must be agreed at the beginning of the contract, and in selecting them the changing shape of the site as the work proceeds must be borne in mind.

It will be necessary for the photographs to 'overlap' when taken to ensure there are no parts missing due to blurred edges on the film. Changing the vantage point when taking the photograph may completely distort the record, since the changing angle of the photograph may miss or change the appearance of some important feature.

Additional photographs can be taken during the progress of the work where the situation suggests it is worthwhile. This may well be in situations where the work is likely to be covered, such as drains, foundations, services within ducts or ceiling spaces, or heating coils enclosed within floor screeds. The possibilities are endless, and it may be necessary to discipline oneself to avoid taking unnecessary photographs.

Defective work during erection procedures or in finishings as the work proceeds can be suitably recorded, as well as alterations to the work under variation orders issued by the architect. Disputes often arise over the performance of materials used in the contract if they have suffered from poor storage facilities earlier in the contract, and photographic records taken at the time will provide greater emphasis later than several pages of documentation.

After the contract has been completed, there are often difficulties proving that the standards of workmanship and quality of finishings were inadequate, since the buildings are then tenanted and damage may be blamed on the occupants. Photographs taken at the time of dispute showing the work appropriately dated can hardly be disputed as evidence and will influence any decisions taken on such matters.

The Clerk of Works who does not have aspirations towards photography can still achieve satisfactory results, for modern cameras are produced quite cheaply with virtually fool-proof built-in mechanisms to take away the difficulties of exposure, etc. A record on film can be obtained immediately by using the high-speed Polaroid camera, making it possible to submit evidence direct to the architect on the same day as any situation requiring his attention arises.

Complete records can be established by marking up the drawings to show the positions from which photographs were taken, and some of the photographs might be included with the maintenance handbook supplied to the client by the architect on completion of the work. Large contracts often progress so rapidly that the architect finds it is advisable to appoint a professional photographer to produce regular monthly progress photographs which may be used for site progress meetings.

The Clerk of Works can assist in this respect by recording the vantage points used by the photographer, and by selecting areas before the photographer's visit he will enable items to be recorded which might otherwise have been overlooked.

CHAPTER ELEVEN

Information

General Sources

The Clerk of Works who seeks information on most subjects within the construction industry will find there is an endless supply of literature available to him. Much of it is provided by trade development groups without any charge to the recipient, but there is an extensive catalogue of inexpensive and informative literature published by government departments.

Most Clerks of Works tend towards creating their own information sources, with manufacturers' instruction booklets and technical papers collected from trade journals. While this is excellent material for keeping up-to-date with general information, the difficulties arise where quick reference is necessary to find an answer to a particular problem. If he is attached to a large architect's office, the Clerk of Works may have access to the office reference library and find the answer to his problem there.

The reference library will be maintained through subscriptions to a proprietary index filing system, or perhaps by a specially appointed member of staff, but whichever method is used it is likely that the filing and classification system will be that known as CI/SfB. Almost all documents, including trade literature, are classified today under this system and though the Clerk of Works is hardly likely to use it, he will find it an advantage to have an idea how it works, not only in order that he may use the reference library but also because it may help him to keep his own catalogues, etc, in more semblance of order.

CI/SfB Classification

The system originated in Sweden. The letters SfB are the initial letters of the words referring to a co-ordinating committee for building, while CI stands for construction index. Apart from the advantages to libraries in working offices where materials and components can be filed more accurately, the system is designed to provide a universal classification which can be used by the professions, manufacturers, and contracting organisations.

The original system consisted of three divisions of information, but this has been revised to four divisions, each division being applied to a single aspect of the industry.

A table of headings is listed within each division, with items being given a reference applicable only to that division.

A standard box is printed in the top right-hand corner of all documents, pamphlets, leaflets, catalogues, etc, in which the reference number is printed.

The box is divided into two halves, the lower part mainly for the use of large libraries, and the upper half further spaced into four parts to receive each group reference.

The divisions are referred to as Tables and the Clerk of Works can obtain a copy of the headings listed within each table which will help him to identify the items initially.

Table 0: Built Environment

This division relates to the following categories:

(a) Natural Environment, which includes town planning, landscaping etc.
(b) Structures, involving Industrial Buildings, Housing and Office Blocks.
(c) Spaces, which refers to the functional application of space.

Items within this table are listed from 0 to 9 and divided and sub-divided into double and treble numeral headings to identify the specific item. To find secondary schools under this system one would find relevant literature identified as shown in the box, and this figure is produced from the sequence illustrated:

713

7 Educational, Cultural, Scientific Buildings
71 Schools
713 Secondary Schools

Table 1: Elements

This distinguishes parts of a structure or site, references being identified by numerals enclosed within brackets, and additional numerals being added to provide further headings, as with Table 0.

Information on curtain walling for secondary schools could be found by reference to the following headings, while identification on the literature would be shown in the box:

713 (21.4)

(2–)   Primary Elements
(21)   External Walls
(21.4) Curtain Walling

Table 2/3: Construction Form and Materials

Both these groups are distinctly related and have therefore been retained in the same table. They are listed separately under alphabetical headings, with the main group under capital letters and sub-divided by adding a small letter and a numeral as shown.

To find the reference to stainless steel curtain walling for a secondary school, check the box shows for the identification, and the sequence which produced it appears as follows:

713 (21.4) Hh3

H   Sections, Bars, etc.
Hh   Metals in General
Hh3   Steel Alloys

Table 4: Activities and Requirements

'Activities' relate to organisation – training – information, etc, while 'Requirements' refer to performance criteria, and the reference is given as a capital letter in brackets. The reference is further divided by the addition of a numeral and a small letter, and as an example the identification for building controls and forklift trucks are shown together with the sequence of producing these references:

(A3j)

(B3h)

(A)   Administration – Management
(A3)   Planning – Design
(A3j) Building Controls

(B)   Construction Plant
(B3)   Transport
(B3h) Forklift Trucks

British Standard Specifications

These are detailed specifications issued by the British Standards Institution to cover materials and components throughout some twelve divisions of industry, including the building and construction industry. Other divisions affected are the chemical industry, electrical, mechanical, photographic, and many others.

BSI, as it is better known, is financed by a subscribing membership, sales of their numerous publications, government grants, and fees for carrying out tests on manufacturer's products to certify they comply with the standards as laid down by the Institution. Where products are successful in passing the tests, the manufacturer is authorised to mark his product with the BSI symbol and the reference numbers of the relevant British Standards. The symbol of course is the well-known 'kitemark', and manufacturers are naturally anxious to acquire this seal of approval for their goods, as it is the recognised acceptable standard of quality.

Specifications included in building and engineering contracts rarely go into details in respect of materials and are content to quote the relevant British Standard Specification, although care must be taken to ensure that the revisions have been considered when quoting current issues of standard specifications.

The standards are compiled by technical committees formed from those who are representative of the particular interests concerned with the work. Draft specifications are issued to various institutions and interested parties for their comments before the appropriate standards committee approves the final draft. Copies can be obtained direct from the BSI sales office in the form of booklets which are revised as required by amendment slips or revised editions.

A really useful issue of the British Standard Specifications for Clerks of Works is the *Handbook No 3*, which consists of two volumes containing summaries of all the specifications on building materials and components, as well as codes of practice and draft issues. Up to 1972 these were issued in loose-leaf binders, convenient for inserting revisions, but the revised forms are in paperback bound editions, issued annually.

Membership of the Institution is open to Clerks of Works as well as other members of the industry, and this enables members to buy Standard Specifications, etc, at a discount rate, besides receiving the monthly edition of *BSI News*.

Apart from the BSI Offices in London and Manchester where copies of current Standard Specifications, together with other BSI publications, can be referred to in the BSI Library, most colleges, universities, and public libraries keep up-to-date copies for reference. A list of these sources can be obtained by writing to the British Standards Institution, either in Manchester or London.

Codes of Practice

The Council for Codes of Practice for Building was formed in 1942 and is composed of representatives from a number of institutions concerned with the industry. The Codes of Practice are prepared by technical committees in a similar way to the Standard Specifications, and drafts are published for general comment before they are finalised. Apart from quoting definitions, the Codes of Practice provide guidance on quality, performance, workmanship standards, design considerations, methods for testing, safety precautions, and methods of assembly.

Clerks of Works should try to obtain copies of the relevant Codes of Practice, if only for reference, before the work is due to start on the site, as this could avoid many problems arising later.

BSI Year Book

A *Year Book* issued annually by the British Standards Institution contains the references of all Standard Specifications and Codes of Practice, together with a brief summary of the relevant standard which is very useful in finding the one required. The *Year Book* is issued free to all members of the Institution, and considering the increasing number of standards, etc, which are now being produced, the Clerk of Works would find this publication of immense value for reference alone.

Agrément Certificates

Because of the problems which arise in assessing new materials, a group was set up by the Minister of Public Building and Works in 1966 to perform this function. The system had been in use for some time in France under the French equivalent of the Building Research Establishment, and was known as the Service de l'Agrément, so it is easy to see why the new group was named the Agrément Board and the certificate they issued referred to as the Agrément Certificate.

The certificates are required for materials for which there is no standard issued, owing to its being a new material, and in the first instance the satisfactory performance of the material is covered with the issue of a certificate of assessment, giving design data, methods of use and installation as well as clearly identifying the product. The certificate is valid for three years only and a further certificate will be required at the end of that period to cover a further three years. By that time a British Standard should be available if the material has been successfully established.

Membership is available to Clerks of Works and others in the industry in the same way as with BSI, literature being available to members and opportunities to attend seminars and conferences on new materials.

DOE Advisory Leaflets

First published in 1950 and revised as a second series in 1966, these leaflets contain up-to-date information on good building practices. The information is illustrated with drawings and charts which will be found very useful for the man involved on the site. The leaflets cover a wide range of subjects from concreting techniques, powered hand tools, setting out on site, etc, to painting problems, condensation in buildings, electricity on building sites, and numerous other topics.

The complete list issued to date is shown on various issues of the leaflets, and these can be obtained at the cost of a few pence from HM Stationery Office.

Building Research Establishment Digests

The *Digests* are short summaries of information resulting from fieldwork carried out by the Building Research Establishment. Originally they were published in the form of questions and answers but in 1960 they took on the form which is familiar today to the many members of various institutions who receive them regularly with their journals. They are issued monthly.

The Building Research Establishment is now a part of the Department of the Environment and includes the Forest Products Research Laboratories and the Fire Research Station.

There is an advisory service available on general construction problems from the stations at Watford, Birmingham or Glasgow. Timber queries can be answered by the Princes Risborough Laboratories at Aylesbury, Bucks, and fire and insulation problems by the Fire Research Station at Boreham Wood, Herts.

Clerks of Works will find the *Digests* to be excellent sources of information in helping to keep up-to-date in materials and building techniques, and should either obtain them through their institute or by direct subscription to HM Stationery Office.

GLC Bulletins

The Research and Development Section of the Greater London Council produces an information service for its own use, but professional offices are able to obtain these *Bulletins* by subscription, and a Clerk of Works attached to a large architect or engineer's office will find a great deal of practical information in them.

Building Centres

The first and the largest of the building centres was established in London in the 1930s, but in 1963 it was reformed and now operates under a trust in other parts of the country as well. Regional Building Centres have also been set up in several towns and cities, and generally they provide an information service besides exhibiting building materials, components, and building services. The Clerk of Works can, therefore, see these items and assess their capabilities before he will be required to do so on the site.

Trade Development Associations

Most Clerks of Works should be aware of the excellent literature which is circulated by these associations. The Cement and Concrete Association is an outstanding example of this source of information. Most of the groups are independent organisations which are either Government controlled or sponsored by the Trade Associations for Research and Development.

The Cement and Concrete Association also organises training courses on a practical basis which provide Clerks of Works with an opportunity to increase their knowledge of this aspect of the industry. The Timber Research and Development Association also has advisory services, and literature is available. Others who provide information include the Copper Development Association, the British Ceramic Tile Council, the Research

Association of British Paint, Colour and Varnish Manufacturers, and the Heating and Ventilating Research Association.

Indeed it would be true to say there is a wealth of information freely available to those who would take advantage of such opportunity.

CHAPTER TWELVE

Controls and Regulations

Planning Controls

The Town and Country Planning Act 1971 requires all development apart from specified exemptions to be submitted for the approval of the planning authority for the area in which development will take place. Planning controls are desirable for several reasons. Probably two main reasons might be described as (a) to control land use in such a way that it will serve the best interests of the community, and (b) to ensure that standards of design are not likely to spoil the surroundings in which the proposed development will take place.

For example, it might be difficult to justify certain types of development such as factories in a residential area, while an ultra-modern façade may not be acceptable in the midst of a Georgian terrace. The 1971 Act is an addition to the Town and Country Planning Acts of 1962 and 1968; and besides controlling land, the Acts enable local authorities to make compulsory purchase of any land required for public development.

Buildings of architectural or historic interest are safeguarded under the Acts, and before a 'listed' building can be considered for demolition, or alteration in any way, permission must be obtained from the authority. Where development occurs, the authority has the power to divert highways or suspend 'rights of way' where these are conflicting with the development.

Applications for planning permission must be made on a special form supplied by the planning authority, which must give written notice within two months of its decision.

Where development has been approved, work must proceed within five years, and where the application has been rejected, reasons will be given. Where an application for planning permission has been refused, an appeal can be made against the decision, which may result in the Secretary of State appointing someone to investigate the circumstances.

Public Health Acts

While the Public Health Act 1961 empowers the Secretary of State to create building regulations, there are also other regulations within the Act directly affecting any building proposals.

Building plans submitted to the authority for approval under the Building Regulations might easily be rejected for a number of reasons under the Public Health Act 1936. These reasons have been confirmed by the Act of 1961, which, apart from giving authority to issue building regulations, has introduced regulations concerning costs in providing sewers, drains and sanitary conveniences, and amended the laws in respect of trade effluent discharged into public sewers.

Dilapidated buildings and demolition remain covered by the Public Health Acts, and the authority is given the right to reject proposals for any building to be constructed of materials which are likely to deteriorate rapidly.

Buildings cannot be erected upon a site where the ground has been filled with offensive materials such as animal or vegetable matter, nor erected over an existing drain or sewer, except under special circumstances.

A satisfactory drainage system must be provided, as well as adequate water supplies, and all new dwellings must be provided with accommodation for storing food and approved bathroom facilities.

Wherever a number of people are likely to gather in buildings such as churches, theatres, offices or restaurants, they must be provided with proper entrances and exits, as well as passageways, aisles and gangways to enable reasonable clearance of the building in the event of an emergency.

Where the construction of living or sleeping accommodation is more than two storeys high, adequate means of escape must be provided in the event of fire.

Building Regulations 1972

Introduced in 1965, Building Regulations did not become effective until the beginning of 1966, when they completely replaced the byelaws issued up to that date by the local authorities. Byelaws had been issued under powers granted by the Public Health Act 1936, and the 1961 Act gave similar powers for the Building Regulations to be issued in 1965; these have now been up-dated by the Building Regulations 1972, amended further in 1973.

District councils and outer London boroughs are given authority to enforce the regulations, but school buildings as well as certain buildings erected by statutory authorities are exempt from them. It is suggested that this provides greater freedom for the authorities concerned to experiment with new techniques and materials, thereby providing a service to the industry. Crown buildings are not affected by Building Regulations, while Inner London is controlled by the London Building Acts.

Scotland has its own regulations, issued by the Secretary of State for Scotland under the Building (Scotland) Acts 1959 and 1970.

With certain specified exceptions building regulations apply to all new buildings and extensions to existing buildings, as well as to the installation or replacement of fittings within the buildings. Regulations affecting insulation against loss of heat, etc, are only applicable to housing, regulations regarding insulation to factories, etc, being included in other Acts.

Notices and plans must be submitted to the authority concerned, which checks that they comply with the regulations for the type of building to be erected. Where the plans are not accepted because they fail to comply with the regulations, the applicant may ask for the matter to be decided by the magistrate's court, or both sides may agree to submit the matter to the Secretary of State, whose decision will be final. It is also possible to obtain a waiver in respect of a regulation if it is agreed it would operate unreasonably in that particular instance.

In order that the authorities can enforce the regulations they require the opportunity to inspect the work, and notice must be given in writing at least 24 hours before work starts on site. Further notices must be given before foundations or drains and private sewers are covered in, as well as within 7 days of backfilling being completed.

Where notices are not given the authority has the right to order the removal of the work which contravenes the regulations.

When the building is completed, at least 7 days' notice must be given before it is occupied.

Factories Act

Besides ensuring the safety, health and welfare of persons employed in and around a factory the Act lays down further regulations in respect of employment.

An abstract of the Act together with copies of all special regulations must be posted at the principal entrance to the works. Where the HM Inspector of Factories directs this, copies must be posted in other prominent places within the factory.

A register must be maintained showing, among other information, the particulars of any accident or industrial disease which may occur within the factory.

Where building operations are proceeding, the area is regarded as a 'factory' under the meaning of the Act, whether it be demolition, construction, structural alterations, redecoration or maintenance of a building. There is no exception in the case of operations on behalf of, or by, the Crown; in such instances the regulations must be observed.

Until 1962 the Act authorised regulations under Building (Safety, Health and Welfare) Regulations 1948, but these have since been replaced by the following regulations.

The Construction (General Provisions) Regulations 1961

Authorised by the Acts of 1937 and 1948, these regulations came into effect in March 1962 and refer to all demolition work, excavations, shafts and tunnels, safe access to works, and the appointment of safety officers. Work on or adjacent to water requires certain precautions to be taken, besides work in connection with cofferdams and caissons. Site transport regulations are included, as well as reference to the use of explosives.

The Construction (Lifting Operations) Regulations 1961

Authorised by the Acts of 1937, 1948 and 1959, these regulations also came into force in March 1962 and refer to the testing and operation of cranes and hoists. They also provide for safety precautions in respect of chains, ropes and lifting gear, besides consideration of safe working loads applied to lifting operations.

Records of all inspections and tests carried out must be maintained and made available for inspection by HM Inspectors of Factories.

The Construction (Working Places) Regulations 1966

These regulations came into effect in August 1966 and were authorised under the Factories Act 1961. They provide a comprehensive reference to

matters in respect of scaffolding as well as ladders, gangways, platforms
and crawling boards. Boatswains' chairs, cages, skips, etc, are also referred
to, besides the loading or depositing of materials on scaffolding.

The Construction (Health and Welfare) Regulations 1966

Again authorised by the Factories Act 1961, these regulations came into
effect in May 1966. Requirements are stated in respect of the first-aid
measures to be provided on site, and varied according to the numbers
employed on the site. While the provision of a suitably equipped first-aid
box will be sufficient on a small contract, it may be necessary to provide
a properly equipped first-aid room on a site where a large number of
persons are employed, besides retaining a person qualified in first aid to
deal with such instances.

Accommodation for taking meals and facilities for drying clothes must
also be available, besides washing facilities and adequate and proper
sanitary accommodation.

Fire Precautions Act

The Act of 1971 provides the Secretary of State for the Environment with
powers to include in the Building Regulations further requirements for
means of escape from buildings in case of fire. Certificates will be required
for all buildings where people are likely to gather in numbers, such as
hotels, boarding houses, and places of entertainment. These certificates
will only be issued by the fire authority when it is satisfied the regulations
have been complied with.

Plans submitted to the local authority for approval under Building
Regulations must also be approved by the fire authority, although it is
the responsibility of the Building Regulation authority to ensure this.

Where Building Regulations do not apply, however, it is important that
approval of the proposals is obtained from the fire authority. Hose reels
and other fire-fighting equipment should be tested before the building is
completed, as it is quite possible these may be required before the building
is completely handed over to the client, since fire risks are always present.

Highways Acts

The Acts grant powers to the local authority to take action where an obstruction is caused to safe passage along a street, or where vehicles are crossing over footpaths, etc.

Excavations in the streets, where connecting to a sewer, and the erection of barriers, or the depositing of materials or builder's skips in the street, are all affected by these Acts.

Certain sections deal with building lines, and others with erection of hoardings and gates around a construction site, or any matter likely to affect the public safety.

Clean Air Acts

The height of industrial chimneys and the emission of smoke likely to cause pollution is controlled by these Acts, which also order the installation of proper plant to deal with grit or dust that would otherwise be projected into the surrounding countryside. The adaptation of fireplaces and the control of smoke from houses is also covered by these Acts.

Electricity and Gas Supply Regulations

These regulations are laid down by the Electricity Acts 1947 and empower the electricity undertaking to withhold supplies unless it is satisfied with the installation within the buildings.

Gas supplies can be withheld also where the gas undertaking is not satisfied with the installation, and its authority is given in Schedule 4 to the Gas Act 1972.

IEE Regulations

Electrical installations generally must conform with the Electricity Supply Regulations and, in the case of factories, with the Electricity (Factories Act) Special Regulations. Other types of installations may be required to conform with additional special requirements.

The Regulations for the Electrical Equipment of Buildings are issued by the Institution of Electrical Engineers and is intended for contractual purposes to supplement the statutory provisions. Part I of these regulations states the safety requirements which must be applied, and the electricity authority would be unlikely to supply a power supply to an installation which did not conform with these requirements. Part II sets out in detail the methods and practices which are necessary to meet the requirements stated in Part I, and where there is any departure from the requirements, this must be clearly stated on the completion certificate issued by the electrical contractor when he completes the installation.

Notices and Approvals

Provision is made in the contract for the contractor to make all the necessary notices and obtain approvals before proceeding with the work controlled by statutory regulations. Before starting work upon the site he must notify the local authority building surveyor of his intention to start on a given date, and subsequent notices must be issued to the surveyor when it is proposed to commence foundation work, and the installation of the drains. These notices must be submitted before the work starts to give the building surveyor the opportunity to inspect, and where necessary to test the work to satisfy himself it is in accordance with the regulations.

CHAPTER THIRTEEN

Site Administration

Site Office

The Clerk of Works' site office should be treated as an extension of the architect's organisation and never regarded as just a site cabin. As his own attitude to the office will be reflected in other people's approach to it, the Clerk of Works must pay heed to this from the moment he takes up residence on the site.

A well-organised office may also demonstrate the competence of the Clerk of Works in other respects, and both architect and consultant will have more confidence that he is a responsible colleague, able to safeguard matters of interest to them as well as the client. Most contractors respect a Clerk of Works who proves himself capable in his job, and an efficient site office will create a good impression right from the start of the contract.

Details of the size and construction of the site office will be found in the contract bills, but the siting of the office must be arranged by the Clerk of Works himself. A position should be selected close to the site entrance, where the Clerk of Works can observe deliveries of materials, etc, as well as visitors to site, when he is working in the office.

It is also important to study the contract programme carefully before siting the office to make sure that it will not later obstruct work on drains, services, roads or footpaths. This can happen on sites where space is restricted, and in this case consideration should be given to a portable form of accommodation which can be resited later.

The office windows should always be arranged to provide an uninterrupted view of the construction area, and if this can also be achieved while remaining adjacent to the contractor's site office, then good communications will be more easily established.

A suitable area for the office would be 18·58 m² with floor to ceiling height not less than 2·286 m. Walls and ceilings should be lined with plasterboard or insulation board and decorated in a light coloured emulsion paint, while the floor should be covered with linoleum. Adequate lighting and heating must be available from the outset, together with a telephone, which must be a separate line and not connected with the contractor's office lines. Owing to the delays which arise on most contracts, the Clerk of Works would be advised to raise the question of services at the pre-contract meeting to make sure that orders for them are placed immediately.

Apart from the time spent by the Clerk of Works on the site, he has visitors to the site who must be catered for, and an additional area should be attached to the office for a WC and a washroom-cum-kitchen. Hot and cold water, together with soap and towels, must be provided; plus facilities for heating food and boiling water, both of which can be met by installing a small stove and an electric kettle. Sufficient coat hooks should also be provided for the Clerk of Works and any visitors to site.

The main door to the office should be fitted with a mortice-lock and a letter aperture, and the exterior of the office painted in a selected colour, with a board showing the title CLERK OF WORKS painted in white or black letters not less than six inches high fitted close to the door. The office should be raised clear of the ground, with a paved footpath providing access and sufficient hard standing to provide parking for four cars.

Attendance and cleaning is included in the contract bills, and all arrangements should be clarified as early as possible and a suitable routine established.

On construction sites in built-up areas it is sometimes necessary to erect the office accommodation on a gantry due to lack of space, and in such instances the area of office floor space will be restricted; but it is still advisable to ensure the uninterrupted view of the construction area so far as this is possible.

In all cases the Clerk of Works' office must be easily identifiable to enable visitors to find it when they arrive on site. The Clerk of Works must ensure his office is kept clean and tidy: unwashed cups and cigarette ends lying around do not enhance the image of a Clerk of Works, and care in returning files to the cabinet and drawings to their rightful place will establish a good habit for the future. It is often put forward as an excuse that muddy conditions on site, especially during the excavation period, make it impossible to keep a clean office. This is not true, and a boot scraper near the door entrance, together with a drum of water and an old brush, help to remove excess mud from rubber boots and only take up a few minutes of anyone's time.

The amount of furniture required will depend upon the size of contract and the amount of drawings and paperwork involved, but the following items should be included.

1 desk with lockfast drawers. 1 Plan chest with six drawers
1 office chair. 4 chairs. 2 office stools
1 six-drawer steel filing cabinet
1 lockfast steel storage cabinet
1 set of shelving
1 drawing bench

Filing Procedures

On a large contract where a great deal of paperwork is likely to be circulated the lever arch type of file is recommended as being the most suitable, enabling papers to be inserted or extracted with ease. Ordinary ring files or box files are quite suitable also, but where there is an excess of paperwork several binders may become necessary for each subject.

The size of the contract will also dictate the number of files required. Where AIs (architect's instructions) and VOs (variation orders) are issued under the same numbering system, these may be kept in one file, but it is most important that the Clerk of Works bears in mind the essential difference between these two forms. A basic list of files which should be maintained will include:

Correspondence – incoming and outgoing
Architect's instructions
Variation orders
Site instructions
Site minutes
Labour returns
Dayworks sheets
Piling records
Site progress reports

Each file should be properly named on the cover to provide easy reference, especially as it may be necessary for someone other than the Clerk of

Works to refer to the system at any stage of the contract. This might easily occur if he is on holiday or sick, and the replacement will be working at a disadvantage through being unfamiliar with the system.

Office Stationery

Apart from those special forms required for reporting progress, etc, the Clerk of Works will require a generous supply of carbon paper to ensure that the copies of the reports that he writes are legible. It is most disconcerting for anyone faced with reading carbon copy reports to find they are indistinct in parts, generally in the important sections of the report.

Rubber stamps and an ink pad will also be required. A date stamp is needed to mark all incoming drawings and correspondence, and a stamp marked with the words 'For Record Purposes Only' to be applied to all dayworks sheets before the Clerk of Works signs them.

To maintain progress records and charts, he will also require graph paper and coloured pens or pencils, while a stapling machine and a paper punch will be essential to maintain a neat filing system. Paper clips should be used for securing sheets of paper in lieu of a stapling machine, and pins should be avoided wherever possible. Rubber bands are useful for retaining a number of papers together, and can also be used to retain amended drawings which are folded up and placed in racks within the office. The drawings should be clearly marked on the outside with their reference number and title.

Bulldog clips help to retain papers and charts which can be hung on the wall for easy reference, and adhesive tape can be a useful repair kit for site drawings, which can be subjected to a great deal of use under adverse conditions.

Stationery will be supplied by the architect or the employer in most cases, but in some circumstances the Clerk of Works will be expected to provide the stationery and will be reimbursed for the expenses by the architect.

Record Books

An A4 size book with a hard back and lined pages will be most suitable for use as a site diary, and a duplicate book of the same size will suffice for writing letters and reports to the architect.

Routine notes during site inspections are best kept in an A6 size notebook with hard back and lined pages, while measurements taken on the site should be recorded in a surveyor's notebook commonly referred to as a 'dim-book'.

The method for recording levels depends on the Clerk of Works' preference, either rise and fall or collimation, but all levels must be entered in the level book whenever they are checked on site, as they will be required later.

All books should be appropriately named, the contract designation being added also, and they should be numbered whenever additional books become necessary, to avoid confusion at a later stage in the contract.

Drawings

Drawings must be filed in a sequence which will provide easy reference, and while experienced Clerks of Works may have found methods over the years which are suitable to their requirements, those less experienced would be well advised to group the drawings into distinct phases of construction.

The system can be developed further once the main phases of operations are established and the Clerk of Works is more familiar with the system. It is quite obvious that even the best system will be of little use if it is not maintained correctly, with drawings returned to their correct place in the plan chest after use. The Clerk of Works who keeps leafing through the drawings in the hope of finding the correct one is using up a great deal of his own valuable time, which could be put to better use elsewhere, apart from the inherent danger of overlooking vital details when he is pressed for a quick reply on a problem. Examples are shown of typical drawings to be included in each group, but this is not a complete list and the Clerk of Works must refer to his schedule in order that he can prepare his own list:

(a) *Site Information*
   Site plans
   Setting-out details
   Piling layout
   Site services
   Drainage plan
   External works

(b) *Substructure*
   Foundation plan
   Piling details
   Foundation details
   Basement details
   Service entries
   Ground-floor construction

(c) *Superstructure*
Frame construction
Cladding details
Elevations
Floor and roof plans
Stairs, lifts and ducts
Motor room

(d) *Services*
Service carcassing
Drainage details
Waste-disposal system
Lift and motor room details
Boilerhouse and plant room
Air conditioning and refrigeration

(e) *Finishes*
Wall, floor and ceilings
Special finishes
Joinery details
Sanitary ware
Service installations
Service equipment
Built-in furniture

(f) *External Works*
Service roads and footpaths
Manholes and service points
Fencing
Lighting
Landscaping details
Signs and notices

Drawing Register

The Clerk of Works must be sure to date stamp all drawings on receipt and enter them in the drawing register. When a revised drawing is issued, it will be given the reference number and a letter which will change with each issue of the drawing; this letter must be shown in the squares on the right of the register in order that the most recent issue will be easily identifiable.

Showing the scale as well as the reference number of the drawing makes it much easier to look through the register for the correct one before resorting to the plan chest.

A register may be prepared by the Clerk of Works, or sufficient blank sheets can be provided by the architect's office.

Site Instruction Register

Delays often occur between the Clerk of Works issuing site instructions and the contractor carrying out the work, since the architect may forget to confirm the site instruction or not agree that it should be issued.

The Clerk of Works himself may give verbal instructions several times before feeling it necessary to issue a written instruction, and complications can easily arise later because of this, especially if the contractor continues with sections of the work which should obviously have been rejected by the Clerk of Works.

There is no doubt that keeping a register of instructions issued will be in the best interests of the Clerk of Works, especially where the contractor remains unco-operative in these matters, and the register can be produced to support comments at the monthly progress meetings. The architect will also find this a useful reminder to confirm site instructions when discussing the register before progress meetings.

In considering the form suggested for the site instruction register (see Appendix), it will be seen that the date upon which the instruction is first issued, either verbally or in writing, must be entered in column 1, with a brief but clear description of the instruction given in column 2. Verbal instructions should be noted by placing a tick in column 3 and subsequent verbal instructions for the same item can be recorded with additional ticks. If no response is achieved following the second or possibly third verbal request, the Clerk of Works should obviously put the matter in writing on an official site instruction form. The site instruction number should be entered in column 4, and when confirmed by the architect on an architect's instruction, this number should be recorded in column 5. Under remarks in column 6 the Clerk of Works should note whatever action the contractor takes in the matter, and column 7 should be used to record the date upon which the work is completed.

More detailed information will obviously be recorded in the site diary and cross-reference with these entries can be obtained by noting the site diary page or date of entry in column 8.

Wall Charts

The Clerk of Works can easily produce wall charts for himself of information which will enable him to provide ready answers to any request from the architect or the quantity surveyor on these matters. The charts can be recorded on a monthly pattern, providing valuable reference for monthly progress meetings, after which they can be filed away for future use where required.

Graph paper should be used, with the days of the month arranged along the top and bottom of the paper and the quantities or numbers down either side. Dots at the intersection of co-ordinates will record the situation on that date, and the dots can then be linked together with straight lines to present a visual picture of the position throughout the month. The Clerk of Works can choose the type of information he wishes to record in this manner, and charts of the labour employed on site, weather records, concrete test cube results, and deliveries of important materials are only some of the items to be considered.

Programme

The contractor issues the programme, the architect will consider this to see that it is acceptable in the interests of the client, and the Clerk of Works is expected to maintain a record of the progress on site related to the programme. He should mark the programme up daily, the marking up depending upon the type of programme submitted, and record the position in his site diary. The bar chart programme is best kept up by recording a coloured bar below the programme bar, but with flow charts and critical path methods it is better to use a length of coloured string or cotton to indicate the position. This will be secured at the top and bottom with drawing pins and the position of the line regulated by small mapping pins.

Labour Returns

Besides helping to estimate the progress of the contract, labour returns can give guidance on the financial aspect of the contract, and will be required where costs are rising, as this will be likely to affect the contract sum. The Clerk of Works should pay heed, therefore, to the labour strength on the site, noting the numbers of various trades and their deployment around the works.

Under certain forms of contract the contractor is bound to provide daily labour returns to the Clerk of Works, and this information should be supplied on properly printed forms to be filed for reference later. It is often difficult to obtain accurate figures, as sub-contractors may not provide these to the main contractor in the first instance, and he in turn may not treat the matter seriously enough. The Clerk of Works should make it clear that the figures must be correct, and he can help to press this point more firmly if he carries out some spot checks on both the main contractor's labour and the sub-contractors'.

Statistical Reports

Housing contracts may require returns to be made to the Ministry, and the Clerk of Works may be expected to supply the architect with monthly progress figures which he can submit. It is important that such information is accurate each month, and the Clerk of Works should refer to his previous monthly totals before submitting the information. It is better not to submit any information than inaccurate information, which may mislead those who are likely to base their assessment on it.

Correspondence

All communications from the Clerk of Works must be addressed to the architect, but copies of the correspondence may be sent to those affected by the contents where this will avoid misunderstandings or delays.

The Clerk of Works with the ability to use a typewriter and an available machine, will not only save himself time in preparing reports but also save the architect time, as they will be easier to read. Where reports have to be handwritten, however, the Clerk of Works must make certain that his writing is legible. Where a duplicate book is required, good carbon must always be used, otherwise reports may be difficult to read, and experience shows that when details have long been forgotten, otherwise excellent reports are often indistinguishable scribble.

Incoming correspondence must always be stamped with the date when it is received by the Clerk of Works, and a note made on the letter of any action taken in the matter.

Correspondence connected with the contract which reaches the Clerk of Works from other sources than the architect should be referred to the architect for his attention before filing it away.

Situations can arise where suppliers or sub-contractors visit the site, discuss matters with the Clerk of Works, and, upon returning to their office, send a letter confirming the discussion. From the point of view of the letter writer this is quite in order, but it may easily cause problems later if the letter is quoted to support a point and the architect is unaware of its existence. It is advisable, therefore, to make certain that the architect is notified of all such incidents, and they should be noted in the site diary at the appropriate times.

The Clerk of Works should not enter into correspondence with the contractor, but where it is necessary to draw the contractor's attention to a particular matter, this should be given on an official site instruction form. This method ensures that all communication between the Clerk of Works and the contractor is recorded and available to all who may be concerned, whatever the stage of the contract.

It is simpler if all reports and letters to the architect are in the same format, with the name of the contract at the top of the paper followed by the date on the top right-hand side. The subject heading should then be written and underlined, the text of the report or letter should follow, and the whole should end with the signature of the Clerk of Works. The text should be confined to relevant facts, avoiding unnecessary comments, but where the Clerk of Works feels it is important to express his opinion, he should confine this to the final paragraph – making it clear it *is his* opinion. This will enable the architect to assess the facts in the first instance before noting the comments of the Clerk of Works.

By the Clerk of Works attempting to fulfil the following points in the specimen report which follows, the architect is given sufficient information to make a decision and instruct the Clerk of Works in the action he must take, or issue an architect's instruction.

(a) Delivery of materials
(b) Error in conforming to specification
(c) Secondary treatment completed
(d) Storage and conditions
(e) Inspection carried out at correct time
(f) Contractor informed of error
(g) Action by contractor to date
(h) Notice of further problem
(i) Further information required.

Melbreak Housing Contract, Westown

17th April 1973

Timber Windows – Preservative Treatment

The contractor has taken delivery today of a load of timber windows which have been given preservative treatment by a 'dipped' process instead of the double-vacuum treatment which is specified in the contract bills.

All the frames have been satisfactorily primed with the paint specified in the bills but no attempt has been made to provide proper storage for the frames, although weather conditions are extremely wet at present.

The frames were inspected by me as they were being unloaded and the attention of the contractor's agent drawn to the error in preservative treatment, which was apparent from the certificate issued by the supplier.

In view of the weather conditions and the type of preservative treatment, the agent was advised to provide suitable protection to the frames, but no action is being taken, and the contractor himself claims he has provided frames in accordance with the specification.

According to the programme, work should commence on Monday next 'building in' the window frames and I await your instructions in the matter.

A. T. Square & Partners,   Signed : T. Break
Chartered Architects,   Clerk of Works
18 Brown Square,
EASTOWN

CHAPTER FOURTEEN

Programmes and Planning

Pre-planning of Contracts

The need for planning requires no explanation, but it is very easy to over-look the fact that the contractor's programme is merely one part of the whole operation, and that all those involved in getting the contractor actually on to the site must also programme their own efforts in the first instance. Even the client must programme his requirements, which will vary according to the type of project concerned: for example, an industrial complex will demand a great deal of detailed planning so that production can start as soon as possible, and this will involve purchase of plant and equipment before the building is started, and may even mean changing the type of machinery by the time the building is nearing completion to keep up-to-date with production methods. Similar programming will be necessary where people are concerned: hotels will have accommodation booked in advance, education authorities will have programmed for more space by a given term-period, and housing authorities will be committed to arrangements in many ways.

Once he has accepted the commission, the architect will have to begin producing a programme to cover the preparation of drawings and bills of quantities, the invitation to contractors to tender for the work, and the implementation of the project. He must also take account of those suppliers and sub-contractors with whom he may be concerned, as they will be obliged to fit in with the programme produced by any one of the contractors submitting a tender.

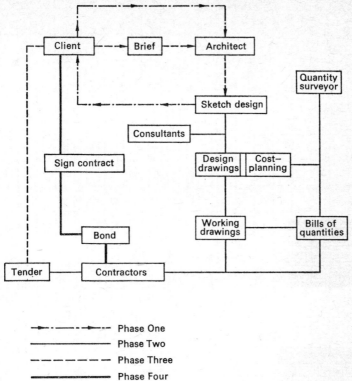

Fig. 2.

The quantity surveyor and all consultants will in turn have to prepare a programme of their own work to meet the dates agreed with the architect. Consultants may also be involved with specialist firms for supplying materials and sub-contractors who specialise in their particular branch of construction.

The contractor will need to prepare a programme of activities before he can consider his own prices for the work, as this will involve suppliers of materials and sub-contractors who in turn must go through similar procedures. The contractor will also be obliged to programme his work-load in the event of his tender being successful.

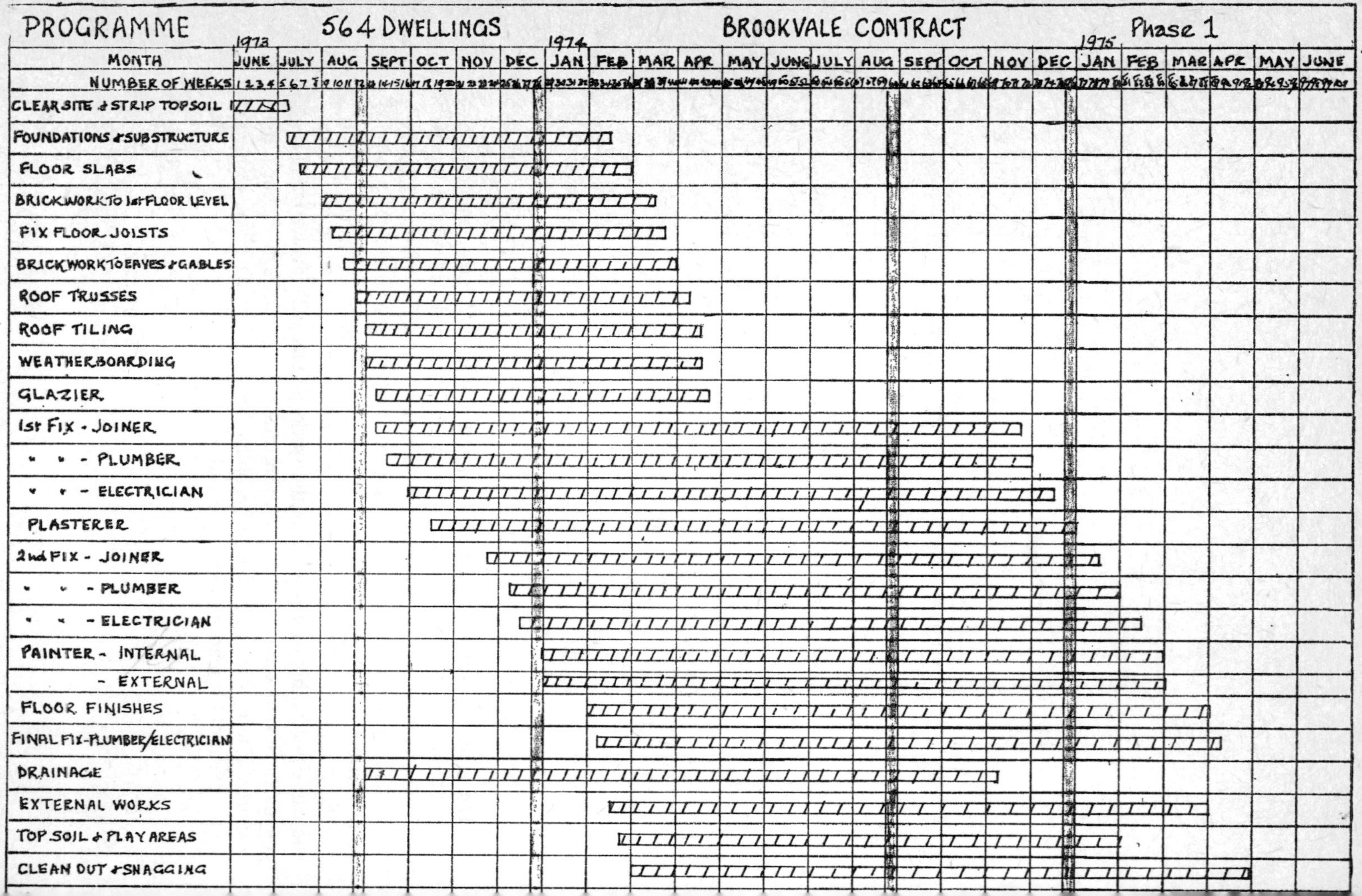

PROGRAMME 564 DWELLINGS BROOKVALE CONTRACT

1975 Phase 1

MONTH	1973		1974																1975					
	JUNE	JULY AUG	SEPT	OCT	NOV	DEC	JAN	FEB	MAR	APR	MAY	JUNE	JULY	AUG	SEPT	OCT	NOV	DEC	JAN	FEB	MAR	APR	MAY	JUNE
NUMBER OF WEEKS	1 2 3 4 5 6 7																							

CLEAR SITE & STRIP TOPSOIL
FOUNDATIONS & SUBSTRUCTURE
FLOOR SLABS
BRICKWORK TO 1st FLOOR LEVEL
FIX FLOOR JOISTS
BRICKWORK TO EAVES & GABLES
ROOF TRUSSES
ROOF TILING
WEATHERBOARDING
GLAZIER
1st FIX - JOINER
"   - PLUMBER
"   " - ELECTRICIAN
PLASTERER
2nd FIX - JOINER
"   "   - PLUMBER
"   "   - ELECTRICIAN
PAINTER - INTERNAL
"   - EXTERNAL
FLOOR FINISHES
FINAL FIX-PLUMBER/ELECTRICIAN
DRAINAGE
EXTERNAL WORKS
TOP SOIL & PLAY AREAS
CLEAN OUT & SNAGGING

Fig. 3.

Bar Charts

These are sometimes referred to as Gantt charts after the person credited with introducing this form of programming, and are probably the best known form of programme used in the construction industry. They are a graphic indication of the progress for each operation on the site, and besides being easy to understand they are also fairly simple to produce. Unfortunately they are not always accurate, and fail to give any indication of a breakdown in any particular operation or to reflect this in the total programme.

Safety factors are built into the programme, but often these are related to only certain operations, and if this safety period fails, the whole programme can be completely upset. There is also a danger of underestimating or over-estimating and trying to speed up operations at the expense of others, which may provide short-term results but will probably cause difficulties later. Experience suggests that many bar charts carefully assessing the preliminary operations on the site are produced, but when drafting the finishings, the completion dates are used as a basis and the sequence of operations worked back from that point, with the result that there is a certain imbalance around the middle of the programme.

The chart is formed by placing the various operations in the order of progress down the left-hand side of a graph, and dividing the sheet into columns, with the names of the months along the top of the sheet. Each square in the graph represents a week, and the estimated number of weeks required for each operation is then hatched in along the paper. Progress is marked in the squares immediately below each of the lines hatched out as the proposed progress, and while the length of the actual bar should coincide with the hatched bar, this rarely happens, sometimes because the starting dates of the operations are not always the same.

Bar charts are useful as a basis for producing more detailed charts, and can help in providing a ready guide to the site agent for the dates upon which he must order his materials.

The Clerk of Works will receive a copy of the programme from the main contractor early in the contract, and he must take care in marking the progress of the work below the estimates on the chart. This will enable the architect to assess the points which must be stressed when attending site meetings, but, as stated, it can be difficult to be definite that the contract is lagging, as some operations will be ahead and others behind, which will allow the contractor to suggest he is more or less on programme.

Network Analysis

Because of the tendency to refer to this form of programming under several headings, there can be confusion in discussing the system, and the Clerk of Works might find it easier to consider the alternate titles and the origins.

Critical Path Method (CPM) is a system of programming produced by two men, J. E. Kelly and M. R. Walker, in the 1950s for the Dupont Corporation, which was constructing several large chemical engineering plants. The system is based upon activities required to carry out the work, and gives one estimate of the time required to carry out that activity.

Programme Evaluation and Review Technique (PERT) was developed for the United States Navy around the time the CPM was published, and was used very successfully on the 'Polaris' project. Instead of 'activities' it referred to 'events' and provided three estimates for the time required to complete each 'event', these times being possible, probable and optimistic.

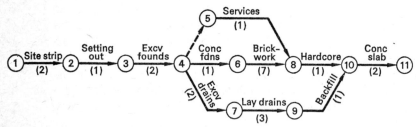

Fig. 4.

Network Analysis is the term applied to any system of programming which uses an arrow diagram to show the sequence and relation of events or activities in any project.

The Clerk of Works is unlikely to be called upon to prepare a network analysis, but he will be expected to be capable of reading and also interpreting charts prepared by others.

Network analysis is sometimes used on work of a repetitive nature that would be served better by alternative methods of programming. On complex contracts where many activities are interrelated network analysis will provide better communications and improved co-ordination between those involved, and a clearer picture of the objectives. The information can also be fed into a computer and analysed for further information, and where the project has more than 200 events, it may be necessary for a computer to produce such information. A list of operations essential to the completion of the project must be drawn up first, and this list will be referred to as the network analysis schedule.

Each of the operations is known as 'an event' and is identified on the chart by a small circle containing a number; an arrow connects each of the 'events' and is referred to as an 'activity'. The activity indicates the time taken to carry out an operation, the tail representing the beginning of the operation and the point of the arrow signifying the completion.

The estimated time required to complete each activity is shown in brackets either above or below the line of the arrow, which makes it possible to determine the sequence of activities taking the longest time. This is the minimum duration of time required to complete the project, and therefore becomes the critical path to follow.

When the arrow has been drawn up, the events are numbered from left to right and from top to bottom. A dotted arrow is a convenient way of showing the link with other activities and is referred to as a 'dummy activity', as there is no time involved.

It must be remembered that all previous activities are to be completed before the next activity begins, and that certain events are critical and must be completed on time if the programme is to be maintained.

The arrow diagram shown is for the sub-structure of a small factory and will provide a guide to the comments already made.

Activity 1–2 requires 2 days for the site to be stripped of topsoil, and 1 day for the setting out to be completed under Activity 2–3. A further 2 days will be required to excavate the foundations under Activity 3–4, and it will be noted that neither Activities 4–5 nor 4–7 can proceed until 1, 2 and 3 have been completed.

Several activities can run on parallel lines from this stage; the ducts for the services within the building can be laid in 1 day during the completion of the concrete foundations and the erection of the sub-structure brickwork, which takes 8 days in all. The drains within the building can be laid and continued externally in 5 days and backfilled in 1 day to allow hardcore to proceed immediately. The whole of the activities must be completed before 10–11 can be started, and in this example the critical path is along the continuous horizontal line, although it might equally occur on any of the lines if the duration of these activities totalled up that way.

Line of Balance Programming

This is a method of programming first applied to factories where there are a number of repetitive operations due to mass production methods. Because

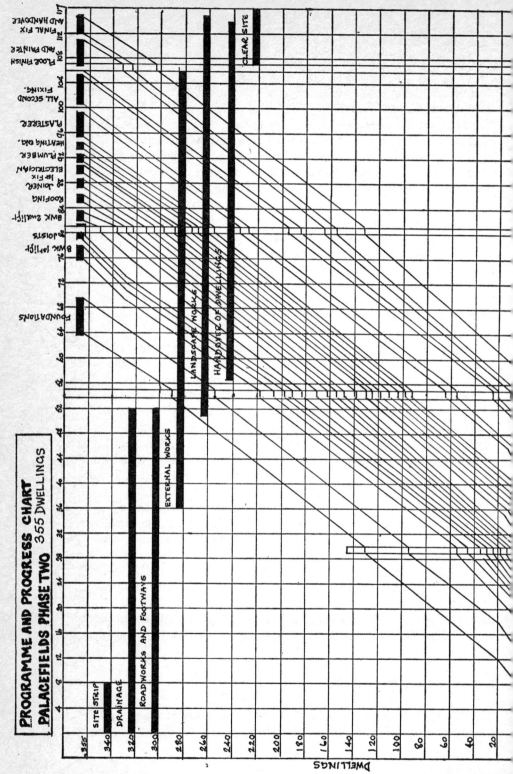

Fig. 5.

it is relatively easy to follow once the principles are understood, line of balance programming provides information quickly to most of those involved.

It was recognised that as housing was a repetitive form of production, line of balance programming could easily be applied to it, although there was one major difference from factory production in that the product often moves along on a belt system in factories with the operatives stationary, while in building it is the products which are stationary and the operatives mobile.

To build at a set rate, it is necessary to estimate the speed at which each operation can be achieved, and this will be affected by the number of men involved.

Once these estimates have been made, they are transferred as lines or bars on to graphs in a similar manner to bar charts, except that the bars in this instance are drawn at an angle from bottom to top of the sheet.

Any errors in the estimates should be highlighted, as the lines or bars will tend to move closer together when the operations are plotted on to the graph. It is usual to introduce a period of time between each operation to accommodate any delays, and this is referred to as a 'buffer'.

Two lines are drawn to show the start and finish of each operation, the space between representing the time taken to carry out the work, and each line will be repeated according to the number of houses – resulting in a band running from bottom to top of the sheet for each operation. Obviously these lines cannot run at a constant angle throughout, as there are holidays and weather conditions to be taken into account; also some operations will move quicker at certain times than others and this must be recognised.

The programme shown opposite is for 355 houses to be constructed in a contract period of 117 weeks and scheduled for a handover rate of six dwellings per week. These figures are shown on the programme. The number of houses is listed down the left-hand side of the chart and the number of weeks along both top and bottom.

Foundations mean all sub-structures up to damp-proof course and floor levels, commencing in week 6 and completed to the first house by week 12. This period of six weeks for each sub-structure continues to the latter half of weeks 64 and 70, when the last house is completed.

A 5 week 'buffer' period is shown between sub-structures and super-structures which begin in week 17, taking 2 weeks to complete the brickwork up to first floor level. Brickwork to the superstructure of the last house will start in week 76 and be at first floor level by week 78.

All subsequent operations can be followed in the same manner up to final fix and handover, when it will be noted there is a gap of one week between these operations.

Weeks 29–30, 54–5, 80–81, and 106–7 are all periods affected by holidays and lack of progress is recorded by showing a break in the angle of the bars.

A bar chart is overprinted at the top of the sheet, providing a quick reference to other activities which affect the programme. By filling in the band for each activity with a coloured pencil as the work progresses, and using a piece of coloured thread fixed with two drawing pins to mark the weekly periods, the Clerk of Works will have an immediate and accurate record to refer to when providing this information to the architect.

The Clerk of Works should also be in a position to make use of this method of planning to provide the architect with advance warning of delays in various sectors which might easily be misread on a larger chart.

CHAPTER FIFTEEN

Site Meetings—Reports—Feedback

Pre-Contract Meeting

The Clerk of Works may not always have the opportunity to be present at the pre-contract meeting, or contract briefing, as it is sometimes called. Where he does attend, it is important that he understands the reason for the meeting, and that he fits into the team.

To allow those who will attend the meeting to prepare themselves for discussion the architect will circulate an agenda a week or so before it takes place. He may also consider it advisable to hold a briefing meeting with the Clerk of Works and others representing the client before the main meeting. The agenda may vary according to the type of contract and the relationship between the parties, but certain items are common to most contracts.

The architect will chair the meeting and the Clerk of Works should note the importance of each of the following items as they are discussed.

Management Structures

The architect will introduce any other architectural staff who are likely to be in communication with the contractor's organisation; he will also introduce the Clerk of Works, the quantity surveyor and the consultant engineers.

The contractor will explain his management structure and introduce his representatives present – probably one of the firm's directors, the regional contracts manager, the site agent, site surveyor, site engineer, and the costing surveyor. It is useful if both sides submit the names of those concerned, together with telephone numbers, on paper in the first instance.

Contract Drawings

The architect will hand a complete set of drawings, together with a copy of the contract bills, specifications and schedules to the contractor. Generally the contractor is supplied with three sets of the drawings and two sets of bills, etc; he will state the number of additional copies he requires, and he may be obliged to meet the cost of these.

It is important that the Clerk of Works is supplied with copies of the drawings and bills at this stage if he is not already in possession of them. Issuing drawings to the Clerk of Works a little ahead of the time the contractor receives them will give him an advantage in studying the information before he is expected to comment on queries raised by the site agent.

Starting Order

The date to be written into the starting order will need to be agreed at the meeting; the contractor may not be prepared to start immediately as he will obviously require time to put his organisation into operation. Apart from notifying his sub-contractors and suppliers to proceed, the contractor must organise his site-office accommodation, including all temporary services, movement of plant and equipment, disposal of excavated materials; notify the local authority on matters of statutory obligation; and prepare a draft programme for the architect's approval.

The contractor will no doubt have inspected the site before the meeting, and may have reservations about accepting possession if it is not in the same condition as when he submitted his tender. This can easily occur when demolition or engineering works have been carried out under a separate contract, and in view of the fact that the completion date for the works is related to the date the contractor takes possession of the site, it is understandable if he approaches this situation with some caution.

On the other hand, if he has already been issued with a starting order and is unable to take possession of the site on the date stated, he will be entitled to a variation order extending the date of the contract.

Communications

In view of the various professions who are involved with the architect, the contractor will require instructions on the lines of communication between his staff and the architect. He will also give the address to which drawings and correspondence are to be forwarded for his attention.

When his head office is nearby he may wish all correspondence, etc, to be sent there direct, but if it happens to be in a different area he may prefer one copy to head office and one copy to the site office. Naturally all communications to the sub-contractors must be directed through the contractor, and the lines of communication at site level clearly defined as being via the Clerk of Works in the first instance.

The situation regarding instructions should also be clarified, especially those in which the Clerk of Works may be involved.

Programme

Confirmation of nominated sub-contractors and suppliers will require early consideration, as these will affect the contractor's programme. Certain sub-contracts, such as piling, may be required urgently, and negotiations may already have been made by the architect, but the contractor is responsible and will be involved with access and disposal of materials as well as bearing responsibility for the setting out of the contract.

Statutory undertakings will also affect the programme, and while it is the contractor's responsibility to deal with them, he may request the Clerk of Works to 'sit in' on all services meetings.

Sub-Contractors

Lists of all sub-contractors engaged by the contractor must be submitted to the architect for approval at this stage, and where necessary, arrangements should be made for examples of the sub-contractor's work to be viewed.

Materials

A reserve order placed for bricks by the architect will require confirmation by the contractor. The question of ordering materials direct from the bills will also require clarification at this stage to avoid any unnecessary misunderstandings arising later.

The procedure for submitting materials for approval should also be explained, and while the testing of concrete cubes or other materials is already laid down in the bills, it is advisable to explain the requirements.

Any other matters concerning treatment or deliveries of materials should be thoroughly clarified at this point, and the contractor should be informed of any factory inspection which will be necessary, in order that he can make such arrangements with the manufacturer.

Insurances

The contractor must take out certain insurances under the contract, and arrangements must be made for the policies, etc, to be inspected and approved by the client's legal adviser.

Valuations

The date for submitting valuations to the architect, as well as the dates for interim payments to be made, will be agreed at this meeting, and as the Clerk of Works may be expected to confirm the materials on site, sufficient time must be allowed to enable him to check these.

Offices and Site Works

If the pre-contract meeting is well handled, most of the initial points of importance will be covered, so that the first site meeting should be merely a confirmation of the agreements made. Accommodation will be required, however, for the first site meeting so that the layout for offices and site compound should be available for discussion at the pre-contract meeting. If this cannot be done at this stage, it should be dealt with as soon as possible afterwards.

Telephone requirements should also be emphasised at this point, especially with regard to separate lines to the contractor's office and the Clerk of Works' office, as this often proves to be difficult. Noticeboards and directional signs should also be discussed to avoid any problems arising from local planning regulations, and though site access, demarcation of boundaries, protection of any special features, etc, may be referred to in the bills, it is advisable to deal with these points in the meeting.

Before any site strip begins, it is useful to prepare a grid of levels, which should be agreed by both parties.

Finally an inspection of the site should be made jointly by the representatives of the architect and the contractor immediately after the meeting, any points of disagreement being listed and noted in the minutes when these are issued.

Contractor's Progress Meetings

During the progress of the work the contractor will hold regular meetings with his own staff and with sub-contractors and suppliers to organise the progress of the contract.

Statutory authorities may be asked to attend a separate meeting to discuss the arrangements for providing services to fit in with the programme of work.

The contractor may choose to hold his meetings before the monthly progress meetings, as this can assist him to reply to matters likely to arise under the agenda issued by the architect. Alternatively he may prefer to wait until after the progress meeting, when he can implement any agreements which have been reached with the architect.

The contractor's meetings do not concern the Clerk of Works, but as previously stated he may be invited to 'sit in' on the meeting with the statutory authorities.

Monthly Progress Meetings

Sometimes these are held in the Clerk of Works' office, sometimes in the contractor's offices, but on reasonably large contracts a room sufficient to accommodate a number of people is set aside for progress meetings.

In general these are organised monthly, but circumstances may require more frequent meetings, especially where a complex contract is involved. While the Clerk of Works may feel he is in no position to influence the arrangements for progress meetings, there is no reason why he should not be aware of good practice in conducting such meetings. After all, the time may arise when he will be in a position to offer advice to an inexperienced young architect involved in his first contract.

Representation

The architect may be supported by other members of his staff, as well as the Clerk of Works, the quantity surveyor, structural engineer and any consultants to the contract.

The contractor will be represented by a principal of the firm, the site agent, a surveyor, and possibly the programmer or similar member of the contractor's management team.

Nominated suppliers and nominated sub-contractors can expect to be in attendance at various stages throughout the contract, especially where it may be considered they are in any way responsible for delays to the progress of the works. Sub-contractors and suppliers engaged by the contractor will only be present at these meetings when the contractor requires them to be in attendance to support particular points he wishes to express.

Agendas

Agendas will vary according to the size of the contract and the manner in which the architect wishes to conduct the meetings. They should be circulated at least one week before the meeting to enable those attending to prepare their information; it also helps to overcome to a certain degree procrastination from some who are expected to provide direct answers to questions.

A typical agenda for a site meeting on progress should include the following items, and the Clerk of Works should prepare himself in the same way as others attending the meeting, to comment or reply to any matters raised under the agenda:

(a) Minutes of the previous meeting.
(b) Matters arising from previous minutes.
(c) Contractor's report on progress.
(d) Correspondence.
(e) Information required.
(f) Issue of additional drawings.
(g) Instructions and variations.
(h) Reports on/from sub-contractors.
(i) Reports on materials and suppliers.
(j) Delays and shortages.
(k) Statutory works and services.
(l) Date of next meeting.

Site Minutes

The minutes of the meetings should be recorded by the architect or a member of his staff and circulated as soon as possible after the meeting to all those in attendance, besides others who may be concerned with the information contained in them. An 'action' column should be provided to apportion the responsibility to appropriate individuals, who can then reply to these points when they attend subsequent meetings.

Upon receiving his copy of the site minutes, the Clerk of Works should first date-stamp them, and then read the items through carefully, making notes on any matters likely to be affected at subsequent meetings. The minutes should be filed in the relevant binder so as to be immediately available for reference later.

Contractor's Report

The report will most likely be compiled by the site agent for presentation to the meeting, and like most individuals he will not take kindly to his report being challenged. Obviously this will be more than possible unless certain basic facts are agreed, such as the date the report is made up to, and where percentages are quoted, whether these have been accurately measured.

In the interests of good relations it is best if the Clerk of Works is supplied with a copy of the report before the meeting for his comments and agreement. This can save a great deal of time in the meeting over the figures presented, leaving more time to discuss the progress of the contract. Apart from the site agent, the Clerk of Works is most likely the only person present who is in a position to comment upon the progress of the works, and because of this he should ensure he is fully briefed to reply to any questions which might be raised during the progress meeting, especially those items referred to in the agenda. A complete inspection of the works should be made by the Clerk of Works before the site meeting if he is to be in a position to confirm or correct the report produced by the site agent.

Programme

Discussion will be required to relate the progress report to the programme, and the Clerk of Works should be sure he is keeping his copy of the programme up-to-date. A little time spent before the meeting can clarify the true position.

Clerk of Works' Report

The Clerk of Works can assist the architect by preparing a report on the contract before the progress meeting. This report should not be confused with the normal weekly progress report, as it will be more in the nature of a briefing similar to the one the site agent will no doubt be giving to his principal before the meeting.

Besides referring to progress, improvements could be suggested, and delays mentioned if they have resulted from lack of information. The condition and the quantity of materials delivered to site should be given, and where delays in deliveries apply, these should be noted. A report on the suitability of materials used on site should also be given, especially with the increase in the use of new materials and products; often the architect hears of problems with new materials when failure has actually occurred.

Feedback

It is difficult for the architect to maintain complete contact with the site to supervise the implementation of his design, with the occurrence of problems which might easily have been averted if noted at the correct stage of the contract.

New materials and new products are very often dependent upon the way they are handled or fitted, and several failures have been recorded where improper use has largely contributed to that failure. The craftsman naturally applies those techniques most familiar to him when he is presented with a new product or material, adapting them to meet the situation. Very often the complex instructions accompanying the product are lost or ignored, and indeed they sometimes seem to be compiled by persons with a limited knowledge of the industry.

By observing the various activities carefully, the Clerk of Works is presented with the opportunity to note the advantage or the shortcomings of these new processes, and can channel the information direct to the designer.

Constant and accurate feedback of such information can only advance the valuable role of the Clerk of Works within the construction team.

Site Diary

This is the most important document with which the Clerk of Works is involved; he compiles it as the work proceeds, and it should therefore provide a complete record of operations during the contract.

If it is to be of value later it is important that events are entered each day in a careful and legible manner, giving an accurate assessment of daily progress, together with the total labour and plant involved in the work. Strikes and other forms of delay are bound to affect the completion dates of the contract, and these must be accurately recorded, showing the period when work was either slowed down or suspended.

Weather conditions can play a major part in the progress of the work, and this must be recorded, especially where it causes a delay or suspension of the work.

Alterations to the design as well as variations to the contract can affect the contract sum, and while the written instructions issued by the architect should be sufficient to resolve these matters, the reasons why such variations or alterations were thought necessary are not always so clear at the end of the contract. The Clerk of Works can help to provide information if he notes in the site diary many otherwise trivial decisions and methods of working.

Visitors to site should always be recorded, especially those who come to make decisions or deliberations affecting the work.

In assessing the site diary at the end of the contract, the information that should have been included but was not is always obvious. Only the Clerk of Works, however, can really assess the priority of his information, and he should take every precaution to see that he has assessed this correctly before entering up the events each day.

Progress Records

The architect will require weekly reports of the progress on site from the Clerk of Works, for which he will supply printed forms in pads of a hundred or so.

Using carbon paper the Clerk of Works will complete the report and retain the carbon copy for his files, the original being forwarded direct to the architect.

The report should provide an accurate assessment of the total labour involved on the site, including all sub-contractors whether nominated or otherwise. The state of the weather during the period between reports must also be shown, together with any delays or any other information which will assist the architect.

It is advisable to restrict the information on the report to facts which can be easily amplified by reference to the site diary later; long, garbled reports are unnecessary and often obscure the essential information. The section of the report covering 'Information Required' must be treated carefully, as this could well be a point for dispute at a later stage in the contract.

An assessment of the progress in relation to the programme must also be given, and this will reflect the accuracy with which the Clerk of Works maintains his copy of the programme.

Visitors to the site must always be listed, as well as deliveries of materials and their condition when inspected by the Clerk of Works. Delays in deliveries of materials are likely to affect the progress of the contract, and the architect must be kept informed of this through the weekly report.

Part Three

CHAPTER SIXTEEN

Preliminaries

Surveys

Before the drawings can be produced for a contract it will be necessary
to carry out a survey of the proposed site. There are several ways in which
this may be done, depending upon the extent of the site. An aerial survey
may even be carried out for a large development.

On the majority of sites, however, the survey will be carried out in a
traditional manner, using a theodolite, level, staff, ranging-rods, measuring
chain, steel tape, and field-book.

The boundaries of the site will be established first, before continuing
to record the topography of the site, which will include buildings, cellars,
watercourses, ponds, hedges, trees, filled in areas, etc. Existing drainage
and other services must be accurately located, care being taken to note
any special mains crossing the site, which might occur where large industrial
concerns are close to the area.

Existing plans held by the local authority can be extremely valuable
in providing information, and in mining districts the National Coal Board
may be able to supply useful data.

In establishing the levels for the proposed structure it will be necessary
to study the existing contours carefully, as floor level and basement levels
can affect the cost of the project seriously. In carrying out the survey many
other important factors must be taken into consideration, matters such as
the limitations on the land, the question of wayleaves, easements, and
leases, rights-of-way, etc. Old maps will provide information on some of

these points, but the detail must be recorded on the survey if it is to be accurate.

Site Investigations

The Clerk of Works does not always have the opportunity to be involved in site investigations, but it is still important for him to understand the procedures which are necessary before work can begin upon the site.

The objective in site investigation work is to establish the nature and strength of the soils within the site. This sounds obvious enough, but it must be remembered that interpretation of site investigation results is a highly skilled job. It is important, therefore, that the Clerk of Works is capable of recognising during the excavation any departure from the ground conditions assumed by the designer.

A copy of the borehole report, together with piling details and foundation drawings will be issued to the Clerk of Works as well as to the contractor, and it is important that the former is capable of interpreting the information given. It will help him to recognise anything unusual in the strata during excavations on site, and where this does occur, he should report the matter immediately to the architect and the engineer.

It is not unusual where satisfactory borehole readings have been supplied for the site to find isolated pockets of highly unsuitable materials during excavations. Where this does occur, it may be necessary to amend some of the detail to the foundation drawings, and if delay is to be avoided, the sooner the problem is recognised, the quicker the solution will be found.

Investigations on a small site may amount to little more than digging a few trial holes to some predetermined pattern and assessing the load-bearing capabilities of the ground by visual inspection of the subsoils. On larger construction sites, however, it will be most important to carry out a thorough investigation, and this is generally achieved by taking test boreholes and submitting the bore extractions to the laboratory for analysis as well as testing the strata encountered *in situ*.

The boreholes will be taken near the proposed foundations on most sites, but on a large development where the area is extensive a widely spaced grid of boreholes will be taken, and penetration tests made within the grid. The number of boreholes required will be related to the ground conditions, as the more taken, the wider the information will be, but costs will also have to be considered.

Testing of the soils in boreholes is carried out by either extracting a sample and sending it to the soils laboratory for testing, or testing the soil

LOCATION : ...CASTLE PARK...............

GROUND LEVEL : ...13.411 O.D........

DIAMETER OF BORE : ...150 mm...........

INCLINATION ...VERTICAL..............

DATE STARTED ...4 MAY 1969.......

DATE COMPLETED ...6 MAY 1969.....

TYPE OF BORE : ...SHELL & AUGER....

DESCRIPTION OF STRATA	Depth below Surface	Legend	Thickness	Reduced Level	SAMPLING		REMARKS
					Type	Depth	
TOP SOIL	0			13.411			
	300 mm		300mm	13.106			
Black and dark grey very soft organic CLAY							Water Table
	900mm		600mm	12.497			
Black fibrous PEAT					U	1.372m	
	1.830m		900mm	11.582			
Light grey medium and fine SAND					S(24)	2.440m	
	2.740m		900mm	10.668			
Red-brown medium and fine SAND							
	6.100m		3.353m	7.315			
Red-brown medium and fine SAND with a trace of CLAY							
	7.010m		900mm	6.401			
Brown stiff very sandy CLAY							
	8.840m		1.830m	4.572			
					S(85)	9.450m	
					U	9.450m	

General Comments:

   U indicates undisturbed sample

   D indicates disturbed sample

   S indicates Standard Penetration Test

   (24) Figure indicates number of blows.

.... **Engineer.**

Fig. 6.

in situ. The type of soil encountered determines which test is more applicable.

There are two types of soil sample required for investigation: (a) undisturbed samples and (b) disturbed samples. The former must represent as closely as possible the *in situ* structure and moisture content of the soil. In cohesive soils, that is, soils which are or have some clay content, it is possible to extract a sample intact by driving a thin walled tube into the ground and withdrawing it together with the soil within the tube. The ends of the tube are capped and then labelled for despatch to the laboratory in properly constructed protective wooden boxes.

Disturbed samples are taken from the boring tools and placed in airtight containers for despatch to the laboratory. The information to be given on the labels for both types of sample must state the borehole and the depth from which the sample was obtained, together with the date.

When the soils encountered are non-cohesive, such as sand, and it is impractical to retrieve an intact sample, the soil is tested in the borehole by means of a standard penetration test (SPT) or a dynamic cone penetration test.

The SPT is made by driving a standard 50 mm split-spoon sampler 450 mm into the ground, and recording the number of blows required from a drop-hammer weighing 62·5 kg and falling a distance of 750 mm to drive the last 300 mm of the sampler. The contents of the tube can be retained as a disturbed sample for analysis.

The dynamic cone penetration test is made by driving a special cone into the ground with a drop-hammer and recording the number of blows per foot of penetration.

Where rock is encountered, it may be necessary to have samples for testing, and these will be taken with a rotary core drill which produces cylindrical cores for analysis.

The laboratory will analyse each sample to determine the moisture content, the bulk density, particle distribution, and the liquid and plastic limits of the soils.

The result of the analysis will be provided in a report which will include a diagrammatic review of each borehole showing the strata at each level and giving a general description of the site. This report will be assembled in the form of a booklet and supplied to each contractor submitting a price for the construction work on site. Site investigations should establish the level of the ground water, which is generally referred to as the water table. Because of the difference in subsoils the water table is not always constant, and the Clerk of Works should note this fact, as his experience in other sectors of his site may mislead him in assessing the actual water levels.

The water table can have a serious effect upon the cost of the works, not only because of pumping during construction but because of the tanking required to waterproof the building, especially where the design includes a basement. It may be necessary to use de-watering or freezing techniques, which will require a specialised contractor and can be very expensive.

Site Boundaries

When the contractor takes possession of the site and before any other work is begun, the site boundaries should be checked and established with marker pegs. These marker pegs must be painted in an easily recognised colour so that they can be identified from any other pegs fixed in the vicinity of the boundary. The Clerk of Works should note the position of the boundary marker pegs on his setting out drawings and these should be checked at intervals during the contract to see they have not been removed. Any irregularities arising in connection with the boundary of the site must be noted at once, and referred to the architect for clarification before proceeding any further.

When the boundaries affect the public highway, minor variations can easily be resolved by the Clerk of Works in consultation with the local authority surveyor, but the architect must be informed.

It is worth repeating that where the Clerk of Works has any doubts concerning the boundaries of the site, he should check again until he is satisfied. The dangers of litigation which could arise through encroachment upon the boundaries of an adjacent owner would be extremely serious where the boundaries coincided with the building line. It might be worth noting the wording of Clause 18 of the JCT Standard Form of Contract, which states 'unless due to any act or neglect of the Employer or of any person for whom the Employer is responsible'.

At the same time as the boundaries are being established, any reference in the contract bills to protection of special features must be considered. Trees and shrubs, ponds, and even existing buildings should be adequately protected by fences, and prominent notices posted and maintained throughout the contract.

Stern measures must be taken by the Clerk of Works at the first signs of carelessness towards items which are to be protected. It has often been noted that notices have been provided and then careless handling of site plant has savaged the main limbs of a tree to such an extent that it has eventually died. Mature trees cannot be replaced, and this should be made clear to all who are likely to overlook this point.

Site Hoardings

The boundaries of town and city sites will require the erection of hoardings to enclose the site before any work begins on the excavations. Such hoardings must be constructed in a proper manner, so that they will not endanger any pedestrians passing by the site. As the erection of the structure proceeds, it will also be necessary to form protective fan scaffolding overhead to safeguard the general public from anything which might fall from the scaffolding or the structure.

Properly constructed walkways and canopies will be needed to provide access for pedestrian traffic where the normal route is in any way interfered with. Access must include all ramps, steps, handrails, etc, necessary for the safe conduct of those likely to use such access.

Gates and doors giving access to the site must be constructed in accordance with the regulations affecting the highway: for example, doors must not open outwards or constitute a hazard to pedestrians or to vehicular traffic.

Adequate lighting must be provided where this will be necessary for safe passage, and warning lights erected at positions where hazards arise. Such lighting must always be maintained and the responsibility for it should be delegated to a particular person.

Viewing platforms and portholes are often provided these days within the hoardings to construction sites to enable interested passers-by to watch the foundation work proceeding. Apart from the publicity value to the contractor carrying out the work, such practices can only foster good public relations for the construction industry as a whole and give a better understanding of the importance of the work.

Demolition Work

Before construction work can proceed it is sometimes necessary to demolish existing structures, and this operation is generally awarded to a specialist contractor. The demolition work is invariably completed before tenders for the main contract work have been accepted and confirmed.

Where the Clerk of Works is involved in the demolition contract, it is essential for him to see that any remaining property is adequately supported and weatherproofed before the demolition contractor leaves the site.

During the demolition the Clerk of Works must also see that basements are filled in correctly, not merely by collapsing debris. Old foundations and bases must be grubbed up and removed, together with any other materials which are likely to interfere with the main contract. Carelessness in the supervision of demolition work can result in unnecessary expense to the main contract through buried debris having to be removed when site excavations are proceeding.

Precautions must also be taken with regard to shoring of existing buildings, especially where piling or excavations are likely to occur nearby. Responsibility for shoring may well be the main contractor's, but where it is included in the demolition contract, it should be enforced. If the Clerk of Works has not been involved in the demolition contract, he should check all these facts before the main contract proceeds too far, thus avoiding any unnecessary problems arising later.

Site Access

All access points to the site should be clearly defined on the drawings issued by the architect, and the matter fully discussed with the contractor at the pre-contract meeting. The contractor will be preparing drawings for approval showing the site offices and compound, and these drawings should outline any arrangements he is taking to comply with restrictions concerning access to the site.

It will be important for the contractor to give full consideration to the type of plant and equipment using the site entrance, in particular low-loaders, tracked vehicles, road rollers, etc.

The local authority must be notified before any work starts on the site entrance which may affect the boundaries of the public highway. Where alterations are required to pavements, kerbs or carriageways, the local authority may prefer to do this work themselves, charging the contractor with the costs involved.

Adequate safety precautions must be taken to prevent accidents occurring through traffic entering or leaving the site, and this may require the erection of warning notices on the public highway at some distance on either side of the site entrance. It is advisable to contact the police authority beforehand on these matters, since such prior discussions can often overcome any difficulties and useful advice will be obtained.

Vehicles must be prevented from carrying mud on the tyres from the site and along the approach roads; not only is this illegal, it is also sure to build up resentment among occupants of adjoining properties. Under the same heading it is advisable to give consideration to the route which is likely to be used by traffic making regular deliveries to the site.

Notices will be required for the guidance of delivery vehicles approaching the site, and restrictions may be placed on the type and the size of such notices. They may be restricted to a coloured arrow board, but again it is advisable to discuss such matters with the highways authority or the planning department of the local authority.

Name Boards and Notices

Contractor's name boards, noticeboards and directional signs must be given full consideration and approval before they are erected.

In the first instance they must be correctly positioned, not only to obtain full publicity value, but to avoid causing any obstruction to traffic or private rights. Secondly, noticeboards must not be allowed to develop into a proliferation of signs which may then become a matter for the local planning authority. Thirdly, when erecting signs and notices, it is important to see that they convey the correct information to those likely to be using them. The names of the main contractor and sub-contractors are now generally confined to one board, rather than, as previously, each one erecting his own board.

A separate name board is usually included in the contract bills for the client. This shows the name of the development and often includes the names of the architect and the consultants, although they often exhibit professional nameplates.

Directional signs for the guidance of visitors and delivery vehicles will also be required, as well as warning notices where employees or visitors may face unexpected hazards.

Clear warning signs must be displayed to warn the general public of any dangers which may affect them at any time because of the work in progress, especially work proceeding overhead, or where vehicles are entering or leaving the site.

If the boundaries of the site interfere with any rights-of-way or pedestrian access, adequate notices must be maintained for the duration of the contract, or until such access is no longer obstructed.

It must be recognised from the outset that failure to display warning notices of possible dangers arising through construction works may prove costly in terms of personal safety, thus entailing legal liability; so while adequate notices may be erected, they must also be properly maintained.

Site Services

Careful consideration must be given at the start of the contract to all existing services adjacent to the site entrances to avoid unnecessary damage
from loaded vehicles entering or leaving the site. Precautionary measures
must be taken or services must be re-routed wherever damage is likely to
occur.

Overhead telephone or electric cables are easily damaged by vehicles
with high jibs, but plastic bunting strung at a lower level than the cables
or the erection of goalposts may well prevent such damage if reasonable
care is exercised by plant drivers or lorries with high loads.

Applications must be made as soon as possible to the various authorities
where service connections are required into the site from the main supplies.

Telephones and water will be required almost immediately, and either
electricity or gas for the contractor's offices and welfare arrangements, as
well as the Clerk of Works' office.

Service generators may be used to provide the power for small electrical
tools on the site, or the ordinary service power supplies may be used. Where
concrete mixing equipment, tower cranes and workshop machinery, etc, are
used and powered by electricity, high power cables and switchgear will be
required, and additional regulations will have to be met.

Setting Out the Works

The contractor is completely responsible for setting out the works in
accordance with the drawings and information provided by the architect,
but it should always be appreciated that mistakes can easily be made by
either of the parties. It is not very helpful at an advanced stage of the
work to find the structure is on the wrong building line or out of square,
even though the fault may be attributable to the main contractor.

A temporary benchmark (TBM) must be immediately established on
the site before setting out any part of the structure, and the level for this
will be taken from the ordnance datum shown on the setting-out drawings
provided by the architect. Once the benchmark (TBM) has been established, it must be protected from anything which is likely to alter the level
it represents; site traffic is probably the greatest hazard, especially track
vehicles.

A useful method to adopt is to cut a large oil drum in two parts and
sink the upper half into the ground; this can then be filled with concrete

and the datum level established by bedding a piece of rail or similar bar into the concrete to form a flat steel surface. This method will provide a reliable benchmark resistant to the most severe traffic, and will certainly outlast the normal wooden pegs surrounded with concrete.

For the ordinary setting-out points, wooden pegs surrounded with concrete should be quite adequate, but the Clerk of Works is advised to provide an additional peg occasionally, positioned as an offset from the main setting-out pegs. This additional point will serve as a quick reference when checking intermediate pegs, and can be used when disputes arise over agreed levels.

The Clerk of Works should certainly record the positions and levels of setting-out points on his copies of the setting-out drawings, as this information can be of vital importance where pegs have been disturbed, or even disappeared. Whenever he is checking any setting-out points with the site agent or with the engineer, or even where he is carrying out routine checks, the Clerk of Works would be well advised to use his field level book to record the date and the levels checked.

To the experienced supervisor the following information may sound too elementary for comment, but where level pegs are fixed to give a reading several feet above datum level, the Clerk of Works must check these levels carefully: 'boning-in' pegs may be set at 2 m or more above the bottom of the excavation. Any error in calculations might easily result in under- or over-excavation. If such an error occurs when sewers are being laid in sectors, a serious problem would present itself when it comes to linking up the sectors.

Subsequent erection of the structure will be obviously affected by the initial setting out, so it is well worthwhile the Clerk of Works spending extra time over this to ensure accuracy.

Once the setting out has been completed, rechecking the main points may avoid future delays and save both the Clerk of Works and the site agent any embarrassment if any happens to be wrong. Whether the Clerk of Works decides to recheck the setting out after the contractor, or considers it more advisable to work jointly with the site agent, is entirely up to himself. It is worth remembering, however, that two responsible persons are more likely to avoid serious errors, on the basis that two heads are always better than one.

It is always an advantage to use the correct equipment in carrying out a task, and this certainly applies to setting-out instruments. The contractor will be obliged to provide the necessary instruments for setting out, in accordance with the contract bills, not only for his own use but in order that the works can be checked as they are proceeding. Where such resources are available from his employer, and the Clerk of Works is able to use his own particular level, it is possible to find errors in the setting out which are caused not by human failings but through a contractor's faulty equipment.

The equipment which should be available to the Clerk of Works will include a theodolite, dumpy-level, measuring staff, ranging rods, steel tapes and an abundant supply of stout wooden pegs. The work will be further assisted by having a long straight-edge and spirit level, as well as a builder's square; the last can easily be produced on site, and should be a right-angle based on the 3:4:5 method. Additional angles can be set out in multiples of 30 degrees, by forming an equilateral triangle with sides either 1 or 1·5 m long.

In setting out on sloping ground, it should be remembered that ranging rods must always be kept plumb and the steel tape horizontal, otherwise the dimensions will be inaccurate.

Piling Operations

Where the load-bearing capacity of the ground near the surface is insufficient to sustain the load of the structure, or perhaps when ground water would make excavation difficult, it may be necessary to support the structure on piles. Looked at simply the pile may act in either of two ways: it may transfer the load imposed on it down to a hard stratum into which its toe is resting (this is known as an end load-bearing pile), or it may distribute its imposed load throughout the strata by means of friction between the pile shaft and the ground (a skin friction pile). Both types of pile may be driven or bored.

Driven piles may be steel or concrete, in one long length or in sections, and they are generally termed displacement piles because in driving the ground is pushed out of the way, whereas for bored piles the ground is excavated. With displacement piles in groups, ground heave may occur. As can be imagined, when a number of piles are driven into a small area, all of them are pushing the ground out of the way, and the easiest way for the ground to move may be upwards! This can in some instances cause an already driven pile to be lifted off its 'set', that is, in the case of an end-bearing pile, out of the stratum into which it was driven. If this is suspected the engineer may require the piles to be redriven.

Piling contractors almost always operate their own particular patent system of piling, and engineers generally recommend the system to be used because of ground conditions. It will be necessary to set out the position of each pile before any piling starts, and while the main contractor is still responsible under the contract conditions for all setting out, the piling sub-contractor's surveyor will probably do this work himself.

If it becomes necessary to set up a test pile, the Clerk of Works will probably be required to take readings of the test gauges at regular intervals, and produce a record of these for the engineer. In such instances the Clerk of Works should always agree the readings with the piling sub-contractor's representative on the site, where this is possible, to avoid any disagreement later.

A suitable access road will be necessary for the piling sub-contractor to bring piling frames and rigs on to the site, and he will also expect a hardcore surface covering to the area to be piled. This will mean site strip must be completed first in order that hardcore may be laid, and of course the topsoil will need to be placed in a stockpile for later use.

Apart from checking the site strip and hardcore blinding as it proceeds, the Clerk of Works must assure himself of the correct setting-out positions for the piles. He should also check on the setting up of the piling frames, as the pile will be wrong where the frame is not set up correctly, and in the case of raking piles the angle must be correct. A single pile slightly out of position may not always be important, and therefore may be acceptable to the engineer, but a cluster of piles similarly affected could mean additional piles having to be driven, with all the consequential delays.

Where piles are driven to a firm base, the Clerk of Works will record the depths, and length of each pile, and where a given 'set' is specified, the number of blows and the penetration achieved must be recorded. The piling contractor will normally supply a daily record showing the number of piles driven, together with all relevant information, such as length of pile, depth, and 'set' achieved.

A useful record may be maintained by the Clerk of Works if he uses a piling layout drawing and fills each pile in with a coloured pencil as it is completed, placing the date alongside.

It will be necessary to pay attention to reinforcement cages, and concrete mixes used in forming the piles, although in most cases the piling contractor will be giving a guarantee for his work.

CHAPTER SEVENTEEN

Excavations and Foundations

Ground Conditions

The conditions on site should have been thoroughly inspected by the contractor before submitting his tender for the work, and he will already be in possession of the borehole report, which will give him additional information. This information should also help him to plan his methods for supporting the sides of the excavations, besides selecting the correct type of equipment to carry out the work.

Despite all the information available, it is still necessary to ensure that the person responsible for the excavation work on site is sufficiently experienced in this class of operation, as ground conditions can vary so much. There is always the danger of 'slip' occurring to the sides of the excavation, sometimes owing to pockets of clay or sand which lie behind the exposed face; but it can occur without warning, and where the sides are unsupported, it can often produce fatal results. Timbering to trenches is sometimes avoided by working closely behind the excavator with pipelaying, and backfilling immediately to reduce the amount of open trench. This is a dangerous practice which can be seen clearly in Plate 1, and is a method which prevents the Clerk of Works from checking the jointing as well as the line and level of the pipes. The land drain which can be seen on the right hand side of the picture is a potential hazard as the bank might easily collapse from this point.

A variation in the expected rainfall may increase the moisture content of the surrounding ground, which will create movement in the soils and affect the trenches in the area that is still left open.

Waterlogged Sites

One of the problems arising from waterlogged sites is that they present a weakened sub-stratum; in that case the site must be properly drained or the water controlled, if it is to be satisfactory for construction purposes.

Wherever land drains are exposed during excavation they must always be diverted, and it is important that backfill materials to trenches do not produce watercourses which direct the ground water to the foundations and basement.

Regular pumping may be necessary to keep the excavations free from water, but it will be of little use pumping the water out of the excavations and discharging it upon the surfaces of the surrounding ground, as it will merely seep back into the excavations.

Heavy rains can quickly overcharge the area, thus increasing the problem, but so long as the topsoil is left undisturbed, it can act as a sponge in absorbing intermittent rainfall. Once the topsoil is removed from the site, the surface can become hard during dry weather and this can be exaggerated by site traffic, creating a large watershed which directs the water to the lower levels where inevitably the working areas lie. Where this is likely to be the case on site, some thought should be given to forming a trench pattern to channel the excess water to a suitable disposal point.

Where the water is allowed to lie in the excavations, it will be necessary to excavate still further to establish a firm base after removing the water. If the water is likely to accumulate again quickly, it is easier to excavate beyond the specified depth in the first instance, and lay a blinding thickness of concrete with a sump at the lower end of the excavation to facilitate pumping out. Careless use in handling of standpipes and water storage on site does not help in many instances, and anything which can be done to overcome this problem will be an advantage.

Excavations and Timbering

The sides of an excavation may be retained by cutting the bank to form a slope, providing a safe angle of repose; and in very large excavations such as basements, storage tanks, etc, this may be the most suitable method to use, providing there are no surrounding buildings or sewers left unsupported. This method has been adopted in excavating the basement shown in Plate 2 although sheet piles have been used in the extreme left of the picture where the bank has already collapsed. The unsupported face of the bank can also be reduced by stepping the excavation and this is shown in Plate 3 although collapse has occurred where the full width has been excavated to accommodate the manhole in the foreground. It will be noted the next manhole has been properly timbered in the top of the picture. Generally the sides of an excavation must be fully supported, and depending upon the conditions of the ground and the depth of the excavation, either timber poling boards or steel sheet piling will be used.

Details of the timbering which the contractor intends to use should be investigated by the Clerk of Works at the beginning of the contract, and where there is any attempt to avoid using sound procedures, this should be reported to the architect. Obviously the responsibility must lie with the contractor, but where there is danger to the works because of the methods of timbering, this might be interpreted as 'not being carried out in a workmanlike manner' and the contractor instructed accordingly.

There is a great deal of skill involved in timbering to deep or large excavations and the younger Clerk of Works will find an opportunity to learn from many of the older men physically engaged in this class of work, provided he cares to take advantage of this opportunity.

Timbering consists of driving poling boards behind timber walings with the toe of the boards penetrating the base of the excavation, with timber or adjustable metal props acting as struts across the excavation width to brace the sheeting. Instead of timber poling boards, interlocking sheet piles will be used where pressures are great or ground conditions poor. Sheet piles have been used on a fairly narrow trench in Plate 4, where the poor conditions are obvious by the settlement of the banks even with support. Greater pressures such as are found in city excavations, where the weight of adjoining buildings must be retained, may require concrete piles to be driven around the perimeter of the area to be excavated to form a caisson; the whole centre can then be excavated, exposing the face of the piles.

Where the method of timbering is too weak to resist the pressures on the sides of the excavation, collapse will be inevitable, and several other factors can increase these pressures even further. Collapse can occur through creating a working area around the perimeter of the excavation, allowing dumpers and other vehicles to operate close to the edges, or by storing building materials near where they are to be used in the excavated area. It is quite common to allow excavated materials to be stockpiled alongside trenches, and this will also put undue pressures upon the banks. Where the excavation has been carried out during wet or damp weather and is allowed to remain open for a long period, subsequent dry spells will cause shrinkage and settlement of the bank, putting a strain upon the timbering. Similar settlement will occur if heavy rains develop while trenches remain open for long periods.

The Clerk of Works must check the size of the excavation as it proceeds to ensure adequate working room is being provided, especially where brick or asphalt is to be applied to the external face of the structure.

Plank and Strut

This item is always included in the contract bills to provide timbering to the sides of the trench even for shallow trenches, but it is entirely up to the contractor whether he prices this item, let alone makes use of it.

Normal house drainage is invariably laid in shallow trenches, and provided the contractor excavates no more than he can deal with at a time, and does not leave trenches open for an unnecessary period, then he may be able to operate successfully with the minimum of timbering.

Safe Working Conditions

The regulations covering excavations are found in The Construction (General Provisions) Regulations 1961 and one important item refers to the appointment of a safety officer on the site.

The regulations refer not only to the provision of timbering to excavations but also to the quality of timber used; it is further stated that the work should be carried out by a person competent in planking and strutting to excavations.

Unfortunately there is a tendency among many persons responsible for excavation work to treat the less complex operations with undue familiarity, and this is where many accidents occur. Where the Clerk of Works notes any failure on the part of the contractor to maintain reasonable safety precautions, he should draw the contractor's attention to the fact, and also record this in the site diary at the time.

Excavations in Sand

Some types of sand can be self-supporting to some extent, so long as they are damp or mixed with a cementitious material, but it is advisable to support the sides when excavating in this material.

Where the sand lies below the water table, it can be eroded and carried along by the flow of ground water; the bottom of the excavation shows a boiling effect, generally referred to as 'running sand'. Failure to recognise this situation may result in pumping extracting the sand together with the water, undermining the surrounding area. It is quite easy to continue pumping operations and suddenly find the whole of the timbering beginning to move in the excavation, but it is much more serious if adjoining buildings are affected.

On a small scale it is possible to deal with this situation, but it requires experience on the site as well as speed in dealing with the operations. Larger operations will call for ground water lowering systems which draw the water to selected filter points from which it can then be pumped away.

Dealing with Water on Site

The contract bills generally call for the excavations to be kept free from water, but the control of ground water can sometimes be an almost impossible task and a very expensive one; therefore, the Clerk of Works must pay close attention to this situation throughout. If adjoining properties became affected by withdrawing water and subsoils from around their foundations, the client would be involved in liability claims, especially where settlement of the buildings occurred.

Where the water table affects the site to such an extent that pumping from the excavations becomes an unreasonable solution, it may become necessary to resort to other effective, although more expensive, systems. By sinking a series of tubes or well-points around the excavation it is possible to reduce the water level sufficiently to allow the work to proceed in reasonably dry conditions. The tubes are linked to a pipeline which is itself connected to a pumping unit, filters being incorporated into the tubes to overcome the extraction of fine soils in the water levels. If the excavation is deep, this will make it necessary to sink the well-points in two or possibly three different levels to allow the work to proceed in stages, as the extraction of water will be limited by the suction-lift of the pumps.

A further method of de-watering the ground is known as the electro-osmosis system, which consists of using an SC current to flow from anodes to cathodes, taking the water along with the current. The anodes are steel rods driven into the ground, while the cathodes are formed as filter wells from which the water is then pumped away. The system is very effective but it is also expensive to install and maintain.

If none of these systems is likely to be effective because of the conditions, an injection system can be used, filling the pores in the subsoils with other materials, such as cement, clay slurry, bentonite, etc, but this system is so effective that the grout can travel for some distance, and close watch must be kept on basements and drains in the area. A further process known as 'freezing' can be used, but this is very expensive as it involves sinking a ring of boreholes around the excavation and lining these with steel tubes sealed at the bottom. A smaller diameter pipe is inserted into each of the bores and these are all connected to a refrigeration plant, which then circulates chilled brine, freezing the ground and creating an ice wall to retain the water. This system takes several months to freeze the ground, but another method makes use of liquid nitrogen, which speeds up the operation.

A chemical injection system makes use of sodium silicate and calcium chloride, which react to form a 'gel' of calcium silicate, providing what is well-known as silica-gel. The injection may be carried out using two pipes, but it is now possible to use a single pipe and an additive to prevent the chemical reaction taking place immediately.

Pumping

The Clerk of Works should note that during excavations it takes double the pump capacity to lower the ground water level as it takes to maintain the water at the existing level. This fact becomes very evident when unexpected storms arise, but it should be catered for previously and not left until the situation occurs.

It is advisable to check that the contractor has standby pumps available during excavation works, especially where there is a possibility of damage to partly completed work.

Foundations

Undoubtedly the best foundation is that founded upon rock, but the Clerk of Works must appreciate that what appears to be solid rock could be a thin shell overlying an entirely different type of base. The rock may also contain voids and fissures which could seriously affect the strength of the foundations, and only test bores will reveal this information, which must be considered by the design engineers.

The rock formation existing below the site may have certain other characteristics which could make it necessary to provide quite expensive designs in foundations, especially in those areas where there is a geological 'fault' in the formation.

Chalk varies considerably as a foundation base, so hard in certain areas that it is necessary to use cutting tools, yet soft and loose in others. Soft chalk usually denotes the presence of water on the site, and it would be

PLATE 1. A dangerous practice – pipelaying in trenches without proper support to the banks

PLATE 2. *Left* Reducing the need for supports by raking the bank to a large excavation

PLATE 3. *Above* Stepping the excavation to drain trenches

PLATE 4.   Pipelaying in poor ground conditions

PLATE 5. Settlement crack in brickwork

PLATE 6. *Left* Installing bar reinforcement to duct walls and floor

PLATE 7. *Above* Timber formwork to column

PLATE 8. *Left* Incorrect setting out of substructure

PLATE 9. *Above* Damage to brick facings

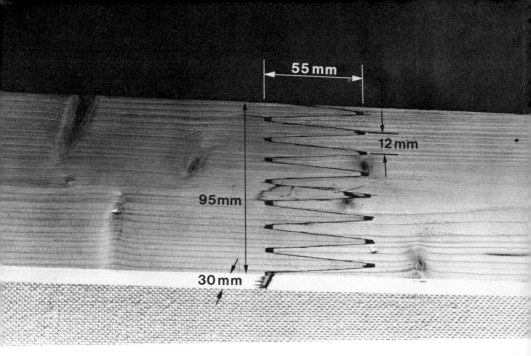

PLATE 10. *Left* Damage to brick facings

PLATE 11a. *Above* Typical finger joint

PLATE 11b. *Below* Recent advance on finger jointing principle

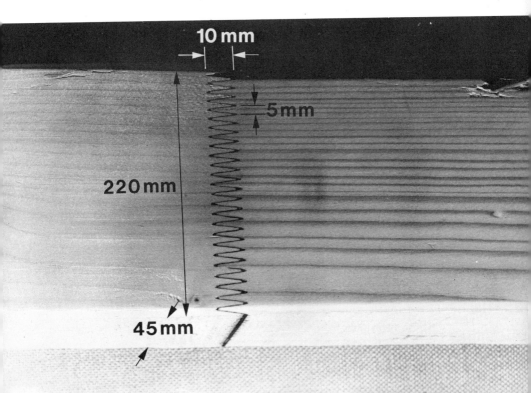

PLATE 11c. *Above* Metal plate joint used in roof truss construction

PLATE 11d. *Below* Early attempt at mechanical jointing

PLATE 12a.   *Above* Poor storage of door frames

PLATE 12b.   *Below* Poor storage of window frames

PLATE 13. Careless treatment of windows

PLATE 14a. *Above* Brickwork cut away to cover flashing

PLATE 14b. *Below* Faulty flashing to finished roof

PLATE 15. *Above* Ineffective roof-securing bracket

PLATE 16. *Below* Debris accumulated on area prepared for landscape contract

advisable to give consideration to the existing drainage of the area. Chalk is susceptible to frost damage and must be given sufficient cover in foundations to avoid this liability.

Gravel is an excellent base to receive foundation, having a high bearing capacity, but it is also necessary to ensure it is not a thin layer covering some lesser strata. Clay lying immediately below a thin layer of gravel would retain the water channelled through the gravel, and produce dampness if it occurred below a building.

Sand forms a good base so long as it remains dry and firm, but it must be retained laterally, otherwise any water will be likely to erode the base in the same way as ground water affects the sub-strata. While the site may be perfectly dry when construction takes place, it is wise to consider future events if this possibility exists.

Clay sites are capable of absorbing moisture, which causes expansion, the subsequent drying out being excessive and irregular. If the movement is constant and measurable, it may not be too serious in certain circumstances, but any structure built upon clay must be designed to overcome differential movement.

Where clay subsoils occur upon a sloping site, there is always a danger of the building sliding, unless the foundations are designed to take this into consideration. It is useful to consider clay particles as small thin plates resting one upon the other, and imagine water collecting between each of the plates. This makes it easier to see the principle involved, where one plate floats or slides upon the one below it.

Although it is known probably before starting on site that infilling has taken place, it is still necessary to investigate and establish the line of infill, especially where this crosses any foundations. The type of materials used for infill to the area must also be checked, as this might conflict with the requirements laid down in the Building Regulations, besides increasing the cost of the structure. Subsoils containing impurities will require special cements to be used in the foundations to combat the corrosive elements which would affect ordinary Portland cement.

The design should take account of any differential settlement, but where alterations and extensions are concerned, or perhaps where variations occur in the load-bearing capacity of the ground, there is always the danger of unequal settlement taking place with any structure. While it is possible to calculate settlement to less than 25 mm, this is still sufficient to cause extensive damage to finishings. Settlement does not only occur to large heavy structures: there have been many cases of lightly constructed buildings such as houses and schools being severely affected.

The soils engineer's definition of rock differs slightly from that of the quantity surveyor drawing up the contract bills. While the bill only accepts a valuation for excavation in rock where it is necessary to use explosives or special tools, the soils engineer regards rock as 'a hard rigid deposit' and soils as 'loose soft materials'. Soils may include gravel, clay, sand, silt and peat, with rock consisting of sandstone, limestone, hard shales, slate, basalt and granites.

Inspection of Foundations

The most important part of the building must be the foundation bearing the weight of the structure, and it must therefore be given adequate supervision.

While concentrating upon all aspects concerning the foundations, the condition of the sub-base must be checked before any concrete is allowed to be poured, and the dimensions of the concrete as well as the reinforcement pattern compared with the detail drawings before the Clerk of Works satisfies himself that work may continue. Whenever he is dissatisfied with any of the foundation works carried out by the contractor, the Clerk of Works should inform the contractor or his agent immediately, and where no action is taken to rectify the situation, the architect and the engineer should be notified in writing. Even slight settlement can create disfigurement in the superstructure, and the brickwork in Plate 5 shows a typical example of settlement of the foundation.

The Clerk of Works may occasionally note certain aspects of the foundation design which he considers are not in keeping with the situation existing on site. In such instances he should inform the architect and the engineer at once, explaining the reasons for his views.

It is not suggested that the Clerk of Works can be regarded as a possible safeguard against faulty design, but his full-time presence on the site should enable him to observe facts which are not always available at the design stage.

The architect or the engineer can always draw their own conclusions from the information passed to them, but because they decide to take no action, this should not prevent the Clerk of Works from reporting any future situation.

In checking the foundations the Clerk of Works must bear in mind that they should be excavated to a level to provide protection against frost, as laid down in the Building Regulations.

On sloping sites it is important to see that the foundations are stepped to provide cover and the correct overlap formed to each step. Although the dangers from building on infill areas of a site have already been mentioned, the Clerk of Works should pay particular attention to this possibility during excavations on site, as records do not always supply the complete answer.

Formwork to Sub-structures

The same degree of care is not always applied to formwork in the sub-structures as it might be to the remainder of the work, presumably because the operator is often expected to work under extreme conditions in ground works. The accuracy of the finished sub-structure has a strong bearing upon the whole of the superstructure, and the Clerk of Works must not allow anything other than recognised methods of craftsmanship.

Formwork for pile-caps, column bases and foundation beams must be accurately formed and assembled, and the bracing must be strong enough to resist not only the ordinary concrete pressures but those additional pressures which may be created by sudden earth slips. In basement construction it is advisable to provide continuous bracing between walls to produce additional strength, and where strong enough this bracing can often serve to support a working platform.

Even though the setting out for the formwork may be correct, there is always the possibility of an error during assembly, and the Clerk of Works should ensure that the line for formwork is finally checked before any concrete is poured. Column bases are generally formed in groups, and it is not unusual to find one or more of these slightly out of line when the time comes to erect the structural steelwork.

The Clerk of Works can always obtain a quick reference by establishing his own setting-out pegs here and there to be used with boning rods as the work proceeds. Sometimes in sub-structures, formwork cannot be removed after the concrete has been placed and there will be an allowance for this as 'permanent shuttering' in the contract bills. The Clerk of Works should investigate the type of shuttering to be used, as timber will possibly decay in certain circumstances and may affect other parts of the work.

Sub-structure Reinforcement

Generally the reinforcement in the sub-structure is provided in the form of cages for pile-caps, column bases, and ground beams, but for basement walls and floors the reinforcement will be assembled in place in the normal manner.

Apart from checking that the bars are of the correct diameter, and the cages assembled in accordance with the drawings supplied by the structural engineer, there should be very little difficulty for the Clerk of Works with this part of the works. Installation of the bar reinforcement is shown in Plate 6, where a concrete blinding has been laid to provide a suitable base for working on. It is worth noting that the excavation has been made through rock, which is clearly visible on the left-hand side of the picture.

It is important to see that correct spacing is achieved between the formwork and the bars when placing the cages, and that cages are properly supported at the base on plastic or concrete spacers to ensure that the specified cover is given to the steel.

Starter bars and holding-down bolt boxes must be correctly positioned, and the latter secured to prevent displacement during placing of the concrete. Where the reinforcement is placed direct into trenches, the excavation must be free from water and the base blinded with a 50 mm layer of concrete.

Concrete to Sub-structure

The formwork must be checked for alignment and cleaned out with water or compressed air to remove any debris remaining, the steel reinforcement correctly positioned and secured to prevent movement as well as being free from mould oils; only then should the Clerk of Works agree to concrete being placed in the formwork. The concrete mix must be checked and the concrete placed in a continuous pour without repeated interruptions for meals and similar reasons. Where the volume of concrete makes it necessary to pour in stages, proper working joints must be provided, with the positions agreed and approved by the engineer beforehand.

Where vertical formwork is to be filled, the concrete must be brought up in layers and not discharged into one part of the formwork to find its own level. Vibrators should always be used for reinforced concrete, but in those instances where they may not be included in the specification, hand methods should be used to consolidate the concrete and completely encase the reinforcement bars.

Before placing concrete in trenches and excavations, pegs must be fixed to establish the level of the finished concrete, and then withdrawn after the concrete has been placed.

Backfilling

When the formwork has been removed and the concrete approved, the trenches should be backfilled as soon as possible with suitable materials from the site. Water must be removed before backfilling and the materials compacted in layers with proper tamps to avoid creating pockets. The ramming is often carried out in certain situations with the bucket of the excavating machine, and in this case care must be taken to see there is no damage to the concrete.

A clay material will obviously prevent water accumulating around the concrete wall of a basement, while a gravel material will act as a channel for water, points which should be considered when selecting materials for backfilling.

CHAPTER EIGHTEEN

Formwork and Concrete

Formwork

The Clerk of Works should investigate the intentions of the contractor regarding the formwork he intends to use and should also assure himself that the proposed design will be adequate. This will avoid subsequent misunderstandings and can prove to be advantageous to both parties if they act and react in the right spirit. It is the contractor's responsibility to design the formwork so that the structure can be erected according to the drawings, but the client's consultants also have a responsibility to see that the design is adequate. Where the structure is a complex one, the engineer will expect drawings of the formwork to be submitted for approval, although such approval will not remove the contractor's liability.

The formwork must be designed to resist the pressures it will be subjected to, and these will always be greater as the depth of concrete increases – for example, in columns and walls.

Joints must be secure and tight to prevent loss of moisture, yet they must be designed to allow the formwork to be dismantled without damage to the finished concrete.

The whole of the formwork must be capable of carrying the total weight of the concrete and reinforcement as well as those loads applied through carrying out the work. The pressures will be increased where vibration is used, and bracing must be sufficient to withstand these pressures, besides being sufficiently rigid to resist any movement during the placing of the concrete.

Although the concrete must be supported until it has gained sufficient strength to withstand its own weight, it will be necessary to remove side formers to beams, etc, as soon as possible, and these panels must be designed to provide easy removal. Where the formwork is prefabricated, it should be produced in sizes easy for handling, and so far as possible the panels should be interchangeable.

Vertical shutters should be provided with access pockets to enable the operator to clean out the formwork before pouring takes place, as well as for tamping or vibrating the concrete.

Modern finishes to concrete call for special linings to the formwork, and where timber is used in the form of ribs, care must be taken not only to see these are accurately fitted but also sufficiently splayed to provide easy removal. Synthetic rubber sheeting which is also lightly reinforced, expanded plastics, and reinforced plastics are all used to achieve special finishes to the concrete face, but these should be properly designed in with the formwork.

Formwork is now available in convenient steel panels, as well as in glass-reinforced plastic, but external quality laminated plywood panels are so convenient if properly braced and supported that their use in concrete formwork has become very extensive. Plywood panels braced with timber framing have been used as formwork to the column in Plate 7. This formwork is divided internally to produce twin columns that will carry two bridge beams spanning a dual carriageway, and the special patent clamps to secure the formwork can be seen with bolts at the bottom of the picture. Pockets have been left in the formwork, and one can be seen at the bottom of the column, plus steel cube moulds for checking the concrete used.

Where continuous pouring is desirable, such as with concrete chimney-stacks, multi-storey blocks, etc, special sliding formwork is used, and this sort of shuttering can also be used to concrete tank structures at ground level.

Economics demand that as many uses as possible must be obtained from the formwork, but there is often a tendency to expect more uses than is commensurate with good concrete surfaces. Repeated use of formwork beyond the limits of its capacity is often the reason for poorly finished concrete, and the Clerk of Works should give close attention to this matter. It is not easy to lay down the number of uses, as this will depend a great deal upon the quality of the timber face as well as the manner in which the formwork is treated on site; so each case must be judged on its merits.

Plywood panels which have a plastic surface are also available, and they produce a very good surface to the concrete, but again such panels require care in handling. Polyurethane varnishes or mould oils are used to achieve good surfaces as well as to enable the formwork to be removed more easily when striking the shutters, but the Clerk of Works should investigate the type of mould oils to be used, as there are advantages and disadvantages to be considered with the various types that are available. Retarders are also used to allow removal of the shutters, as well as to achieve special finishes, such as exposing the aggregates in the concrete; if not carefully handled, however, these materials can cause problems with the concrete and the reinforcement. Where retarders are to be used or suggested by the contractor, then the Clerk of Works should discuss the matter with the engineer beforehand to establish the procedures to be adopted.

The specification will give the minimum periods for striking the formwork, but when there is frost these times will need to be increased. It is always good practice to remove the side sheeting, but removal of the supports should be delayed as long as possible, and care taken when removing these eventually that the concrete is not disturbed.

Special bolts and cramps are available for securing formwork, as well as metal banding which can be stressed and cut with a special tool. Where fixing blocks, channels, brackets, etc, are fitted to the formwork to be included in the concrete, then care must be taken not to pull the shutters away in the partly cured concrete.

Reinforcement

The Clerk of Works will be supplied with a set of detailed drawings prepared by the structural engineer, together with a set of bar schedules giving the shape and sizes of the reinforcement bars. The length, shape, bar diameters, and the quantity of bars will be clearly identified on the schedules, with a reference number for each bar, and this number will also be shown on the detail drawings to assist the steelfixer in distributing the bars. In his calculations the engineer will take account of every one of the bars shown, and while it is the responsibility of the contractor to see they are assembled correctly, the Clerk of Works must also check the work on behalf of the client; it will be of little use to find errors when the only way to rectify them is by repeating the whole operation.

The size and shape of bars are often amended during the construction period, but this does not always account for the surplus of shaped bars to be seen around the site after construction work has been completed. Reinforcement is supplied as mild steel and also as high tensile steel, and as the latter has a far higher strength, the Clerk of Works must see that the correct steel is being used on site.

Tensile steel requires additional resistance to prevent it being pulled through the concrete when loads are applied, and the surface of the bar is indented or given an irregular pattern to produce this grip within the concrete. Mild steel in its normal use does not require the same resistance to retain its bond within the concrete. The reinforcement is delivered either as bars or mesh, the bars being in bundles and the mesh in mats or rolls, but all having a metal tag attached to identify the type. This identification should be noted by the Clerk of Works.

When reinforcement is placed in position, it should be thoroughly checked by the Clerk of Works to see all bars and spacings are in the right order. In heavily reinforced sections it is also advisable to check the work periodically with the steelfixer as the work is proceeding. If errors are not discovered until the whole of the reinforcement is fixed, expense and delay will result, affecting both the client and the contractor. Errors, as we have said, are not always the fault of the contractor, and stripping out complete sections of reinforcement does not improve site relations at any level, irrespective of who is to blame.

Floor areas generally involve the use of fabric reinforcement, which can often produce perhaps more difficulties than bars when one tries to get the right amount of cover. Spacers and stools should be provided to position the reinforcement correctly, laps should be checked, and where additional bars are specified to resist extra loading, these must be noted. In checking the reinforcement for correct cover it should be noted whether wire is being used through the formwork to retain the bars, for this will produce rust stains on the finished surface of the concrete, and is unnecessary now that plastic spacers are available.

Concrete Work

Techniques as well as design in the use of concrete have advanced during the past few decades, and this is reflected in the new skills demanded of craftsmen.

The Clerk of Works must devote a considerable degree of study to this subject, keeping abreast of new procedures; he must understand the principles underlying it, and be able to cope with the supervision of what amounts to a speedier form of construction. As new ideas are introduced, added precautions become necessary, and the specification for each succeeding contract needs closer study. Standard concrete mixes have almost been replaced on contracts by design mixes and performance specifications for structural work, and this calls for the Clerk of Works' close attention to materials and mixing procedures.

Aggregates

In assessing the suitability of aggregates it must be remembered that they comprise all the constituents mixed with cement to produce concrete, fine aggregates being sand and coarse aggregates described as gravel, crushed stone, etc. When combined, they are referred to as ballast.

Apart from the compressive strength of aggregates it is important to obtain the correct gradings, and where the type of contract demands close supervision of the concrete work, the Clerk of Works should have a set of BSS sieves available on site. Alternatively, samples of the aggregates (taken in accordance with the recommendations of BS 812:1967) can be submitted to the laboratory for a report on their suitability. Before any concrete work begins on the site, the aggregates must be approved either by the engineer or the Clerk of Works, and once agreed, deliveries should be checked regularly to see that the standard is maintained. In checking aggregates which are washed at the plant the Clerk of Works must always be alert, as good supervision is equally necessary there. Good water supplies must also be available. Occasional loads get by without adequate washing, and sometimes the residue from previous washings is included in them. Balls of clay can often be found among coarse aggregates, and these can cause pockets or voids in the finished concrete, leading to weakness in the structure if they are excessive. Coal and pyrites are among other impurities to watch for. Pyrites cause staining, which creates problems where facing work is important.

Cement

If ordinary Portland cement is specified in a contract to be carried out in the winter, the contractor may ask permission to change to rapid-hardening cement. If he does, it must be remembered that while the setting-time for both types is exactly the same, rapid-hardening cement gains strength much more quickly and its use will speed up the job.

For some time, where it has been necessary to achieve increased strength over shorter periods than could be provided by ordinary Portland cement, high alumina cement has been used. Its process of manufacture is quite different from that of ordinary Portland cement, and it is more complex in character. The structural engineer has invariably required a note to be included in the specification calling for his approval before high alumina cement is used on site.

Manufacturers have used this type of cement to speed up production of prestressed concrete beams, but recent failures have resulted in a ban on high alumina cement for structural work. This decision is likely to affect the 'deemed to satisfy' conditions under Building Regulations for foundations and structural work.

The manufacture of cement is carried out under very stringent conditions, and while laboratory tests may be called for by the engineer, there should be no reason for site tests to be applied, though a certificate will be supplied where requested.

It should be noted, however, that the guarantee in supplying the cement in paper sacks refers to the whole consignment being the correct weight, although it is inferred that each bag contains approximately 50·8 kg.

Concrete for structural work should be mixed with a weigh-batcher, and bags of cement should not be assumed to contain 50·8 kg; it is quite possible for faults to develop with loading machinery at the plant, with the result that the bags may contain more or less than the quantity suggested. On contracts where a large quantity of cement is required, a silo will be erected and cement delivered by special vehicles which pump the cement directly into it.

Additives

These can take the form of accelerators to improve the setting time of the concrete, plasticisers to increase the workability, and air-entrainment agents to increase the voids and produce a lighter concrete. Calcium chloride is often used in various forms with concrete as an accelerator, but as the quantity which should be used is very slight (2 per cent), it is always possible that too much may be added; approval of the structural engineer should be obtained before the Clerk of Works allows it to be used on the site. In some cases the specification states that calcium chloride cannot be used without the express permission of the engineer or architect.

Water

The supply of water should come from the mains, but where there is any difficulty in obtaining mains water, it must be of the same degree of purity as drinking water. The reasons are fairly obvious, in that water could contain organic matter or salts which would effect the setting properties of the concrete.

Siting the Mixer

Perhaps the Clerk of Works may not at first appreciate why he should concern himself with the siting of the mixer, but indiscriminate use of vehicles transporting the concrete to various areas of a large development may affect site conditions to an extent which may cause delays to the contract.

During concrete operations he may also find that long hauls have developed, producing unsatisfactory concrete at the point of placing.

The type of contract and the amount of concrete required will dictate the mixer arrangements; one central source may be best, or a number of smaller mixers at vantage points. If only one source is available, it is important to see there is continuity in the event of a breakdown.

Access for deliveries of aggregates and cement, both bulk and in bags, will be required, and this may affect the number of mixers if a temporary road system cannot be installed initially.

Mixing the Concrete

The strength of concrete can be seriously impaired by the methods adopted for mixing, and the Clerk of Works must give attention to this matter when the first mixes are being prepared. The initial mixes are often used for preparatory works around the site and are not critical, but once they have been agreed, it means that the quantities have been settled when the mix for structural work is required.

Mixing times may vary according to the design mix, although the specification may stipulate that the drum must be rotated for not less than two minutes after all materials have been placed within it. Aggregates are generally measured by weight, but where volume is adopted as the measurement, precautions must be taken against the 'bulking' of fine aggregates.

Aggregates should be protected from the weather, especially from low temperatures, and should be stored in bins or compartments on a clean hard base laid to falls to drain off excess moisture.

The amount of water added to each mix will have a bearing on the ultimate strength of the concrete, and must be controlled not only at the mixer but right up to the time it is placed in the final position. Where the water is connected to the mixer via a supply tank, the water gauge must be set to the correct proportions and checked at regular intervals, but where the water is added by manual methods, strict control must be maintained by taking slump tests and cube tests at regular intervals.

Where the design mix gives a water/cement ratio, allowance must be made for the moisture contained in the aggregates, and where washed aggregates are used, this could be a considerable quantity. To check the amount of moisture in the aggregates it will be necessary to dry a sample and weigh this for comparison with a sample direct from the materials to be used.

Cement should be introduced first into the mixer along with the water in order to prepare a paste which will adhere to the aggregates, but because a certain quantity of cement will adhere to the blades and the internal surface of the drum, it is essential that initial mixes each day are reduced slightly in aggregate content. Mixers should be kept cleaned out at all times, especially at the end of each day's work, to prevent the concrete adhering to the blades and affecting the efficiency of the mixer.

Before there is a change in the type of cement being used in the mixer, it must be thoroughly cleaned and washed out.

Concrete Tests on Site

The Clerk of Works should carry out regular tests on the aggregates to ensure they are well graded and clean. He will be able to see lumps of clay, etc, but to check the grading of coarse aggregates he will require BSS test sieves. The grading limits will be found in the specification, but where these are not available, a table is given in BS 882:1965. Fine aggregates can be tested, as explained under Brickwork and Blockwork, and dirty materials rubbed between the palms of the hands leave an obvious stain.

Sands are also classified into Zones 1 to 4, the lower number signifying a higher proportion of coarser materials, but they can be subject to sieve tests.

Where samples are to be submitted to the laboratory for testing, it is most important that the sample is obtained in accordance with the BSS, otherwise the test is of no value.

Slump tests should be taken at the mixer and also at the point of placing to keep control of the water content of the concrete. The slump cone should be cleaned before each test and placed on a firm level base. A sample of concrete should be taken from the material when it is being discharged from the mixer or when it is being deposited in the formwork. The concrete should then be placed in the mould in four separate layers, each layer being rammed down with twenty-five strokes of the tamping rod, and then levelled off at the surface with a trowel. The droppings must be cleared from around the mould, which should then be lifted clean from the concrete and placed on the base alongside the slumped cone of concrete. The slump is then measured by placing a straight-edge across the top of the mould and measuring down to the top of the slumped cone; this dimension should be recorded in each case for subsequent reference. The size of slump will vary according to the placing of the concrete: for instance, where vibrators are being used, a 25 mm slump may be required, but in a heavily reinforced beam where vibrators could not be inserted because of the amount of steel reinforcement, it may be necessary to have a slump of approximately 100 mm. Test cubes must be made with steel moulds, although there are at present fibre-glass moulds available.

The mould must be cleaned and slightly oiled on the inner surface and the base plate to prevent the concrete sticking. The sample must be obtained from the point of discharge from the mixer or at the point of deposit, and placed into the mould in three layers, each layer being rammed with the tamp rod at least thirty-five times. The surface of the concrete should be levelled off with a trowel and all droppings cleaned from around the mould. At least three cubes must be taken each time and stored under damp sacks or in damp sand for 24 hours in a temperature of 20°C plus or minus 5°.

The cubes must be marked with an identification number in black paint and recorded in the site records. If they are to be despatched to the laboratory for testing on the seventh day, particulars must be entered into the test form, and the cubes packed into damp sand in a wooden box before despatch.

A slump test should always be taken before taking test cubes, and should be recorded in the site records together with the cube results. Cube testing may be carried out by specialist firms who call on the site and take the cubes for test to their laboratories, saving the contractor the problems of packaging, etc.

Transporting the Concrete

Over short distances the concrete may be delivered by hand-barrows, but dumpers are most likely to be used over longer distances. Trucks with containers suitable for carrying concrete are used on some sites, one type being fitted with agitators to prevent the concrete achieving initial set. So long as it is agitated, concrete can be prevented from setting for quite some time, but where there is no means of continuous agitation, the concrete should be placed within half an hour of being mixed.

Dumpers are likely to be used where the work is below or at ground level, but at first floor and above it will be a combination of barrow and hoist or crane. On high level blocks where tower cranes are used the concrete will no doubt be conveyed by skip to the point where it is to be placed. On sites where conditions are poor, and wheel or track vehicles are restricted in movement, a suitable means of transport is the monorail which can provide access to the most difficult position and is a fairly fast system.

Concrete can be transported both horizontally and vertically by means of the concrete pump, which is capable of delivery up to 500 metres horizontally and up to 50 metres vertically, using a 180 mm diameter pipeline. These pumps can be stationary or mobile, and where used in conjunction with ready-mixed concrete provide a rapid method of placing concrete.

Whether short or long distances are involved, it is important that no segregation of the concrete is allowed to take place, and, as stated elsewhere, the Clerk of Works must always be on the alert to see that no water is added to the concrete at any stage between the mixer and the point of discharge.

Ready-mixed Concrete

Conditions at a ready-mixed concrete plant enable better control to be exercised over the batching of concrete than is possible on the majority of construction sites: storage of aggregates can be better achieved, weighing of materials done more consistently, and testing facilities are easier to provide.

It is more expensive for the contractor than producing his own concrete on the site, but there are conditions which make ready-mixed concrete economical to use. On confined town and city sites, where there is difficulty in storage of materials, or where the demand is for large quantities of concrete within a limited period, ready-mixed concrete may provide the answer. It is also useful for foundation work if the vehicle can get within reasonable distance and the chute attachment is used to discharge the concrete.

Where ready-mixed concrete is being used on a large pour, it is advisable to have an alternative source available in the event of a breakdown in supplies, which is always possible in these days of traffic jams and accidents. The alternative could be either another depot or a small standby mixer.

The contractor must obtain approval from the engineer before using ready-mixed concrete on the site, and where possible it is advisable for the Clerk of Works to visit the plant before deliveries are made. The storage of aggregates, as well as the source of supply, should be noted, and the methods of weighing, batching and mixing should also be observed. Discussions should be initiated on documentation, as queries may arise later regarding particular deliveries, upon which the plant should be expected to provide information. Arrangements can be made for certificates to be supplied with each delivery showing particulars of the mix. Test cubes must still be taken, whether the concrete is site or ready-mixed.

Placing the Concrete

Before any concrete is placed, the Clerk of Works should inspect and approve both the reinforcement and the alignment of the formwork. The reinforcement must be assembled in accordance with the engineer's drawings and spaced within the formwork to allow the specified amount of cover. Where mould oils are used, there must be no evidence of the fact on the reinforcement.

Besides checking the formwork for alignment, it is important to check that there is adequate propping and bracing to support the formwork when it is loaded with the wet concrete.

Shavings, wood chippings and surplus wire ties must be removed and the formwork washed out with a hose or cleaned by air pressure. Where temperatures are low, it will also be advisable to check that there is no ice or frost within the formwork, and that there is sufficient heating provided to maintain the concrete at a suitable temperature.

Proper working platforms must be provided where beams or vertical work is concerned, and on floor or roof slabs care should be taken to see the reinforcement is not used to support barrow-runs, etc.

The Clerk of Works must ensure that the concrete is not deposited in such a way as to cause segregation to occur, especially where chutes and skips are used.

The formwork must be evenly filled throughout, and where vibration is not specified, concrete must be tamped with bars and slices to ensure that the reinforcement bars are completely surrounded and all areas of the moulds completely filled.

Great care must be taken to see that the concrete is fully compacted; otherwise, when the formwork is stripped, a honeycomb effect may be present on the face of the concrete, and this could also be repeated within its mass. Voids in the concrete will very seriously affect the strength, and where vibration cannot be applied, hand tamping must be carried out.

Vibrators properly used will reduce the voids and allow a drier mix to be designed, giving greater strength to the finished concrete. Immersion or poker vibrators should be used at fairly close intervals along the line of the concrete as it is poured, and should only be withdrawn when air bubbles have ceased to rise to the surface. Poker vibrators must not be allowed to come into contact with either the reinforcement or the formwork, in case they are disturbed. It is also worth paying attention to the manner in which poker vibrators are sometimes dropped in the mud while another task is performed, and then thrust back into the concrete, mud included.

External vibrators should be securely fitted to the formwork, which must be stronger to resist pressures greater than those from other means of vibration.

Additional checks must be made on the alignment of the formwork while pouring of concrete is continued, and additional bracing should be available in case it is required.

The position of all construction joints may be shown on the drawings, but any additional joints required must be agreed beforehand with the engineer or Clerk of Works.

Joints should be straight and not staggered. Horizontal joints in beams and slabs should be formed in the centre or middle third of the span, and in columns at the haunching to the beam. Vertical joints should be kept to a minimum and formed by placing a stop-edge within the formwork. A groove can be formed in horizontal joints by fixing a batten at the top of the formwork so that the concrete will be forced up against it during compaction.

Before continuing with the next section of concrete it will be necessary to remove the laitance from the construction joint; this can be done with a stiff brush if the concrete is still green, but where it has been allowed to harden, it has always been considered necessary to hack the surface, though modern views suggest it is better not to do this, as it affects the aggregate. The first layer of concrete should be slightly richer with cement to assist the bonding, but where colour tone is important in the finished concrete, it may be better to wash the joint well. This is better than applying a thin layer of cement grout, as is often recommended.

Concreting in Cold Weather

Precautions should be taken by the Clerk of Works when concreting is proceeding in cold weather. He should pay special attention to recording temperatures on site, both at the place of mixing and at the point where the concrete is placed. Good organisation on the site will enable concreting to be continued quite safely when work on a poorly organised site may have been forced to come to a standstill, and as it is in everyone's interests to keep the work proceeding, more thought should be given to cold weather working before the occasion arises.

Precautions must begin with the materials to be used; aggregates should be kept constantly free from frost by covering them against cold winds, and winter conditions can be anticipated by forming steam coils below the base of aggregate stockpiles. Provisions should also be made to heat the water for mixing to be sure there is no frost in any of the aggregates. Rapid-hardening cement may help to overcome the delay which will be caused during cold weather in striking the formwork, and where approval of the engineer is obtained, a percentage of calcium chloride may be used with ordinary Portland cement.

Where concrete is to be placed into excavations, protection must be given beforehand to see the frost has not penetrated the ground; and once the concrete has been placed, tarpaulins, straw, polystyrene or similar insulating materials should be used to protect it. No concrete can be placed into formwork until one is sure no ice or frost is present. Salamander heaters, flame guns, steam jets and many other aids can be used to dispel frost. A gentle breeze can reduce an air temperature of 3 degrees of frost to 7 degrees, so precautions should be taken to reduce the wind by erecting screens of polythene sheeting around the area to be concreted.

CHAPTER NINETEEN

Structural Steelwork

Steel Frames

The use of structural steel frames in the erection of buildings is not quite so common today as it was in the past, no doubt owing to the advances made in concrete technology. However, where speed and flexibility of operation are the important factors, as in factories, then steel-framed buildings are widely used.

Many single storey buildings are produced with a welded steel portal frame, and rectangular or round hollow tubular steel framing may be used. Where heavy structural framing is required, rolled steel stanchions and beams provide the answer. Rolled steel joist can be cut on a trough-like outline and then welded together to provide a much deeper beam, saving costs and reducing the weight of the frame; these are referred to as castellated beams and are used extensively, especially in school construction.

A steel-framed building can act as a morale booster on the site, the client feeling progress is good when the frame has been completed, the architect noting that the building will soon be weather-proof, and the contractor pleased to be out of the ground works, especially if it is a bad site.

To meet the regulations, steel-framed buildings may require protection against fire, and this will be provided by encasing in concrete or brickwork, sprayed or sheet asbestos, etc. Where beams are likely to be used for lifting purposes, as in factories, it is advisable for the permissible maximum loadings to be painted on each beam.

Steelwork Drawings

The design of the steelwork frame is produced by the structural engineer, who may negotiate contracts with specialist firms on a supply and erect basis, obtain competitive quotes and put a PC item in the bills, or nominate a sub-contractor. Some of the major steelwork companies will quote for designing the frame also, but in any case they will become a sub-contractor to the main contractor.

The supply position has been making it necessary for many years now to place an order for the steelwork at an early stage in the contractual arrangements, and a reserve order which can be confirmed by the successful contractor is generally placed by the engineer.

The structural engineer bases his drawings upon those supplied by the architect, but as a different approach is made, this may cause those unfamiliar with steelwork drawings to find difficulties in reading the information immediately. In the past steelwork drawings were referred to as 'blueprints' because they were printed as a white outline on a blue background, and occasionally these are still found among the drawings issued to the Clerk of Works.

On the plans the columns are shown as I-sections and identified by a number within a circle, sometimes prefaced with S to denote stanchion – thus S29 – while beams are shown as a thick line with the identification as a number within brackets above the line, as, say (291). The section of the beam is shown below the line, together with the weight in kilogrammes per metre, thus:

$$\frac{(291)}{305\times165 \quad 54 \ \text{UB}}$$

The layout of the steelwork is shown on a grid pattern, with each grid line cross-referenced by a letter and a number, making it very easy to identify any particular column or beam. These grid lines can then be continued as a reference throughout the remainder of the contract.

Delivery of Steelwork

A crane will be required to off-load the steel when it arrives on site, and the Clerk of Works should note the methods of unloading and storing the steel.

It will be advisable to study the specification for painting steelwork, as this will sometimes call for priming to be carried out before delivery to site; generally, however, the steelwork is delivered untreated to allow weathering to break down the mill-scale. When priming is carried out before delivery, additional priming is nearly always needed after erection. Where tension bolts are to be used, it is desirable that the steel is left unpainted at these points, to provide more positive contact of surfaces for jointing.

The steelwork must not be allowed to be scattered around the site, especially where muddy conditions exist, for apart from the danger to personnel on site, the identification markings on the steelwork can become obscured, in some instances resulting in beams fitted incorrectly.

Setting Out for Steelwork

The position for the steelwork should already have been established by the work previously carried out by the main contractor in forming stanchion bases and ground beams, including the holding down bolt positions. Before starting erection the steelwork contractor will establish his own setting-out lines as a check against the contractor's work, and the Clerk of Works would be well advised to pay regard to this check, noting any discrepancies which may occur.

Obviously a certain tolerance is provided within the holding down bolt positions, but this is limited; if it is allowed to accumulate, it may be necessary to recast the base. Centre-lines for the steelwork grid should be carefully checked throughout the construction of the bases, since it is better to find an error before erection begins than to delay work in progress.

Erection of Steelwork

The erection programme should be discussed with the steelwork contractor and the site agent before any work begins, and a joint check should be made of the site works prepared.

Steel erectors like to put up a number of columns as quickly as possible, but it is advisable to see that the first two bays of steelwork are erected and checked before work proceeds too far. If the first bays are checked and bolted down, some established point to work from is provided, reducing the risk of the steel erector attempting to 'drift' the columns where one base is found to be slightly out of position. Erectors not only resort to sledge-hammer tactics to 'drift' the steelwork into position but apply block and tackle to 'spring' the steel into position for bolting up. Adequate temporary bracing must be provided during the erection of the steelwork.

Supervision of Steelwork

The Clerk of Works should watch that there are no missing nuts or bolts in the steelwork, and that there is sufficient thread showing in every case to enable the nuts to act effectively. Washers must also be provided where required.

Welding has now almost entirely replaced riveting on the site, and the welding must be examined to ensure it is correctly done. Where doubts exist the engineer should be informed immediately. It is possible to apply X-ray tests to welded joints, but only the designer will be able to decide if this is really necessary.

Wherever expansion joints are provided in the steelwork, they should be checked for correct dimensions, since a great deal of movement can occur with steel frames.

Stanchion bases must have a clearance up to 50 mm to allow grouting up to take place, and holding down bolts must be thoroughly tightened on the base plate once the steelwork has been correctly aligned. All cleats and angle plates must be checked for alignment and correct positioning, and where sheeting rails are provided, these should be checked for line and level, as any variation will be transferred to the cladding lines.

Once the steelwork has been erected and offered as completed by the steelwork contractor, it is the contractor's responsibility to check for accuracy. Generally there may be a tendency for the contractor to rely upon the steelwork contractor's assurance, but the Clerk of Works should insist upon a joint check being carried out by the contractor and the steelwork contractor before the latter is allowed to leave the site.

It may be necessary to see that priming paints and possibly even subsequent coats are applied to the steel in positions which may be difficult to reach later, such as tops of beams, etc. It may be advisable to treat such places with bitumen paint, but this will affect future decisions on the use of oil paints.

CHAPTER TWENTY

Brickwork and Blockwork

Mortar for Buildings

For many years on building sites it was considered that a good mortar was obtained by providing a fat and workable mix, designed to satisfy the bricklayers as well as setting hard enough to enable work to proceed with sufficient speed. It is quite true that mortar should be relatively easy to use, besides setting sufficiently hard to enable work to proceed, but this definitely does not mean using fat mixes. In fact, the best mortar for the purpose is seldom the strongest, and in general it should be no stronger than the bricks which are to be bedded.

Cement mortars are strong; they set very quickly but are prone to severe shrinkage, causing cracks in the brickwork. Lime mortars are weak, their slowness in hardening making them extremely vulnerable to frost damage. By adding a small quantity of cement to a lime mix the advantages of both can be acquired, with setting properties speeded up and shrinkage restricted to a minimum.

Lime may be omitted from a mortar mix in favour of a plasticiser, which produces air bubbles within the mix and provides the same workability as lime. These air bubbles create voids in the mix which accommodate any expansion set up by frost action, even after the mortar has set. Although ordinary lime mortar has little setting power, hydraulic lime may be used instead, and this has the added advantage of being able to set under water.

The practice of re-tempering mortar is still carried out, and should be strictly dealt with whenever the Clerk of Works finds it is happening on his site.

Lime-sand mortars manufactured from non-hydraulic lime can be stored indefinitely, but the addition of cement immediately requires the mortar to be used within two hours.

Sands for Mortar

As sand occupies the greater volume of the mortar, close attention should be given to it at the early stages of the contract. Samples should be obtained and submitted to various tests, and, if possible, a laboratory test should be done. Sands should be obtained from sand-pits or from the river bed, since for building purposes sand obtained from the seashore will cause dampness and efflorescence, as well as eventually corroding the wall ties or any brick reinforcement.

The Clerk of Works can carry out frequent checks on the sand during the contract to see that it is clean and free from loam. By squeezing a sample in the palm of the hand he can find out if it contains too much clay or loam, as it will then remain in a ball; and he may detect dirty sand by rubbing a sample between his palms, for it will stain them.

Clay, iron pyrites, mica, coal and vegetable matter are all types of impurities to guard against when inspecting suitable sands for mortar. Sand obtained from the river bed can contain small globules of oil, probably from shipping using the river.

The grading of sands is most important for all purposes but especially for mortars; where they are too coarse, the mortar will be weak and porous, and where they are too fine, the mortar will be weak.

Testing Sands on Site

The Clerk of Works will only be able to assess the suitability of sand visually on the site and it might help him to check typical samples in the gradings given under BSS Zones 1 to 4.

To check sand for clay or silt, half fill a 2 lb jar with clean water and add sand until it is approximately 25 mm below the water level. Stir the contents thoroughly to expel all the air from the sand and leave standing for fifteen to twenty minutes, when the contents will have settled, showing the amount of silt as a layer on top of the sand. By leaving the jar for a further 3 hours the silt layer can be measured, and where this is in excess of 6 per cent, the sample should be rejected. If the jar is kept for a further

24 hours, it should be possible to see the silt and clay in layers on top of the sand.

Tests for organic impurities can be made by taking a 12 oz graduated clear glass medicine bottle and filling it to the $2\frac{1}{2}$ oz level with a 3 per cent solution of sodium hydroxide (caustic soda), which any chemist will make up. The sand should be added until the volume in the bottle reaches 7 oz, when the cork should be replaced and the bottle shaken vigorously and left for 24 hours to settle. Then if the water is straw-coloured, it is safe to use the sand, but if it is darker, organic matter is present, and if it is very dark, it should be referred to the laboratory for further tests. The reaction of organic matter when caustic soda is added can be seen by adding a small amount of the latter to a little weak tea in a jar, when the liquid will immediately turn a dark brown shade.

Special Mortars

Mortars are available in premixed form, requiring the addition of water only, and they can be obtained in a variety of colours.

Where large quantities are required, lime-sand mortars which merely require the addition of cement for immediate use can be obtained. These mortars have the advantage over site mixes in that they are produced under strict control, and where colour is added, there is likely to be better consistency throughout.

Special cements incorporating plasticisers in lieu of lime are also available, but care should be exercised with the mixes, as there is a wide variation in the amount of sand which must be added to produce the correct mix.

Where plasticisers are used in liquid form in the mortar, the Clerk of Works must pay particular attention to the quantities used, as a very weak mix may result in a breakdown in the jointing. This may not be apparent until a later stage, after the contract has been completed.

Plasticisers are sometimes added to the water butt used for mixing purposes, and this water is used at intervals to soften the mix if initial set has taken place. The dangers of this are too obvious to require further explanation.

A further practice to guard against is adding plasticiser to masonry cement as though it were ordinary Portland cement. As masonry cement already has a plasticiser incorporated within it, the consequent mortar strength is far below that required.

Where colouring matter is added to mortar on site, it should be appreciated that excessive use of pigment can reduce the strength of the mortar, especially if not evenly distributed throughout the mix.

Brickwork

It is remarkable that we are still extensively using bricks as a constructional material after 2,000 years of progress. Modern prophets repeatedly predict the end of this era, through a shortage of craftsmen, economic fluctuations within the industry, and the acceptance of more modern building techniques. But bricks still go on, overcoming the challenge of alternative materials. No doubt the flexibility they provide, as well as their aesthetic appearance, still appeals to a vast majority of the public.

In his design the architect will select the type of brick he wishes to use; this will be stated in the contract bills by name, or a rate will be allowed for bricks to enable the contractor to select within a certain range. In all probability the architect will have discussed the bricks with a particular manufacturer and placed a reserve order for the quantity required. Once the contract has been awarded, the selected contractor will be able to confirm the reserve order to the manufacturer on receipt of an architect's instruction to that effect.

Samples of all types of brick, both commons and facings, to be used on the site should be obtained at the outset, and, after approval by the architect, should be retained in the Clerk of Works' office for future reference. The bricks should be marked and the details recorded in the site diary, as experience shows that memories can be most uncertain when such points are discussed later. A sample panel of facing brickwork will be allowed in the bills, and this should be erected at an early stage in the contract close to the Clerk of Works' office, where it will be convenient for reference.

Manufacture of Bricks

Bricks are produced from clay, shale, brick earth, sand-lime, concrete, breeze and several other materials in the form of facing bricks, common bricks, and load-bearing bricks. The quality of the clay has a bearing on the type of brick produced, but generally the clay or shale is ground and mixed until it reaches a plastic state, when it is extruded in a continuous ribbon which is self-supporting over 1 m or so. The clay travels along on an endless belt in this ribbon state, being cut into approximate brick sizes by carefully positioned wires before the unburnt bricks continue their way to end up as wire-cuts or are directed into a set of dies in a hydraulic press which stamps them ready for firing. Pressed bricks have a frog on one side or sometimes on both sides, which reduces the content of clay, but the brick conforms to a specific compressive strength. Wire-cuts can be perforated and this also reduces the amount of clay used, and heat within the kiln more easily gets to the centre of the brick, giving it a more uniform shape. Bricks in their plastic stage are loaded on cars which then travel at a controlled rate through a continuous kiln, or may be loaded into special chambers which are then subjected to high temperatures on a particular cycle of events.

Older methods consisted of forming layers of plastic bricks and layers of fuel within a clamp and then firing the whole together. This produced bricks which are much admired today because they were less mechanical-looking – their shapes and sizes were varied and different colours resulted from the position of the bricks within the kiln.

Calcium silicate or sand-lime bricks, as they are better known, are produced by mixing sand or crushed siliceous rock with lime, and subjecting this in a mould to a high pressure to form the brick. These bricks are then stacked on pallets and removed to an autoclave where they are stored under high-pressure steam for several hours. Sand-lime bricks are well shaped and of a regular size, but the importance in manufacture lies in the correct grading of the materials.

Concrete bricks are manufactured in a similar way in that the concrete is subjected to high pressures in the mould and then removed to autoclaves for steam treatment, although they could be left to cure as ordinary concrete.

Brick Deliveries

Where the bricks have been nominated by the architect, there is always the possibility that the contractor may subsequently claim delays owing to poor deliveries or quality of bricks. The Clerk of Works must keep close watch on this situation, as both deliveries and stocks may be affected by the 'call-off' rate which the contractor has established with the manufacturer. If the contractor fails to accept deliveries because he is behind with his programme, this fact must be noted at the time to balance against any future claims.

The area where the bricks are to be stored should be level and dry, or eventually the bottom layers will be unusable because of mud, etc. Adequate covers must be provided to restrict the effect of rainwater on the bricks, for this will cause discoloration in certain areas, especially where the bricks are stored indefinitely. Bricks should be used in rotation as they are delivered, and this will allow better liaison with the manufacturer.

Deliveries of common bricks will be made with tipping lorries, and the bricks deposited in stacks around the site at convenient points; but facing bricks and engineering bricks must be offloaded carefully and stacked properly, using straw or building paper between layers to avoid chipped arrisses. Delivery of banded or palleted bricks is now increasing, providing ease of unloading and site handling under good site organisation. The bricks are packed in layers bonded to produce brick packs of 250 or 500 bricks, which can be handled by crane or forklift truck. Care must be taken to see the packs are tightly banded or movement during transport can affect the brick arrisses. The practice of opening the packs on site by breaking the bands with steel putlogs should be discouraged.

Testing and Approvals

Field tests on bricks will be restricted to checking the sizes according to the BSS, inspecting any overburnt or misshapen bricks, and looking for any appearance of free-lime, variation in colour and any damage to facings, etc. A ringing tone indicates sound quality when two bricks are struck together, but underburnt bricks give a dull sound. It is not unknown for underburnt common bricks to disintegrate when left in a heap exposed to the weather, and obviously such an occurrence would produce disastrous consequences if it happened in the sub-structures of a building.

Colour variation in facing bricks may not be quite so obvious in assessing deliveries, especially where some may have a higher moisture content than others, but this problem can become particularly difficult if not attended to during the construction. The Clerk of Works would be well advised to keep a close watch on the way in which bricks are being used, so that newly delivered supplies are not used indiscriminately with old stocks that have been on site for months.

Where the contractor finds bricks in short supply, there can be many problems, but the variation in brick sizes can produce some situations which are not easily overcome; deliveries should therefore be constantly checked, and where not in accordance with the BSS, the manufacturer should be called in to discuss what can be done to overcome the problem. Samples submitted to the laboratory will require a minimum of ten bricks, which will be tested for water absorption and compressive strength. This is particularly important in the case of structural brickwork.

Brickwork Sub-structures

Conditions are not always good when the work in sub-structures has to be carried out, but this does not justify the tendency to accept it as 'rough work'. Inaccurate formation of foundation concrete is often overcome by bedding bricks-on-edge in the footings, allowing excessive bed joints, or resorting to courses of 'pig' to achieve correct levels. Hard-burnt bricks should be used below the DPC level, and where bricks with deep frogs are selected, it is important that the frogs are laid uppermost and filled with mortar; otherwise the cavity will be susceptible to water at ground level and that may then be subjected to frost action. On a reasonably dry site this may not appear such a problem, but in wet conditions it is anticipating troubles. Where the sub-structure is in two leaves of brickwork, care should be taken to see the ties are properly bedded and inserted at correct centres; some bricklayers resort to building-in headers as ties, which are referred to as 'bumpers'.

Before any hardcore fill is allowed within the area of the sub-structure, concrete should be placed within the cavity and allowed to set; if not, the brickwork can easily be displaced through overloading, which may not always be noted at the time. On a very deep fill the thickness of the sub-structure brickwork should be increased to withstand the additional pressures, a fact which may be overlooked in the design where floor levels can be adjusted on the site without reference to the actual designer of the sub-structures.

Setting out must be carefully checked on sub-structures; there is still the attitude on many sites that adjustments can be made within the first two courses of facings at floor level. This should not be tolerated, and an example is shown on Plate 8 where the superstructure brickwork is over-sailing the sub-structure by 40 mm, with attempts to disguise the fact by making up with sand and cement.

Brickwork Superstructures

The first thing to be checked when brickwork starts at this stage is the bonding, to make sure this works in with all openings without creating broken bond. Discussion with the architect will establish how much tolerance he is willing to accept in adjusting the position of windows and doors, for it is unlikely that he has worked bonding of the brickwork accurately to a few millimetres. It is very important to use average delivery sizes of bricks when setting out. Quite often little attention is paid to this requirement, larger bricks being used, with subsequent difficulties in trying to achieve reasonable perpends with smaller bricks.

There is always a danger on cavity work in allowing droppings to bridge the cavity, even though cavity laths are used. Sometimes this is caused through careless handling when changing the level of the laths. The Clerk of Works should insist upon examining cavities before they are closed, and where droppings are lodged across tie-wires, etc, the mortar must be removed by using a length of reinforcement bar, and bricks removed at DPC level to clean out the mortar. Mortar across the cavity will undoubtedly create either dampness or at the least efflorescence within the building.

The height to which one leaf of brickwork may be taken will no doubt be specified in the bills, and this must be kept under control, especially where the inner leaf is in blockwork, which often happens today. The practice of pressing the wall ties into the wet mortar should be discouraged also, and ties should be built-in and bedded correctly. Gauge rods should be used to check levels at various stages, such as window sill and heads, floor levels, etc; and where any bearings occur, this should be checked properly with a level.

The brickwork should be correctly plumbed as the work proceeds but the Clerk of Works will find it useful to line up corners and reveals by visual means to see they do not offend. In days past it was considered essential to have a good eye for accuracy, and it is still an asset to the Clerk of Works, one which should be cultivated at all times, as it may save him embarrassment at some time in his career. Flushing up the brickwork as the work proceeds is not always adhered to, and that not only reduces the strength of the work, but affects the insulation values, which can be critical to party walls.

Calculated load-bearing brickwork should be built with the frog up, and all bed joints and perpends built solidly without reliance on flushing-up methods. Great care should be taken to distinguish between brickwork which is designed as load-bearing in an engineering sense and brickwork designed as general construction.

Expansion and Shrinkages

The use of incorrect mortars may result in cracking in the brickwork, and where the design allows a heavy water deposit down the face of the brickwork, this can result in water penetration, especially where there are heavy wind pressures against the face of the building.

Where sand-lime or concrete bricks are used, there will be movement in the bricks themselves, and a strong mortar used in these circumstances will result in unsightly cracks in the brickwork. If a weak mortar is used, it will enable any movement to be accommodated within the area of the brick, resulting at the most in a hairline crack around each brick in the mortar.

The chemical reaction of cement requires water to assist the process, and care must be taken when using bricks with excessive suction to avoid the mortar being dried out too quickly, as this will break down the adhesion between mortar and brick, leaving a clear path for the penetration of water.

Where the tolerances are critical in the height of brickwork care should be taken in the choice of bricks as some brickwork has been known to 'grow' in height, chemical action within the bricks causing them to increase in size after laying.

Scaffolding for Brickwork

The scaffolding arrangement should be discussed with the agent because he may be intending to operate by working overhand, and if this has been overlooked in the specification, it can create a strong difference of opinion.

The question of the height of lifts should also be noted, avoiding the tendency to overreach with courses, which does not help true coursing of the brickwork.

Scaffolding can contribute to defacing the brickwork where planks are not turned back after finishing at lower levels by causing mortar and rain to splash on the facings over a period of time, leaving stains which take years to weather out.

Overloading the scaffolding with bricks can be a dangerous practice, and the Clerk of Works must bear in mind the safety regulations concerning scaffolding, especially as he will be clambering about on it while carrying out his inspections.

Protection of Brickwork

Care should be taken to protect the brickwork after each lift, either by sheeting it over or using planks to throw off rain and dirt. Polythene sheeting is sometimes used to protect it, but unless this is secured, it can cause more damage by flapping against the facing bricks and smearing the joints. Efflorescence at window openings and parapet levels is adequate evidence of a lack of care in protecting the brickwork, and gutters with short lengths of rainwater pipe attached or sometimes none at all are often responsible for large areas of efflorescence appearing on the finished brickwork. The sort of damage that can occur is clearly illustrated in Plates 9 and 10. It could easily have been avoided.

Wall-ties and Cramps

Quite often the correct type of cavity wall-tie is not used on the site because the difference in the gauge of the metal is not always appreciated by those responsible for providing these. Ties are commonly provided in three forms: as strong galvanised metal strips with fishtail ends, as thin wire twisted into a butterfly shape, and as a double-triangle with a straight portion between.

The disadvantage of wall-ties is that they bridge the cavity and trap mortar droppings as the work progresses, and the mortar then contributes to dampness in the structure. The Clerk of Works must see that all the precautions possible are taken to avoid mortar collecting in the cavity, besides checking that the correct type of wall-tie is being used.

Ties may also be required for retaining stone and other claddings, and in such cases wire fixings, cramps, or special fixings secured by dovetailed metal channels to the inner leaf, must be of non-ferrous metals.

By sloping ties towards the outer leaf any moisture within the cavity should be removed from the inner face, and wall-ties are formed with a drip for this purpose.

Where the inner and outer leaves of the cavity wall are taken up at different stages, there is a danger of ties being bent to fit the coursing. Galvanised metal strip ties treated in this way can become loose and ineffective.

Cramps securing window or door frames should be built-in; for if bricks are cut out to accommodate them later, the fixings can be slightly loose. While this may not often be serious, it may necessitate a great deal of maintenance if the site is exposed.

Timber pads are built into the brickwork to act as fixings for window frames and door frames, and these pads should be treated with preservatives as well as being kept slightly back from the face to allow the joint to be properly pointed. A plastic fixing pad which can be built into the brickwork is available, and this provides a positive fixing for door and window frames, besides being rot-proof.

Damp-proof Courses

Most parts of a building depend upon a connecting section resisting either rain penetration or ground water, and in assessing the value of a damp-proof course it should be considered likely that at some time water will appear in that particular area. It is much easier to provide an efficient damp-proof membrane in the sub-structure during the construction of a building than to find a cure for rising damp later.

The practice today of relying upon a polythene sheet, subjected to the traffic of site personnel, to resist rising moisture seems rather doubtful, but the Clerk of Works must endeavour to see it is installed correctly.

The damp-proof course at ground level should be of a suitable material to avoid the bitumen being squeezed out under the load. The damp-proof course to the inner leaf must bridge the joint with the ground floor slab, and the cavity should continue at least 75 mm below the level of the outer damp-proof course.

A damp-proof membrane should be provided above all openings in the brickwork, and be stepped down one course from the inner leaf. The width of the sheet should be sufficient to avoid water affecting any timber frame built into the opening.

Vertical damp-proof courses should be formed wherever the external leaf of brickwork is returned to meet the inner leaf, or vice versa. Where an internal wall becomes an external wall, such as a gable which continues above a kitchen or garage roof, it is important to see that the damp-proof course is correctly formed to cross the cavity and form an apron to the upstand covering to the roof.

At a casual glance damp-proof courses can all look alike, even to the practised eye, and where hessian-based DPCs are being installed instead of those with a metal base, a breakdown of the protection in that area may result.

The Clerk of Works should study the drawings to note the positions for damp-proof courses, and make a special point of examining these before the work has been allowed to progress too far.

Where a DPC is required in a free standing wall, it is better to build-in a course of engineering bricks rather than the usual type of damp-proof course, which may produce a weakness at that point in the wall.

Blockwork

Concrete blocks are manufactured in a variety of forms from cement and aggregates. They can be used for structural purposes, as facing work, or purely as a decorative screen, and are available as hollow blocks, cellular blocks, and as solid blocks. The strength of the blocks must not be judged by their appearance, as all three types may have an equivalent strength, depending upon the block density. The blocks are graded under three types, with Types A and B being suitable for general construction work, and Type C for use as a non-load-bearing partition or as infill to frame construction.

The cavities in cellular blocks are closed at one end, and the Clerk of Works should note this is the portion of the block which should be uppermost as construction proceeds. The cavities in hollow blocks continue through, while solid blocks have minor cavities which enable the bricklayer to handle them more easily.

The use of concrete blocks for facing work has been increasing in recent years, and where good workmanship has been available, the result has been very pleasing, but, as with all concrete work, a decided amount of movement takes place, and unless proper movement joints are provided, the facing will be marred by cracks. The correct gauge of mortar must also be used with concrete blocks, or hair cracks will occur, allowing rain penetration on exposed faces which in turn will produce further problems.

Lightweight blocks can be produced by using additives to the mix to produce aerated concrete, or by using lightweight aggregates such as pulverised fly-ash, foamed slag, clay pellets, vermiculite, and numerous other materials, including graded timber particles.

Clay blocks are manufactured in a similar manner to bricks, clay being extruded in a plastic state and fired in kilns. Clay blocks have many qualities similar to bricks but are unsuitable for facings because of their appearance, and difficulties arise in providing fixtures to clay block walls. They have been used for many years as filler blocks in concrete floor construction, as internal non-load-bearing partitions, and as internal leaf to cavity wall construction.

On the Continent clay blocks are used for general construction, apparently with success, even on high rise buildings with RC frames. The surface of the blocks is ribbed to provide a key for plaster, and blocks are available to be built in where chases are required; but chasing to either clay or other cellular blocks must be checked by the Clerk of Works to see there is no effect to the structure of the wall.

Breeze blocks were used extensively between the Wars, but were often treated with some suspicion because impurities in the aggregate affected plasterwork. The problem was overcome to some extent but breeze blocks appear to be less common, no doubt because of the wide variety of lightweight building blocks available.

A particular type of clay brick, which may almost be considered as a block because of its size, was developed by the Building Research Station as an answer to the problem of two separate operations to form a cavity wall. The blocks were known as V-bricks because of the vertical perforations, with large apertures to the centre of the block to produce a vertical cavity. The nominal sizes were $228 \times 228 \times 76$ mm, and specials were available for returns. Although they are produced on a commercial basis today, they never achieved the success they might have done, because of the care necessary in preventing the cavity becoming blocked with mortar droppings and because they were not popular with bricklayers.

Curing the concrete blocks is usually carried out by normal exposure to the atmosphere, or it may be accelerated by low-pressure steam, but many of the lightweight blocks are cured by high-pressure steam in special chambers.

When blocks are insufficiently cured when they are delivered to site, especially lightweight concrete blocks, there is often excess wastage through handling and stacking. Insufficient curing may occur either because the manufacturer is under pressure from many sources for deliveries, or through indiscriminate ordering from the site. The results are likely to be expensive in either case, and where it is possible delays will be created to the contract, it becomes of importance to the Clerk of Works and the architect.

Storage of concrete blocks on the site should be arranged to allow good circulation of air around the stacks, and sheets should be provided to protect the blocks from rain and snow. The base should be prepared to avoid unnecessary wastage through the bottom layers being affected by mud and site conditions.

The problems of storage and maintaining the blocks in a reasonably dry condition will affect the contractor if he is prevented from building with wet blocks. Because they have a high initial shrinkage, concrete blocks should be allowed sufficient time to dry out after manufacture. Wet blocks create greater shrinkage problems when drying out and will possibly affect the plasterwork on internal walls.

Setting out of blockwork is very important, as coursing will not be so easily adjusted as in brickwork. Bonding must be checked to ensure it is carried out correctly, and as half-blocks and special blocks for return ends are available, the use of common bricks to make up these positions should be discouraged from the outset.

Coursing can be a difficulty where the blockwork is used as an inner leaf to cavity construction and starts at sub-floor level, which will be 50 mm below the outer brick coursing.

Blockwork must not be continued above a reasonable height, which will prevent the wall bulging where the mortar has not set sufficiently. In cavity wall construction it will be necessary to check that wall-ties are being fitted correctly, as there may be a tendency to bend these to suit the coursing either way.

CHAPTER TWENTY-ONE

Carpentry and Joinery

Selection of Timber

Timbers will be selected by the architect according to the purpose for which they are particularly required, and poor selection will result in poor performance, no matter how well the workmanship may be carried out.

Certain timbers have been specified for structural purposes for a long time in the industry, and these include European redwoods, Douglas fir, and hemlock. Improved knowledge and modern techniques have enabled structural timbers to be used on a much more economical basis. Engineering principles have been developed in the use of timber, providing the industry with framed structures, roof trusses, beams, framed floors, and load-bearing partitions, but in all these developments the quality of the timber is equally as important as design principles and jointing techniques.

Timber of good quality should be strong in tension and reasonably strong in compression, and grain should be parallel to the length of the timber member, as any check or slope in the grain can appreciably affect the ultimate strength.

Flooring timber should be selected to provide resistance to wear, and for this purpose it is best quarter-sawn (rift-sawn), although softwood flooring and some hardwood flooring is flat-sawn (slash-sawn). Additional covering is invariably provided to softwood flooring in the way of carpets, etc, but where appearance as well as wearing quality is desirable, hardwood floors will be selected. The flooring can be supplied as narrow strip boards, grooved and tongued for jointing, or wood blocks with interlocking edges to prevent movement after they are laid.

Some hardwoods are liable to splinter, which makes them unsuitable for flooring in certain instances, especially in hospitals, ballrooms or gymnasiums. As central heating conditions are likely to cause greater shrinkage of the boards, care must be taken to specify the correct moisture content.

Seasoning of Timber

Once the timber has been felled, it can be left to season naturally, but the log still contains a large percentage of water, and shrinkage will occur in drying out, setting up unequal stresses and causing the timber to split. Natural seasoning can be improved upon by cutting the logs into planks and spacing them with packings to allow good circulation of air around them, a process generally referred to as air drying.

Logs must be sawn in a certain way to obtain the maximum quantity of suitable timber, and this quantity will be seriously reduced if undue splitting occurs through poor seasoning. Air drying requires both time and space, each of which are at a premium in modern times, so that seasoning is increasingly being carried out by other methods.

Kiln drying is a skilled method of seasoning timber by placing it in artificially heated drying rooms where the humidity is controlled by introducing steam or spray into the chamber to control the rate of drying.

Timber Quality

The Clerk of Works should cultivate a knowledge of timbers, which can only be acquired by experience. Assessing timber purely on the basis of a specification will provide a wide range of interpretations, and a difference of opinion among the 'experts'.

The terms used to distinguish the two main types of trees are deciduous and coniferous, the former being hardwoods and broad-leaf trees, while the others are softwoods and narrow-leaf trees. It is equally important to remember that all hardwoods are not necessarily hard timbers, and neither are all softwoods to be regarded as soft timber.

Timber has been used so wastefully for many years that many species regarded as traditional building materials have now become scarce, and in certain instances almost unobtainable. The Clerk of Works was always able to rely upon the knowledge and experience of timbers he gained as a craftsman within the industry, but the position is quite different today, with many of the timbers having unfamiliar names.

A copy of the current issue of shipper's marks can be useful for recognising the main sources of timber supplies: these marks are stencilled on the ends of timbers in red or blue paint, although Russian timbers may be hammer-marked with various symbols. Timber is also sold in grades, 1–5, and as unsorted, Russian timbers are one grade different from others; for instance, Scandinavian fifth grade is equal to Russian fourth.

The Clerk of Works can avoid many problems concerning the quality of timber at site level by visiting the suppliers with the agent before deliveries are made. Apart from noting the growth rate, shown by the spacing of annual rings, the Clerk of Works should always check the dimensions of the sawn timbers, as errors can occur in sawn sizes. Waney edges and excessive knots can reduce the strength of the timber, and excess moisture may cause severe shrinkage or give rise to fungicidal attack.

Stress Grading of Timber

The difficulties in obtaining suitable qualities and quantities of timber for structural purposes, plus the need to calculate the requirements a little more carefully, has resulted in the demand for timber grading to be specified. Although the specification was introduced some years ago, stress-graded timbers are more generally used today because of the increased application of engineering principles to timber construction. Visual methods are still relied upon a great deal, and there is always a margin of error which can be expected in view of the number of items to be assessed. Visual grading must consider each of the following points.

Rate of growth	Fissures in the timber
Knots in the timber	Resin content
Slope of grain	Fungal growth
Spiral grain	Wormholes
Waney edges	

Mechanical grading is increasing but suppliers must still rely upon visual grading for many points mentioned above. A machine is used to measure the modulus of elasticity in the timber, which is related to strength, and then the timber is stamped indelibly with the appropriate grade. There is also a colour coding for stress-graded timber; it is based on matching a piece of timber of known strength against other timbers. The assessor then grades the other timber as 40, 50, 60, or 75 per cent in relation to the known sample.

Two standard grades have recently been introduced for visually- and machine-graded timber: GS (general structural grade) and SS (special structural grade), the prefix M being used to denote machine grades (MGS and MSS). It is expected that further machine grades will become available. Markings on visually-graded timber should identify the grader or responsible company together with the grade, while machine-graded timber will also show the licence number of the machine, the BSI kitemark and the BS number.

Moisture Content

The moisture content of timber is specified as the percentage of water present compared with the weight of the timber when dry, and expressed as the formula

$$\frac{(\text{net weight} - \text{dry weight})}{\text{dry weight}} \times 100 = \text{moisture content per cent.}$$

The moisture content for timber will vary according to the position in which it is used. Carcassing timbers, such as roof trusses, purlins, rafters, joists, etc, should be 18–22 per cent, timber windows approximately 16 per cent, and joinery for internal use 10–12 per cent, and where central heating is installed, the lower figure should be sought.

Moisture content is reversible, and joinery items delivered at the correct moisture content will quickly acquire the moisture level of the conditions in which they are stored. Once installed, they will again be reduced to the required moisture content, but fluctuations create movement in the timber which affect the quality of the goods.

Where the moisture content in the timber is high, the risk of fungus attack is greater. The Clerk of Works, therefore, must maintain a close watch on timber from delivery to its final position under specified conditions.

Special gauges for checking the moisture content of timber are operated by a small electric current which reacts when a metal probe contacts moisture. A needle is then activated and registers on a dial with a predetermined scale; the reading is then compared with a chart giving readings for various timbers.

Timber Preservatives

Carcassing timbers, window frames and external boarding should be treated with preservatives to prevent decay or infestation.

There are three main types of treatment, which differ in appearance, application and degree of protection, and can be applied either by vacuum/

pressure impregnation, immersion, or brushing. The most successful method is by vacuum impregnation, which carries the preservative deep into the timber. The protection given by immersion will depend upon the period during which the timber is immersed, for the term is used equally whether the timber has been dipped or steeped for several days. Brush treatment is suitable for touching up sawn ends or joints in the timber, the preservative suppliers providing a special organic solution for this purpose.

Coal tar oils are suitable preservatives for such items as fencing, but are difficult to handle and cannot be painted afterwards.

Waterborne solutions can be handled satisfactorily, and, when given time to dry, can be painted or glued without danger. They carry toxic salts into the timber, where the salts remain when the water has been allowed to dry off.

Organic solutions allow decorative treatment to be applied to the timber together with the preservative. Water repellents may also contain preservatives, and these can be applied to cladding boards as a decorative finish at the same time.

The Clerk of Works must check the specified method of treatment in advance with the suppliers of the chemicals. Often a reagent is available for checking the treated timbers.

It should be remembered that the treatment is carried out by the timber manufacturer under licence, and while it is not suggested they are likely to provide the wrong type of treatment if correctly informed, there is often confusion among site personnel regarding the types of treatment available.

Modern Jointing Techniques

Modern production resources in joinery have enabled less complex joints to be developed than the traditional jointing of timber, although of course the latter are used wherever they are best suited to the purpose. Some examples of modern jointing techniques are illustrated in Plates 11a, b and c. Plate 11d shows an early attempt to achieve a mechanical joint.

Combed joints are used a great deal in the manufacture of joinery, and provide strength by creating a greater surface area for the synthetic resin glues used to bond them together.

Finger joints enable continuous lengths of timber to be produced for the manufacture of door and window frames, and, apart from the surface area for the glue, the joint is precisely formed by machine. The length of the teeth on the joint vary, but a recent form has a 5 mm deep joint bonded with resorcinol-formaldehyde, enabling structural timbers to be produced in a continuous length and cut later to the required size.

Lap joints rely upon the contact surface area secured by bolts and timber connectors of varying design.

Butt joints are formed of metal gussets which are either pre-bored to ensure the nailing pattern is correct, or the 'nails' are formed as teeth pressed out of the plate. Trimming joints previously formed with tusk tenon joints can now be made with pressed metal anchor plates.

Timber Joists

Before joists are positioned, the Clerk of Works should check whether these are specified as rough-sawn or cut to size, as the tolerances for rough-sawn joists will be too great to enable the joists to be lined through top and bottom. It is general practice to line the top face of the joist to receive the flooring, so that when plasterboard is fixed to the underside of rough-sawn joists, it will be necessary either to pay for 'dubbing-out' or accept poor angles and wavy ceilings.

Joists must be given sufficient bearing but should not be allowed to project into the cavity in brickwork, and where joist hangers are used, they must be lined and levelled before being built into the brickwork. Unless they are fixed square to the run of the joist, metal hangers can induce twist to the joist, especially where cross-bracing is not provided. There is a tendency to omit cross-bracing, as a false economy, where the span is near the limits.

Joist spacings should be regular, and where packings are inevitable, these should be of slate or similar material, not timber. Faulty packing of joists produces gaps between the skirting and the floorboards when the building dries out.

Where it is necessary to pass services through the joists, the holes should be bored along the axis before fixing, and notching of the joists should be left to the carpenter. Joists should not be notched more than one-eighth of their depth, and this should be done within one-eighth and one quarter of the span from either end. It is possible to notch slightly deeper than this further within this area, but notching should be carefully supervised.

Roof Trusses

Modern roof structures depend more and more upon prefabrication, trusses being made in the factory and delivered to site ready for erection. Metal jointing plates, already referred to, are fixed to roof trusses in the factory both manually and mechanically, and this can lead to variations in the positioning of the plate. The Clerk of Works should check trusses when they are delivered, and where he is not satisfied, he should arrange a visit to the factory together with the agent, where corrections can be seen to. He should arrange to have a copy of the truss manufacturer's drawings, which are usually submitted to the architect for his approval, so that he will be familiar with the timber sections and other details beforehand.

Trusses assembled with bolts and timber connectors will require to be checked when drying out has occurred in the building to see that the bolts are correctly tensioned; otherwise there may be some undue settlement of the roof.

Plywood beam trusses are manufactured with a camber, and while it may seem unlikely, these can be erected incorrectly. Their correct storage is essential. They are often left uncovered, allowing the rain to collect within the framing and upsetting any likelihood of moisture control. Apart from insisting upon protection to roof trusses during storage, it is advisable for the Clerk of Works to note the methods of lifting them into position, and the means for securing them to the wall-plate.

Tongued and Grooved Boarding

Improper storage and lack of protection for tongued and grooved floorboards becomes very obvious when buildings, particularly houses, are ready for occupation. The problem of shrinkage has been increased by the installation of central heating in a greater number of dwellings, and it is not uncommon to see flooring shrink to an extent where the tongue is almost clear of the groove. Many contractors offer to overcome this problem by gluing and pinning strips of timber into the faulty joints, but this provides an inferior job for the client, and a more costly one for the contractor. Proper steps taken to store the timber in the first instance would avoid both problems.

Narrower boards produce less shrinkage problems, so where the Clerk of Works has the opportunity to offer advice on the selection he should recommend boards no wider than 5 in (125 mm).

Apart from general points regarding the fixing of boards with deadknots, waney edges, splits, shakes, etc, the Clerk of Works should note that boards are carried through close to the walls so that a proper joint can be made with the skirting. Boards must not be laid in short lengths, except where access traps are formed, and butt joints should be placed on a joist in each case. Nails should be provided at every joist and punched home, although there is an increase in the use of nail guns which can be adjusted to penetrate below the board surface. Flooring is carried out before the ceiling is plated, and a quick check often reveals a line of nails just missing the joist when viewed from below.

Access points for services should be formed when the flooring is laid, not cut out afterwards. This avoids damage to the flooring by another tradesman, who may be anxious to get on with his own work rather than wait for the carpenter.

Laying floorboards is only part of the operation; equally important is giving a measure of protection to floors. This used to be accepted without question, but now it seems to be reserved for floors with special finishes. The Clerk of Works, however, should ensure that adequate protection is given to all finished floor surfaces.

Roof Boarding

Where flat roofs are boarded to receive built-up roofing felt, the levels should be checked to ensure there is sufficient fall for draining the roof, and where packings are provided, these must be secure.

If tongued and grooved boarding is used, it should be carefully cramped and securely nailed, for sharp or rough edges will affect the felt. For the same reason, angles should be fitted with a splayed fillet. An inspection of the roof will reveal any nails not properly punched home or boards inadequately nailed.

If no provision has been made to provide ventilation within the roof space, this fact should be brought to the attention of the architect in case it has been overlooked.

The boarding should be covered with one layer of felt as soon as possible to avoid the boards becoming distorted, either by rain or sun. Gutters should be fitted as soon as possible, together with rainwater pipes to provide adequate drainage; while aprons and flashings must be completed to ensure the roof is watertight.

Timber Doors

The majority of doors are factory-produced today. The few that are not may be required for non-standard positions, or in buildings of high quality, where they will be specially detailed and produced at a much higher cost than mass-produced doors.

Doors are generally described under three headings – unframed, framed, and flush – each having its own use.

Unframed doors will be restricted to stores and outbuildings. They are entirely dependent upon the nailing for strength, so nails should be punched and then clinched over into the ledges. The size of the ledges will also affect the stability of the door, which will also sag and warp badly if it is not properly braced. Its appearance will be improved by V-jointed boards, or else the gaps due to timber shrinkage will look most unsightly.

Framed doors may be used for stores, but they can be specified for quality works also, and where they are correctly nailed and jointed, they can withstand a great deal of abuse.

Flush doors, which can almost be described as standard doors today, are mass-produced on a very large scale in an assortment of finishes and veneers. They are also made as fire-resistant doors to meet the requirements for both half-hour and one hour resistance.

Stiles and rails are framed with machine jointing, in many cases timber dowel joints, while the core varies from expanded plastics to paper honeycomb, timber slats and coiled shavings. Timber blocks are inserted for fixing hinges, locks and door furniture, and the flush surface can be formed of either plywood or hardboard, coated with glue to receive the framing and core.

Lipping, provided to some doors to protect the edges, can be on the hinge side, hinge and lock sides, or sometimes all round. There is a tendency to omit the lipping today, but apart from protecting the hardboard or thin ply facing, it provides a certain tolerance for the joiner fitting the door into the rebate of the frame.

Exterior quality doors are of more solid construction than interior doors, having a heavier frame and exterior quality plywood finish.

Fire-resistant doors may be formed with a laminated timber core, but cheaper versions may have a stout frame and deep centre rail rebated to receive a plasterboard lining before the plywood facing is applied. Lippings must be glued to provide a secure joint, and it is no longer necessary for these to be throated into the rail.

Panelled doors have been almost replaced by flush doors over the years, but there is a growing market for the former once again. The quality of timber is important in the manufacture of panelled doors as sagging is inclined to occur, causing open joints and loose panels.

Factory-finished doors are available with paint, plastic or veneer face finishes, and they may be delivered with plastic covers for protection. Advances have already been made in producing complete door sets, with frame and pre-hung door; architraves are formed on one side of the frame, allowing the whole unit to be inserted into the door opening and secured by fitting the loose architraves to the other side.

Door frames should be plumbed when they are fitted into openings, to prevent adjustments having to be made when the door is hung. The lipping to doors may otherwise sometimes be planed almost to a feather edge.

Differences arise over the correct fitting of doors, but they should be flush with the frame and rebate, have a clearance which is sufficient to allow a coin to be inserted between door and rebate, and be clear of the floor when fully opened.

Hinges should be set flush with the timber face, and screws correctly supplied and fitted flush in the hinge. One pair of butts may be sufficient for a lightweight flush door but heavy doors should be fitted with one and a half pairs of hinges.

Letter plate openings are often badly cut out when this job is carried out on site, and the operation is much better left to the manufacturer, who can probably do it more cheaply.

The Clerk of Works can reassure himself of the quality by examining samples of the doors on site, which means having them cut open to reveal the construction methods, or by visiting the factory where they are produced. Fire doors have proved to be worth examination on many occasions. Correctly manufactured doors, in fact, show a remarkable resistance to fire.

Timber Windows

The high rate of decay in timber windows has prompted those authorities on the subject repeatedly to emphasise the importance of good design, proper workmanship, suitable storage and, above all, preservative treatment. A basic design produced by BWMA is used to produce standard windows, but many windows produced are variations of this design, some having improved features and some creating further problems.

The quality of timber windows depends a great deal upon the timber selected, but this is often affected by price, so that the best materials are not always available. A minimum standard must be used if the window is to perform reasonably and the Clerk of Works must consider this problem very carefully.

He should study the drawings and specification closely beforehand, so that he is familiar with the requirements before the sample window is provided. It will assist him to understand the quality if he is able to visit the factory where the windows are manufactured. He will then be able to assess the standard of workmanship in the factory in the production of units for other contracts, and examine in detail the arrangements for producing the units for his own contract. Besides examining the timber stored at the factory, the Clerk of Works has an opportunity to see the standards of machining, the jointing techniques, and the type of adhesives used. He will also be able to assess the methods of priming the joinery, as well as the system for applying preservatives. It is true that windows and other commodities can be inspected without visiting the factory, but while one swallow does not make a summer, neither does one sample give an indication of the supply.

Poor communications are often the cause of faulty supplies, and experience shows that manufacturers are more than willing to discuss problems at an early stage of manufacture. If problems are raised at a later date of production, they may be impossible to resolve economically, resulting in dissatisfaction on both sides. Workmanship depends upon a number of factors and can be one of the weakest links in the chain, yet this is the very point at which the Clerk of Works should be able to contribute most. His experience of former failures and the reasons for them will allow him to make useful suggestions this time.

When windows have been manufactured and delivered to the satisfaction of all, this does not by any means imply that all is well, for more windows are probably spoilt while they are stored on site than at any other stage. Poor storage is also a high contributory factor in windows becoming defective later, making necessary the specification of preservatives to provide complete protection.

Proper storage also includes correct stacking methods to avoid distortion of the frames, and this must be given close attention throughout the contract if satisfactory results are to be obtained. The examples illustrated in Plates 12a and b are by no means unusual on many sites. The window frames in (a) are structural elements and the method of completing the mortice and tenon joints does not conform with the specification.

Where the preservative is merely a dipped treatment, it will be important to ensure that priming is carried out correctly. Rebates, throatings, timber drip moulds, jointed sills – these are all places where the first protective coat of paintwork should be checked. The quality of the primer should also be sufficient to do its job; many primers are either sufficient to provide a slightly different colour to the timber, or act as a mud pack which obliterates grain, knots, and jointing. Sample windows should never be accepted like this, as the timber will be unrecognisable and one of the main purposes in calling for a sample in the first place will be lost.

Jointing to windows should be examined to see that they have been formed and glued correctly, and nails should not be accepted in lieu of either timber or metal star dowels. Where throatings are machined and allowed to continue throughout the length of the frame, they may allow water through the sill joints if not properly filled and sealed.

Ironmongery

The architect will select the ironmongery after discussing his requirements with the representative of an ironmongery firm and considering samples, but the Clerk of Works who has taken notes of faults or problems arising during previous contracts can often offer valuable advice on this commodity.

Once the ironmongery has been selected, however, the Clerk of Works should obtain a representative sample on a board, so that he can make himself familiar with each item before the fixing stage is reached. This will reduce the amount of time he will otherwise be forced to spend investigating and checking such matters.

Factory-made windows may be perfectly acceptable in other respects, but close attention should be given to the fitting of furniture, especially with fastener and plate. This is intended to draw the casement fully closed, and where this does not happen on assembly, it can result in a twisted frame to the casement, which may not become apparent until much later.

Casement stays may all look alike from a functionary point of view, but the styling can often affect the life of this much used item. Hinges have not changed much over the years, except that lift-off patterns and nylon hinges are more common, while cheaper versions of pressed hinges are used on lightly constructed internal doors. Spring-loaded hinges should correspond with the weight of the door, otherwise their usefulness will be short-lived. Overhead door closers, where floor springs should have been specified, are often used for cheapness, but where floor springs are specified, the Clerk of Works should note the thickness of the floor finishes beforehand.

Although nylon hinges are suitable in most instances, they are not suitable for fire doors.

Door furniture can be decorative as well as functional, but locks must be capable of doing the work required of them. Where mortice locks are used, it is possible to have the door morticed by the manufacturer before delivery. The Clerk of Works should be familiar with the types of lock as well as the significance of suiting the locks, especially where master and sub-master keys are required. When the handling of doors is described, either in placing an order or reporting to the architect, there often appears to be some confusion over this. The ironmongery manufacturers refer to a left-hand lock as one fitted to the *left-hand* side of the door, when viewed from outside, and the right-hand lock as one fitted to the *right-hand* side of the door when viewed from outside.

To establish the outside may be easy for an external door, but the outside of a room door will be the face outside the room, and that of a corridor door the side from which the hinge knuckles are not visible. The handing of doors must be considered when ordering locks, although lever handles are interchangeable, as are the bolts and latches within the locks.

Continental supplies of ironmongery are increasingly specified, and the Clerk of Works should collect one or two manufacturers' catalogues, which will help in fixing these items.

Adhesives in Building

Adhesives have provided a suitable alternative in many instances to screws and nails for fixing purposes; with sheet materials they have helped to overcome problems of rippling by providing an overall surface fixing.

Adhesives can generally be classified as water-based or solvent-based. They may be derived from rubber, plastics, or casein, although animal glues are still used for some purposes.

The range of adhesives is continually growing, and care must be taken to select the correct one for the purpose by studying the properties of each. Adhesives suitable for floor tiling would hardly be used when bonding wall tiles to plaster, and adhesives giving excellent results indoors may be totally inadequate outside.

The manufacturer's instructions must always be carefully followed. These invariably state that all contact surfaces must be clean, dry and free from dust before applying the adhesives. Adhesives applied to both surfaces are referred to as contact adhesives, and it is most important to allow sufficient time for the solvents to evaporate, in accordance with the instructions given by the manufacturer, or they may be trapped between the surfaces and cause an unsatisfactory bond.

Adhesives are produced for both structural and non-structural purposes, and can be obtained either as one-part or two-part solutions. Once two-part solutions have been mixed together they have a relatively short 'pot' life.

Structural adhesives for timber jointing are only really suited for use under factory conditions as the moisture content of the timber is important and the adhesive requires a minimum bonding temperature of 10 degrees C.

Cold-setting casein glues are used extensively by joinery manufacturers, but mainly for internal work, and where high bonding strength and weatherproof structural joints are required, either urea-formaldehyde or resorcinol-formaldehyde will be the basis of the adhesives used. Adhesives can be obtained either as thin liquid substances for close jointing or as thick pastes with gap-filling properties.

Concrete products can be bonded together with epoxy resin or polyesters, but the working temperature and the moisture content of the concrete make the use of these resins difficult when carrying out repairs to cracks.

CHAPTER TWENTY-TWO

Glazing Procedures

Types of Glass

Although glazing has become a major item in construction, it is not always given the attention on site which it requires, and where he is given the opportunity, the Clerk of Works would increase his own understanding of this unique material by seeing the manufacturing process carried out. The stage in operation at which glazing should be undertaken is often disputed because of the high breakage rate, and while this is probably true in many cases, there is often a lack of supervision, which is illustrated in Plate 13.

The range in types of glass is extensive, but the Clerk of Works will find himself dealing mostly with sheet glass, wired glass, heat-reflecting glass, and float glass (which has now almost replaced plate glass).

Sheet glass is sometimes referred to as drawn glass because of the method of manufacture, and is shown in the specification as OQ, which stands for ordinary glazing quality. This is the glass used normally for housing, etc, and as the two faces are never perfectly matching, criticism may arise on site because of distortion in the viewing qualities. The Clerk of Works must judge whether this is sufficient to reject the glass, and if the question is raised early enough in the contract with the manufacturer, this will help to overcome the problem. Where the quality is not up to the standard required, it may be that the specification is wrong, and special quality is necessary, which would be shown in the specification as SQ.

Polished plate has now been almost replaced by float glass, which gets its name because the molten glass is floated upon liquid metal, which gives it two flat polished surfaces. It is supplied in glazing quality for general purposes, and selected glazing quality where bevelled or high class work is required. The specification will refer to these as GG and SG, and there is a further quality used for mirrors or special work which is referred to as SQ.

Special toughened glasses are produced by applying further heating processes to float glass to increase the mechanical strength, and as the glass cannot be worked after this process, it is necessary to quote the sizes required when ordering. Toughened glass is used for doors and special screens where a greater measure of safety is required than is allowed by wired glass.

Wired glass has a fine wire mesh embedded into the molten glass during the rolling process, and is supplied in one quality only. The wires are electrically welded and can be obtained in square or diamond pattern. Wired glass is used where fire risk occurs in construction or where falling glass would constitute a hazard.

Solar heat-reflecting glasses are produced by tinting or introducing metallic ions into the glass surface during manufacture, and a further type of glass contains a metallic film between two laminated sheets of glass to provide a pleasing appearance.

Coloured glass is also formed in segments of varying thicknesses, and used with epoxy resins to produce specially designed windows and featured panels for churches and public buildings.

To provide a barrier against heat losses and also as a measure of sound insulation against noise, double glazing has increased significantly in both public and domestic buildings. The air space between the two sheets of glass for heat insulation should be around 19 mm, but not less than 100 mm for sound insulation. The thickness of the glazing unit will require a much deeper rebate in the window frame, and the bedding of the unit into the rebate must be allowed for, as must the provision of a fixing bead to retain the unit.

Glass Sizes

The Clerk of Works should give proper attention to sizes, as glass is often incorrectly cut to size by the operative after it has been delivered to site. This may happen when glass is cut to a standard size and variations occurring in the window sizes require some adjustment on site. The tolerance around the glass is necessary to allow the use of spacers and supporting blocks; breakages often occur after fixing because no tolerances have been allowed, and movement of the timber or transmission of shock to the glass from the frame results in the glass cracking.

It is also important to ensure the correct thicknesses of glass are being fixed, as they will vary according to the sizes of the openings.

It is essential to retain the glass by other means than the compound, and while sprigs are used in timber windows, it is necessary to use wire glazing clips in metal frames. Where high wind pressures or suction are likely to occur, as on high rise buildings, the glass should be retained with special fixing lugs. Metal glazing beads should be fully bedded into the glazing compound to avoid water penetration, and care should be taken to see that corner clips are also fitted.

Timber glazing beads are very prone to movement, exposing the compound and causing it to break down, and eventually allowing water to reach the glazing table. The water is then trapped, and unless some action is taken, the timber will rot as the water reaches the joints.

Glazing Compounds

The Clerk of Works must pay particular attention to the type of compound specified for glazing, as this can mean the difference between success and failure in weather-proofing. A glazing compound should adhere to both the glass and the rebate, and retain a measure of plasticity while achieving surface hardness.

In softwood frames it is best to use linseed oil putty, but the rebates must be adequately primed with paint, and, after glazing, the putty should be protected with two full coats of paint brought on to the glass itself in line with the rebate. As linseed oil putty sets partly by absorption of the oil into the rebate of the window, and partly by oxidisation of the surface, it is important that painting is not carried out before the putty has weathered. This interval, however, should not exceed 28 days.

In non-absorbent timbers such as hardwoods it is advisable to use a metal casement putty, as the rebate will be unlikely to absorb any of the oils. Painting to the surface of the metal casement putty should be carried out after two weeks in the same manner as for linseed oil putty.

Glazing into metal frames will be carried out with metal casement compounds, and where the frames are aluminium alloys, it is possible there may be difficulties with adhesion.

Where timber frames have been treated with preservatives, the latter may affect the glazing compound, and the rebate should either be primed or treated with a thin coat of varnish where the frames are not to be primed.

Heat-reflecting glasses are best set in non-setting compounds and carefully spaced into the openings with spacer blocks. All rebates should be sealed first with a suitable sealer.

Polysulphide sealants can be recommended for glazing, but they can be expensive for normal requirements.

Metal Windows

These may be of aluminium alloys, or stainless or galvanised steel. While the last is best left unprotected to allow the galvanising to weather, the other types should be protected with plastic or paper wrappings. The protective coating may sometimes be spray-on plastic, especially with aluminium alloys, and care must be taken not to damage the metal when the coating is being removed. Storage of metal windows is very important, as they are so easily distorted, although this may not become apparent until the windows are fixed into position.

A level base should be formed with timber battens to receive the windows, which must be stacked evenly, care being taken not to damage any of the fittings, pivots, vents, etc. It must be remembered that the weight applied to the windows at the bottom of the stack is more than sufficient to distort them.

Aluminium alloy windows should not be allowed to become coated with mud, plaster or cement, as these may corrode the metal. Such deposits are not always cleaned off galvanised metal windows before they are painted.

Galvanised windows should be checked for rusting, and where this is apparent, it should be removed and the window treated either with a galvanising solution or a metal priming paint. Checks should also be made upon the welding of the frames, and both frame and casement should be checked to ensure they are square. They should be fixed either with lugs or coated screws, and care taken to see there is a small clearance all round the opening, which should be grouted up with cement and sand, before pointing with mastic.

Patent Glazing

Specialist firms are generally engaged to carry out patent glazing, which relies upon the glass being held within special detailed glazing bars, which include cappings to seal the glass. The bars may be manufactured from steel and encased in an extruded jointless lead covering sealed at each end of the bars, or they may be encased in plastic sheathing. Glazing bars are also produced in galvanised steel, as well as from aluminium alloys.

The glazing bed will include a seating made from plastic, neoprene, or greased asbestos cord, and the rebate will vary according to whether single or double glazing is to be fitted, or special infill panels for screening purposes.

The Clerk of Works should study the details for the patent glazing at an early stage in the contract, noting where fixings may be required in the structure to secure the glazing bars. These fixings may be in the form of plugs or brackets positioned at sill or beam level, or in columns or end walls, and naturally will be of little use if incorrectly positioned.

Where a large area of patent glazing is fitted, there must be some tolerances allowed for expansion and contraction, and these matters should be noted by the Clerk of Works when studying the details. Certain areas immediately behind the patent glazing may become inaccessible, yet still visible, after the glass has been fitted, and the Clerk of Works should watch carefully for them. Floor edges, staircase strings, and spandrels are typical instances where plasterwork or decoration can be overlooked until it is too late.

Curtain Walling

This can generally be regarded as a proprietary system of metal framing with glass or sheet materials as infill panels, used to enclose the elevation of a building instead of bricks or similar cladding.

The metal framing is most often constructed as box sections with special extrusions secured to the framing to receive the infill materials. Galvanised metal may be used for the framing, but more often it is produced in aluminium, stainless steel, or bronze. The erection of the curtain walling is carried out on site by specialist fixers who use various mastics to seal the joints as the cladding is assembled. Special fixing points are formed in the main structure to secure the framing, especially at the sill and head, and retained at each floor level by special brackets secured between the mullions and top of floor slab.

Curtain walling is accurately machined and fabricated within the workshops, while site assembly can be expected to remain within reasonable tolerances. These are unlikely to be achieved with building materials, and the fixing brackets are generally designed to accommodate the additional tolerances.

Because of the importance in keeping within these recognised tolerances the Clerk of Works should arrange for the dimensions to be checked regularly during the main construction period, and again before erection of the curtain walling begins.

As the curtain walling is likely to cover a fairly large area, it will be exposed to a great deal of wind and rain, and any failure in design or workmanship will inevitably result in water penetration or movement of the frame.

In the case of failure, an element of doubt is bound to arise regarding the manner in which the curtain walling was erected; the Clerk of Works, therefore, is advised to arrange an inspection system to note all fixing, jointing and mastic procedures. He must check the glass sizes, thickness and glazing procedures, together with the methods concerning the infill panels. A record of the procedure should be maintained in the site diary, together with any comments which may assist in future discussions.

CHAPTER TWENTY-THREE

Roofing

Pitched Roofing

Materials used for roof finishes have always varied from district to district in the past, but this is not the case today, where slate, stone, tiles or thatching can be found in almost any part of the country.

Pitched roofs are less likely to suffer from leaks than those which are flat, but there is always a danger in exposed positions of rain blowing under the tiles, or wind pressures tearing off areas which are insecurely fixed.

Projections in the roof such as vent pipes, chimneys, dormer windows, and hips or steps in roof levels, will need flashings provided to prevent water entering the junction with the roof finish.

Valleys in the roof can be a dangerous source for water penetration if incorrectly formed or damaged in any way, but specially produced valley tiles or lead sheeting laid on felt and boarding will overcome this problem.

The weight of the materials used as a roofing finish will affect the structural requirements of the roof, varying the spacing of roof trusses or rafters and the thickness of the roofing battens.

Certain districts require all roofing timbers to be treated against attack by beetles, but it is becoming more general for preservative treatment to be given to roofing timbers throughout the country.

Roofing finishes will normally be formed by laying sarking felt across the rafters and securing it with large-headed galvanised clout nails. The roofing battens are then nailed at a suitable spacing to receive the tiles or slates according to the specified gauge.

Certain roofs may be covered with tongued and grooved boarding before the felt is laid, and in these instances the battens should be fixed on counter-battens to prevent any water penetrating the tiles, etc, being trapped between the battens.

Slating

Excellent weathering qualities as well as an attractive roof finish are provided by a slate roof, especially where Cornish or Westmorland slates are used and laid in random courses. Since the gauge and the width of slate varies, this form of roof finish calls for skill on the part of the craftsman, the largest slates being laid first along the eaves and the slates diminishing in size towards the ridge. These slates are rough textured, available in up to five grades, and sold in tonnes rather than in numbers.

Generally Welsh slates are of a smoother texture. They are obtainable in standard sizes and may be graded as standard, heavy or extra-heavy. As quarries may vary in their grading systems, the Clerk of Works is advised to check with the quarry concerned for sample grades as specified before any deliveries are made.

Slates can be holed successfully with a sharp point on the reverse end of the slater's hammer, but the operation is more efficiently carried out by the hand machine produced for this purpose. Holes must be formed in the slate by piercing it from the 'bed' side, which will cause the face to spall around the hole and produce a countersunk hole to receive the nail head.

Slates should be sorted on site, and the best time to do this is when the holing procedure is taking place. Flaws and cracks are not always easy to see, but a tap with the hammer will produce a dull sound from a faulty slate and a clear ring from a good one.

Slates are usually centre-nailed and have a double lap to provide good wind resistance. Double courses should be fixed to verge and eaves, with the verge slightly tilted. The final course at the ridge will be head-nailed to avoid the tail of the slate being 'kicked-up'. Ridge tiles are edge-bedded in sand and cement mortar with the joint struck.

Clay Tiles

Clay tiles are produced in much the same way as bricks, the clay or shale being quarried, ground and eventually reduced to a plastic slate from which the tiles are moulded, either by hand or pressed by machine. Tiles are much thinner than clay bricks and therefore more susceptible to frost damage if not correctly manufactured. The Clerk of Works should check tiles on delivery and note any signs of lamination or excess porosity, which could cause later problems.

Clay tiles are manufactured as double lap or single lap fixing, and may be relatively smooth-faced, sand-faced, or glazed.

The specification for nailing should be noted, but this should not be greater than every fourth course, with all tiles nailed at abutments or verges. The nails should be made of copper, zinc or composition.

Battens should be fixed as for slating, although the specification may well state the lap and not the gauge for tiling, owing to the possible variation in length of tiles.

Single lap tiles produced as interlocking tiles enable lower pitches to be achieved than would be otherwise possible.

Concrete Tiles

Concrete tiles can be obtained in sizes and shapes similar to those produced in clay, and are now used extensively, especially on housing.

For some time there were problems in maintaining the colour in concrete tiles, and breakages were high. The sand face washes away to some extent, and the Clerk of Works should note the gutter arrangements, as these will require cleaning at intervals for some time.

The concrete mix for manufacturing these tiles is very fine and dense, and because they are not subjected to a firing process after they are pressed, like clay tiles, concrete tiles are more regular in shape and size.

They are available as plain tiles or single lap tiles, and nailing will vary according to the pitch, although the Clerk of Works should bear in mind those areas of the site which may be more subject to wind suction than others. Suction depends upon pitch of the roof as well as on wind speed.

Wood Shingles

Since shingles are no longer feared as a fire hazard, there has been an increase in shingle roofs in this country. Although shingles can be made of oak, the greater proportion are made of cedar from Canada. They are sold by the 'bundle', the amount of roof covering being dependent upon the gauge.

Wood shingles should be specified as 'edge-grain' to offset curl or warping, as well as reducing their tendency to shrink. They should be treated with a fire-retardant, either before or after fixing, and should be impregnated against fungicidal attack. The shingles are manufactured in varying widths and taper from the base. They should be fixed as plain tiles by nailing them to the roof battens. Non-ferrous nails should be used. As they are only one-tenth the weight of plain tiling, the structural part of the roof may be lightened, with rafters or trusses at wider centres.

Good air circulation is essential for wood shingles to reduce the risk of fungicidal attack, but where the building is in an exposed position driving rain may make it necessary to provide an underlay of sarking felt.

Asbestos Slates

Asbestos slates are light in weight, like wood shingles, and are supplied in similar bundles, though they are available in various sizes. They are finished on the face with an acrylic-silicone. They are secured with two copper nails and a copper disc rivet to the tail of the slate, and laid in the same manner as ordinary slates with a regular gauge.

If they are stored under damp conditions, efflorescence will appear on the reverse side of the slate, and where the tiles remain in bundles, this will be transferred to the face of the slate.

Roof Sheeting

Large rigid sheets are used as roof covering, especially for industrial buildings. They may be made of asbestos or metal, the latter often sheathed in plastic or bitumen to provide a decorative as well as a protective finish.

Care must be taken to see that sheets are not damaged before or during the fixing, for damage to plastic or bitumen coatings could easily lead to corrosion of the metal.

Where asbestos sheets are not completely cured before fixing, they can become distorted, and cracks not immediately obvious to the fixer may occur.

Side laps are controlled by the design of the sheets, but end laps should be carefully checked to ensure that adequate lap is provided. Sheets are fixed to roof purlins either by hook bolts or patent clips, and while it is necessary for these to be secure, they should not be over-tightened, as this may cause fracture to the sheet.

Minimum standards of insulation laid down for industrial buildings make it necessary to provide a further lining to sheet roofing. This may be done by providing a ceiling of insulation materials, or by forming a further layer of sheeting, with the cavity lined by an insulation quilting.

Roofing Felt

Felt is provided (1) to carry away to the gutter any water which may have penetrated the slates or tiling, either through wind pressures or damaged roof covering, and (2) to retain heat within the building. Any break in the material, therefore, is likely to reduce its effectiveness.

The Clerk of Works should always check the felting to be used, as it is often found to be incorrect according to the specification. Felt may be supplied in various weights and types, such as bitumen-impregnated felt, bitumen/asbestos, bitumen/fibre-glass, etc.

Unless it is supported on boarding, the felt will sag between the rafters, and may form a retaining trough for any water penetrating the tiling. Laps must be carefully checked to see they are no less than 150 mm, and the felt should be continued into the gutter and across the cavity at the verges.

The felt should be turned up around any pipes passing through it, and if there are any tears, the felt should be replaced in that area.

The felt should be secured with large-headed galvanised clout nails.

Roof Battens

The battens should be checked when delivered to site to see that they are the correct section and, where this is specified, that they have been treated with preservatives.

They will vary in thickness according to the type of roof material, but in all cases they must be securely fixed to each rafter with a galvanised nail. Joints must always be formed on a rafter, and be staggered to avoid too many joints upon one rafter. Short battens should cover at least three rafters.

To conform with fire regulations at party walls, the battens must not be carried through but should be cut to allow approximately 25 mm bearing on the wall.

The battens will establish the gauge or lap of the roofing tiles, and setting out will be necessary to avoid wastage in cutting the tiles around any projections or offsets.

Chalk lines should be marked from ridge to eaves at intervals to provide a guide to the spacing of tiles over the roof, as some of the courses may creep and an irregular line will be produced when the verge is reached.

Chalk lines should also be struck to establish the line and gauge of the tiling before fixing the battens to this line.

Care should be taken to fit a tilting fillet at the fascia to avoid a sag in the felt causing water to be retained at that point.

Nails

If the wrong type of nail is used, corrosion may ensue and the tiles or slates will become loose and easily disturbed by winds. Galvanised iron or steel nails are unsuitable for this work, and composition nails, copper nails, aluminium alloys, or coated nails should always be used, according to the specification. In exposed conditions nails may be used to each tile in every course, but in other instances fixings may vary up to every fourth or fifth course.

Tiles which are supplied with nibs may only require nailing at intervals, while others are fitted with patent clips nailed to the battens. These clips should be positioned close to the tails of the tiles fitted to eaves and verges.

Flat Roof Construction

The increase in flat roofs has introduced many patent forms of construction and finish, but unless great care is taken with the design and workmanship, maintenance may be difficult. Care must be taken with upstands and flashings, as well as with the deck finish (see Plates 14 a and b).

The structure of the roof may be formed with *in situ* concrete or precast concrete beams, covered with a lightweight cement screen laid to falls and finished with asphalt or several layers of roofing felt bonded in hot bitumen. Lighter roof construction can be obtained with flat sheeting carried on timber joists or steel beams, and finished with a lightweight screed and built-up roofing felt.

There are many systems of roofing on the market which consist of lightweight trough decking in aluminium or steel carried on light steel beams and covered with insulation boards secured with clips or hot bitumen. This is then finished with two or three layers of bitumen roofing felt and dressed with a layer of stone chippings bonded in hot bitumen.

Roof Screeds

The roof screed is required as a means of providing falls to the roof slab, as well as improving the insulation. Because of the importance of this insulation, the screed must be allowed to dry out before any layers of felt are applied.

Pockets of moisture can be trapped within the screed or even drawn from the roof slab itself, and, unless removed, they can affect the roof covering by generating steam and creating blisters in the roofing felt. Patent systems have been devised to help disperse the moisture, one being the 'breather vent', installed to a pattern over the area of the roof. A special type of perforated felt known as a 'breather felt' may be laid direct on to the screed below the final layers of felt, and a further type, similar to a mineral-faced felt, may be laid face down on the screed to provide pores for the moisture to escape through to special vents.

Screeds should be laid to falls of 1 in 80 at an average thickness of 50 mm, and can consist of cement and lightweight aggregates such as vermiculite, perlite, foam slag, or pulverised fly-ash (PFA).

Cement and sand can be used with an additive to aerate the mix, but that is best laid by a specialist contractor.

One way of reducing the moisture in the finished screed is to lay it as dry as possible in the first instance, without losing the workability of the mix or affecting the setting qualities of the cement.

Built-up Roofing Felt

This is a term applied to the binding of several layers of bitumen felt to the roof structure with hot bitumen and surfacing it with stone chippings.

The chippings are bonded to the felt in either hot or cold bitumen, and, apart from acting as a solar reflectant, it is suggested they provide weight and help to resist any wind suction that might otherwise tear off the roof covering.

Three layers of roofing felt should be applied to a flat roof, and, where conditions are exposed, at least one of these layers should be heavy quality felt. The felt should be laid parallel to the eaves, with successive layers laid to avoid the joint in the layer below.

Low pitch roofs only require two layers unless conditions are exposed, and the felt should be laid from eaves to ridge, and carried over to break the cross-joints.

Sand and cement screeds should be primed with a bitumen compound containing a volatile solvent before the first layer of hot bitumen is applied.

The first layer to a boarded roof should be secured with galvanised clout nails at 50 mm intervals along the laps and spaced at 150 mm to the centre of the roll, or well bonded with bitumen.

Three classes of roofing felt concern the Clerk of Works although these are supplied in several weights and thicknesses. Type 1 is fibre-based and is used extensively for roofing where costs are important; but it is susceptible to water damage, and inclined to blister a lot, and much less resistant to decay than the remaining types. Type 2 is asbestos-based, and where fire resistance is important, is more likely to be selected; its use may be restricted to one layer laid immediately over the screed or boarding. Type 3, which is glass-fibre-based, has a high stability to resist movement, and will not decay, is usually restricted to good quality work, though it should be used on roofs with little or no fall in them.

One layer of felt is generally laid as a vapour barrier to prevent moisture rising from the roof screed or through the decking, and is bonded in hot bitumen. This is most important where insulation boards are used within the built-up roofing, as these are by no means resistant to decay and may be affected by the humidity created within the roof covering.

Inspection

The Clerk of Works must begin his inspection as the materials are delivered to site, checking that they conform to the requirements of the specification and seeing that proper storage arrangements are made. The decking must be checked to see it is not damaged in any way especially as there may be areas of this which will remain exposed as a finished ceiling. Because there is a variety of similar materials, it is advisable to check that the delivery is the correct type of material. After checking the type of boards delivered, the Clerk of Works should insist upon proper storage, especially where fibre-board or cork is to be used as insulation material; it is so easy for these materials to become wet during storage and then be included in the roof construction, with unfortunate results.

All timbers included in flat roof construction should be checked for moisture content, especially timber roof decking. If there is restriction on air circulation within the roof, the moisture content should not exceed 16 per cent when the roof is covered over with felt.

Bearing surfaces are always important in roof construction and all bearings should be confirmed. The fixing of decking and roof members is important, especially with patent roofing systems, because of the dangers of wind suction. Where fixing brackets are specified to secure the roof they must be treated with proper caution, and the example in Plate 15 illustrates this. The water service pipe has been routed in such a way that the fixing bracket serves no purpose whatever and might easily result in displacement of the roof at a later stage.

There have been several instances of roofs blowing off because they were not securely fixed at all necessary points, and the Clerk of Works should consider the fact that weakness in any one area may affect the whole roof. In calculating excess wind forces, a period of three seconds is considered sufficient to cause failure to the roof.

After checking that the correct type of felt has been delivered, it is advisable to see that it is stored on end under proper conditions, and not loaded directly on to the roof. Errors can occur in the number of layers of roofing felt applied, and the Clerk of Works must insist that each layer is completed before the next is begun. It is advisable to have the whole of the roof made watertight with one layer before any other work is allowed to proceed.

The alignment and fixing of aluminium edging should not be overlooked. Holes cut for pipes passing through the roof should be cut in a proper manner, and sleeves provided to form a waterproof finish to what can be a suspected source of penetration.

CHAPTER TWENTY-FOUR

Asphalt Work

Roofing

Asphalt may be applied to a number of roofing sub-bases, but all falls in the roof for drainage must be established previously and not formed by the asphalt. Hair-base bitumen felt should be laid between asphalt and sub-base to isolate any movement in the structure from being transmitted to the asphalt. The felt also helps to maintain the period in which the asphalter can spread and level the material on otherwise cold surfaces.

Where asphalt is used on timber roofing, the sheeting may be tongued and grooved boards, resin-bonded sheathing plywood, or chipboard, etc, but these materials should not be less than 25 mm thick and close jointed. The moisture content must be given close attention to reduce movement to a minimum, and a splay fillet fitted to all upstands and abutments should be set slightly forward to allow ventilation around the roof structure.

Where a timber roof slopes more than 10 degrees, expanded metal lath must be nailed to the boarding over the felt membranes, to retain the asphalt. If this work is not carried out properly, the asphalt will sag as it softens from solar heat. The Clerk of Works should be aware that chicken wire is not suitable for the purpose.

On timber upstands it will be necessary to fix metal lathing with galvanised staples, taking care to fit the lathing the correct way up to retain the asphalt.

On metal decking a vapour barrier will be bonded with hot bitumen to the decking and covered with the insulation boards, and this will be followed by the hair-base membrane and the asphalt.

Cement screeds will be formed on concrete roofs, and those formed with wood wool slabs, etc, and the felt membrane will be laid as before and followed by the asphalt.

The asphalt must be laid in two separate layers 10 mm thick, and laid in bays to avoid through joints in it. The joint in the second layer should preferably be set back 152 mm from the joint in the first layer. Joints at abutments and upstands must be dealt with in the same manner, and skirtings should be formed at least 150 mm high and tucked into chases in the abutments. The thickness of the skirtings should be 13 mm, and a splay fillet of asphalt should be formed along all internal angles.

The surface of asphalt roofing can be treated in several ways, but a reflective paint with aluminium base will reduce the effects of solar heat, as will spar or limestone chippings set in bitumen.

Tanking

While it is important to keep the level of water down during general construction operations in excavations, it is fundamental to the successful application of asphalt. Any pressure of water will cause the asphalt to bulge and ultimately fracture, and for this reason it is necessary to load it or restrain it against horizontal or vertical surfaces.

It may be laid directly as a membrane to a suitably finished layer of blinding concrete, and then loaded with a reinforced structural floor slab. Alternatively the asphalt may be applied to the surface of the structural slab and then covered with a 50 mm protective concrete screed.

It should be laid to horizontal surfaces in three separate layers to produce a combined 30 mm total thickness, with each joint cut back 150 mm on the previous layer to avoid creating a through joint.

Vertical tanking may be applied to either the internal or the external surface of the structure, but in either instance a protective skin of concrete or brickwork will be necessary to restrain the asphalt. Where the protective skin is not making contact, the asphalt will be inclined to sag, and the Clerk of Works should check that the brickwork is well grouted up with mortar as the brick coursing proceeds. Vertical work in asphalt depends upon the provision of an adequate key in the surface to be covered; in brickwork this is easily achieved by raking out the bed-joints, but in concrete structures it should be considered in the design.

Vertical asphalt should be applied in two coats to provide a total of 20 mm thickness, and joints on the second coat should be cut back 75 mm to prevent through joints.

When applying asphalt for tanking purposes, it is important to remember that there must be no break in it, and care must be taken over pump bases, stanchion bases, and pipes or fixings which pass through the asphalt into the structure. Internal angles should be sealed with an additional splayed fillet, and external angles formed to ensure that full thickness of asphalt is obtained.

The asphalt in tanking must always be carried high enough to be above the anticipated water level, and sealed by tucking it into a junction in the structure. This will overcome any danger of water seeping into the joint between the asphalt and the structure and affecting the bond between the two.

The Clerk of Works must check that the work is being carried out with the correct grade of mastic asphalt, as tanking requires a softer grade than is necessary for other purposes. The blocks delivered to site should be stamped with the appropriate BS number and the manufacturer's symbol, but where doubts exist, the Clerk of Works can always have a sample submitted to the laboratory for testing.

Reinforcement or other materials must never be deposited on the asphalt, and where reinforcement must be erected over it, adequate protection must be supplied, for any damage to the asphalt would ruin the whole operation.

Oils and solvents must be kept clear of the asphalt, as they can affect the bitumen in it, softening and ultimately breaking down the material.

Flooring

Sometimes asphalt will be used as an underlay for other finishes, such as tiling to kitchens or factory floors, and where resistance to chemical action is of importance, a special acid resistant type of asphalt is available. Care must be taken with asphalting for acid areas, and such work may involve tanking to ducts and manholes within the flooring.

Where asphalt is provided as an underlay, the thickness required may be no greater than 15 mm applied in one coat only. Where it provides the actual floor finish, the thickness will be dictated by the amount of traffic involved, as well as the loading applied by any vehicular traffic. Although in certain cases it may be necessary to lay flooring in two separate layers, it will be generally laid in a single coat up to a total thickness of 40 mm.

Asphalt laid on concrete needs a reasonably even surface and, where required, should be laid to falls. Wherever the thickness is less than 25 mm, the surface should be cleaned and a membrane of hair-based felt provided to prevent the asphalt becoming chilled when it is applied to the floor. Glass fibre will provide a better underlay wherever conditions may be damp, as this type of membrane is rotproof.

The Clerk of Works should look for blows or bubbles in the surface of the asphalt flooring, which may be unsightly. They often result from laying on a damp surface, or from failure on the part of the operator to sufficiently 'work' the asphalt to a smooth polished finish. A matt surface can be achieved by dusting fine sand on the surface as the final float finish is applied, and then brushing away the surplus sand on completion.

Asphalt for flooring is the hardest of all grades, and where it is exposed to frost, it may crack or open at the joints. This fact must be noted, especially where the flooring also acts as a membrane to prevent water penetration to floors below, as in balconies or deck access to blocks of dwellings.

Damp-proof Course

Where asphalt is to be used as a damp-proof course, it must be taken throughout the full width of the wall and laid in one coat not less than 12 mm thick. The surface must be scored to provide a key for the mortar bed-joint, or the surface may be roughened by embedding grit while the asphalt is still molten. It is important to ensure there are no breaks in the continuity of the asphalt damp-proof course, and the Clerk of Works should give this particular attention.

Mixing Asphalt

Asphalt is generally melted in a cauldron on the site, though it may be melted in a mobile mixer with mechanically driven agitators. Whatever the method, the Clerk of Works must ensure that the position of the mixer is unlikely to damage any of the finished work on site.

The temperature of the asphalt at the point of laying should not be greater than 215 degrees C, though it will obviously be affected by the distance the molten material has to be transported from the mixer.

Where asphalt has to be hoisted to a higher level, the Clerk of Works must insist that proper protection is given to cladding already fixed, in particular materials such as brickwork or stonework, where the bitumen is likely to stain the surface. If the mixer is allowed to be used at a higher level, the dangers arising from fire should not be overlooked, since molten asphalt can itself cause a great deal of damage.

CHAPTER TWENTY-FIVE

Plastering

Modern Plasters

Plasterwork is an old craft which has been successfully adapted to meet modern requirements by reducing the 'wet trade' problem and introducing new lightweight plasters and plasterboard lining techniques. Besides increasing the insulation values within buildings, the new plasters have enabled decoration to be speeded up.

There are two types of plaster available – thin wall plasters, which have an organic binder and are used exclusively as finishing plasters; and gypsum plaster, which is manufactured in four classes.

Class A: Plaster of Paris

This is produced by heating the gypsum sufficiently to drive off some of the water, with the creation of a rapid setting plaster when water is added. This plaster is not used much today on sites, but is popular in fibrous-plaster workshops and in the dental and medical fields.

Class B: Retarded Hemihydrates

By adding retarders to the gypsum when it has reached the plaster of paris stage, the setting times can be controlled when water is again added, a factor that may account for this being the most widely used plaster on the site. It is available in two particular types – (a) gauged with sand to provide a backing coat of plaster, and (b) used as a finishing coat on sanded undercoats or as a finishing plaster on plasterboard.

Class C: Anhydrous or Hard-burnt Plaster

Driving all the water from the gypsum when it is heated produces a plaster with no setting qualities, but the addition of accelerators allows controlled setting times to be fixed. This type of plaster is used for finishing work only.

Class D: Keenes or Parian Cement

This is a hardburnt plaster similar to Type C which is used on highclass work. It was used for many years on a sand and cement backing to provide a hard external angle, but metal angle beads have now made this function obsolete.

The Clerk of Works should note that up to 25 per cent of lime can be added to finishing plasters on sanded backgrounds, but finishing plaster applied to plasterboards should be used neat.

Premixed plasters consist of gypsum plaster with lightweight aggregates such as expanded perlite and exfoliated vermiculite, and require the addition of water only to enable them to be applied direct to the wall or ceiling.

Thin wall plasters do not set but harden by drying. They are sprayed on and levelled with a spatula, but require a fairly even backing surface to be effective.

Sand for Plasterwork

Where sand is used as the aggregate with gypsum plasters, it must be carefully selected, as a sand containing too many fines will produce a weak friable mix. Where this is combined with a strong finishing coat, the result will be a highly unsatisfactory plastering job.

Sands are graded into zones, those recommended as plastering sands falling into Zones 1 and 2. Generally a plastering sand should be clean, well graded, and free from hygroscopic salts; such sands can be obtained from the river-bed or from sand-pits. A good plastering sand will reduce the shrinkage which occurs when the plaster begins drying out, thus avoiding crazing and cracking to the finished plaster. Impurities in the plastering sand will have a serious affect upon the finished plasterwork. Such impurities as silt are not serious in small quantities, but clay must be avoided.

Where clay is present in the plastering sand, the mix will be easy enough for the plasterer to use, although more water may be necessary to retain plasticity during application; but once the work has been completed, it will be slow in setting, then cracking, and its adhesion to the wall surface will very likely be poor.

The occurrence of lignites in the sand can lead to pitting or blows in the finished plasterwork, while iron pyrites may cause staining. Sea salts will cause dampness and efflorescence, as well as corroding any metal fixings to the plasterwork.

Before accepting a sand for use on site with plasters, the Clerk of Works should submit samples to the laboratory for testing and grading, and where the tests are unsatisfactory, the contractor should be asked to submit further samples.

Bonding Agents

Where the surface for the plaster is too smooth to provide a good mechanical key, it will be necessary to use a bonding agent. Two are available. The first is suitable as a damp-proof membrane on walls as well as a bonding agent, and is a bituminous solution or emulsion, usually applied in two coats and sprinkled with sand while the final coat is still wet to provide a mechanical key. This type of bonding agent is not recommended for application to soffits, and in such cases an emulsion of PVA or other polymers should be used. This second type of bonding agent can be used on a glazed tile surface to provide a satisfactory key for plasterwork, and it also has the ability to reduce the suction on dry backgrounds needing to be plastered.

Lime for Plasterwork

The lime used for plasterwork is delivered to site either as rock lime for slaking into lime putty or as bagged hydrated lime in powder form.

Rock lime is produced by burning limestone or chalk in special kilns to remove the carbon dioxide and leave calcium oxide, which is referred to as quicklime.

Hydrated lime is produced by adding a controlled quantity of water to the rock lime so that it disintegrates into a powder, which can then be air-dried and bagged for delivery. Before using hydrated lime with gypsum plaster, it should be soaked overnight, but the powder form can be gauged with sand to produce lime-sand mortar.

Owing to an increased use of bagged lime, rock lime is only used occas-sionally on construction sites nowadays, but where it is used it must be slaked correctly into lime putty. First a large pit is formed on site, with a smaller pit or tank alongside. The small pit is filled with water and a quantity of rock lime added. After a short time the water begins to boil and the rock lime to disintegrate, producing a rich creamy fluid. The contents of the pit must be stirred to ensure complete slaking of the lime, and then the liquid is poured through a small mesh sieve into the larger pit. There it should be left to mature for at least a fortnight before any of the lime putty is used for plasterwork. The purest lime will be obtained from the furthest point away from the sieve, while the lime nearest the sieve is best used for lime mortar rather than plaster finishes.

The skill of the operative when slaking lime lies in his assessment of the time at which to pour the contents of the small pit, as partly slaked quan-tities of lime create dangers from pitting and blowing in the finished plaster-work, besides being uneconomical in the use of the material.

Plasterboard

Various sizes and thicknesses of plasterboard are available, but the standard thicknesses are 9·5 mm and 12·7 mm and the main types are wall-board, lath, and gypsum plank. Lath, baseboard and wallboard are all designed to receive a finish coat of gypsum plaster, but the reverse side of wallboard has a special surface to receive decoration direct.

Gypsum plank is manufactured in a constant width of 600 mm and a thickness of 19 mm. It is intended to form a solid partition, once a back-ing coat of gypsum and sand has been applied to both faces and it has been finished with a skim coat of plaster.

Where insulation is required the boarding may be supplied with a metal foil backing, and in such cases it is important to check that these boards are being applied to the correct areas. The Clerk of Works should also check that boards of the correct thickness are being used on the recom-mended spans – for instance, 9·5 mm boards should not be fixed to spans in excess of 450 mm or 12·7 mm boards to spans in excess of 600 mm.

Paper-covered edges to plasterboards should always be at right-angles to the bearing surfaces, and a clearance gap around the edges of the board should be kept at approximately 3 mm wide.

Boards should be secured with galvanised nails at 150 mm centres and at least 13 mm from their edge.

Boards which are damp when they are fixed are likely to develop a sag between bearing points, and will dry out with this deformity, producing an unsatisfactory finish, especially to ceilings and internal angles.

Metal Lath

Metal lath has been in use for many years. One of its many uses is as a suspended ceiling, where lath incorporating stiffening ribs is often chosen. The lath is fixed ribs uppermost and the longway of the mesh across the bearers, with laps not less than 25 mm, and secured with 18 SWG galvanised tying wire (1·22 mm). Where the fixing points are to metal rods suspended from ceiling hangers, the mesh must be secured with 18 SWG galvanised tying wire, and where the lath is fixed to timber joists or bearers, it must be secured with galvanised staples. Metal lathing is used as a backing for plaster to provide fire protection to steel columns; to make certain that the column is completely encased, it is advisable to fit loops of steel wire around it before the metal lath is fitted, to ensure that plaster will penetrate to the face of the steel on the rib. It is also advisable to see that the strands of the mesh slope inwards and downwards to provide a satisfactory key for the plaster.

Metal lathing should always be kept as rigid as possible for strength, and, of course, that makes it easier for the craftsman applying the first coat of plaster. Laps occurring between bearers must be properly secured with tying wire, and all cut ends or damaged surfaces of the mesh should be treated with bitumen paint before any plasterwork is applied.

Drylining

This is a technique of fixing plasterboards direct to the wall and finishing the joints with tape and gypsum plaster to produce a smooth even surface for decoration, instead of applying two coats of plaster.

The boards are fixed to the wall in one of three ways:

(a) timber framing cast in or nailed to the wall;
(b) metal channel bedded in a proprietary adhesive;
(c) bitumen-impregnated fibre pads bedded in gypsum plaster dabs.

With method (a) the boards are fixed directly to the timber framing with 30 mm (14 SWG) nails at 150 mm centres; with (b) the boards are fixed to the metal furring channels with 22 mm self-tapping screws at 300 mm centres; and with method (c) a series of gypsum plaster dabs are applied between the fibre pads, and the plasterboard pressed against them until it is firmly against the pads, when it is secured with double-headed nails. The advantage of the double-headed nails is that they can be removed without damaging the boards when the gypsum plaster dabs have set.

The boards must be securely fixed before proceeding with any jointing, and where any damage has occurred to the boards or gaps appear greater than 3 mm between the joints, these must be filled with the patent filler provided. The tape is then applied to all joints and angles and smoothed over with a special jointing finish, external angles being treated with tape having a special metal insert to act as a protection against damage. When the taping is completed, the whole surface is treated with a slurry coat of special finishing plaster and smoothed with a sponge. Each operation must be carried out separately to allow the materials to set before proceeding.

Special tools available for taping and jointing enable skilled men to work speedily and provide a finish difficult to distinguish from a plastered wall.

Preparation for Plasterwork

Before the contract reaches the plastering stage, the Clerk of Works should study the detail drawings and make notes of the type of background to receive plaster. He should also check the specified thicknesses and the relationship between them and other details and features.

Door frames and casings fixed into partitions must have sufficient cover to both faces. Conduits and switch boxes may be difficult to cover with 13 mm of plaster, and chasing will be required in the backing surface. Service drawings will provide further information regarding pipe-runs and brackets which may overcome the problem of cutting or chasing plasterwork after it has been completed.

The programme must be carefully watched to note when the plasterwork is due to start, as there is always a tendency for it to start too early and interfere with tradesmen on other jobs, even though the starting date may be sometimes later than the programmed date. Glazing should be finished before plastering begins, because of the problems attendant upon drying winds, frost and heavy rain.

The Clerk of Works is advised to check all areas to be plastered before the work begins to confirm that all the backing surfaces have been correctly aligned and finished to receive the specified thickness of plaster. Where there is any discrepancy, he should notify the contractor that this must be corrected to avoid delaying the plasterwork. Two-coat work does not allow much tolerance in the backing, as on general surfaces this will be 13 mm thick and on concrete work only 10 mm thick, and too many plastering faults can be traced to poor preparation or misuse of materials. It is much better for the Clerk of Works to bring the problems up at this stage rather than after the plasterwork has been completed.

Attention should be given to the storage of plastering materials. Unless adequate precautions are taken, gypsum plaster may set partially, thus reducing its effectiveness.

Mechanical Plastering

Plastering by mechanical means is much more common on the Continent where the method of application by hand is generally a throwing method, not the technique applied in this country.

For mechanical application of plaster to be economical it must be used on areas that are reasonably large and accessible, and it must be continuous, that is, the machine cannot return to areas already worked in. Any delays or congestion caused through involvement with other trades will reduce the efficiency of the machine, for which adequate space to operate will also be required.

Thin wall plasters are used for spraying, but most gypsum plasters are suitable. It will be necessary to keep the machine clean, or else the plaster will be contaminated by previous mixes and the setting periods will be lengthened.

Sands used in spray plastering must be evenly graded, with no more than 3 per cent through a No 100 mesh BS sieve.

The machines in general use in this country operate on compressed air, worm screw drive, or piston. The wet plaster is forced from the container along the hose to the nozzle, where it is atomised by compressed air and spread on the surface to be treated. In piston-pump machines and screw-drive machines the materials are fed into an open hopper, but with compressed-air machines the material is loaded into a sealed container.

Spray guns generally have removable nozzle caps which enable different sized orifices to be fitted for the application of backing coats or finishing coats.

After the plaster has been sprayed upon the ceiling or walls, it is levelled off with straight-edge or darby, and finish plasters are smoothed off with spatulas. As with other operations, the degree of finish with spray plaster depends upon the skill of the operators, but it seems fair to say that it does not equal the finish produced by trowel methods correctly applied.

Inspection

The Clerk of Works must keep a close watch on plastering during each stage of the operations if his supervision is to be effective. He must note the mixing methods for plasters, especially where mixes are specified to contain no lime. Surfaces to be plastered must be clean and free from loose materials and mould oils. The Clerk of Works should remember that a high suction background will affect the adhesion of the plaster, and consider this point beforehand.

Where finishing coats are applied over backing coats which have not dried out, there is a danger of blistering and shrinkage occurring, and a backing coat allowed to become too dry before the finishing coat is applied may affect the adhesion of the skim coat, besides causing crazing of the surface. Plasterwork can become too dry on both finishing and backing coats where drying winds are allowed to find their way through open doorways and windows.

Skim coats are not to be over-polished, as this will affect the subsequent decorations. It is better to brush off the surface after the final trowelling.

Jointing to plasterboarding is sometimes specified with jute scrim or bandage scrim, although paper scrim is used on some dry lining contracts. The Clerk of Works should note that the jute scrim requires a full coat of plaster, whereas bandage scrim is much easier to cover. Metal angle beads are in general use today and other metal beads have been introduced to enable plaster to be stopped at door frames and casings, skirting levels and ceiling angles – allowing a slight check to be provided and overcoming shrinkage cracks in these areas. Temporary lighting should be considered before the shorter working days are reached, as difficulties in setting times for plaster may result in the operators finishing off plaster surfaces the following day by application of water and trowel.

Wall Tiling

The manufacture of wall tiles is a complicated process. Various clays are ground into a fine dust, mixed with water to provide a slurry and then mixed with finely ground limestone and flints to produce a rich creamy substance know as 'slip'. Removing the water from the slip leaves a fine plastic clay which is then ground once again to produce a dust from which the tile is formed and fired. It is then known as a 'biscuit'. The biscuit passes through a glaze and is fired once more to produce the finished tile.

Tiles are available in several sizes, but generally internal wall tiles are 152×152 mm and either 5 mm or 6 mm thick, with small nibs on each of the edges which assist in ensuring the correct joint size as well as taking any compressive strain transmitted through the tile surface.

Sand and cement backings are usually provided for wall tiling. They are allowed to stand in order that shrinkage may take place and suction be reduced before tiling proceeds. Tiles must be soaked in clean water and allowed to drain before they are used. They are bedded by first buttering them with a sand and cement backing before bonding them to the wall surface. An alternative method of bonding is to butter the tiles with a ceramic fixing compound in place of the sand and cement, and a further method consists of spreading a tile adhesive over the surface of the finished wall with a trowel having a serrated edge, and sticking the tiles straight on to the adhesive.

Tiles must be thoroughly grouted up after fixing with a proper grouting compound. Neat cement should not be used, as it will only shrink, causing cracks on the surface which will admit any water present, and creating problems with the backing.

Inspection by the Clerk of Works will involve checking the initial backing of sand and cement to see that it is sound, and the method of bonding the tiles. Setting out is very important in avoiding too much cutting. Tiles must be bedded flush with each other and bonded joints should be reasonably true.

Where there is a reasonable amount of tiling to be done, a specialist contractor will be appointed. He will guarantee his work but this will not relieve the Clerk of Works of the need to check it as it proceeds.

Asbestos cement sheeting or exterior quality plywood can be covered with tiles provided these materials are securely braced and fixed to the framing. Boards are more stable if secured with screws rather than nails, and both asbestos and plywood must be painted on the reverse side and all edges to reduce distortion of the boards.

Tiles should be fixed with a rubber or resin adhesive to these surfaces, but on less even surfaces cement-based adhesives will allow a thicker bed to take up irregularities.

Water-resistant grouting must be used and the manufacturers' recommendations followed carefully in such instances.

Exterior Tiling

This presents many more problems because of the danger from frost, and care will be necessary in designing this form of surface finish if it is to be successful. Movement joints must be formed both vertically and horizontally between 3 m and 4·5 m centres, and also where the tiles are carried over different backing materials. On a structural concrete frame the joints should be formed either side of beams and columns, and should be at least 6 mm wide as well as the full depth of tile and bed. Movement joints should be filled with polysulphide compounds, but as these are expensive materials, it may be advisable to fill deep joints with either polyurethene or neoprene foam strip before sealing with polysulphide. The choice of backing materials can be very important, as brickwork which is subject to sulphate action will transmit excess movement to the tile surface, causing possible failure at the joints.

Sand and cement renderings applied to take up irregularities in the backing create more weight on the surface and subsequent movement. One method of overcoming this is to fix metal lath to the backing and render over this to form a reinforced skin, which is then tiled with a thin bed adhesive. An alternative method is to apply direct to the brick or concrete surface a grout made up to thin bed adhesive, and while this is still moist to bed the tiles with a thick application of sand and cement to their backs. This provides a surface where each tile is separately secured to the backing, and because of the small cavities created between the bedding materials any slight movement is accommodated. Grouting should not be carried out until the backing has had time to dry out, and then it must be forced well into the joints, over small areas at a time. Water-resistant materials must be used for grouting, and double grouting helps to ensure that defects in the first application are remedied.

CHAPTER TWENTY-SIX

Floor Screeds and Finishes

Monolithic Screeds

It is useful to consider floor screeds as (a) those which act as an underlay for other finishes and (b) those which are floor finishes in themselves.

The Clerk of Works should study the detail drawings at sub-structure stage to confirm the various floor finishes, as the designer may have provided for different finishes by adjusting the levels of the structural slab. Alternatively the structural slab may be the finished floor level by incorporating a surface finish as a monolithic construction.

Monolithic screeds are those laid within three hours of the base slab being formed, and should be laid at an average thickness no greater than 20 mm or the slab may be liable to curl. The object in creating a monolithic finish is to obtain good adhesion between the screed and the base slab, as well as providing a dense wearing surface. The use of this construction on industrial buildings will not only reduce costs but also speed up the progress. If the surface is treated with a disc power float instead of hand trowelling, a smooth dense surface suitable for normal factory traffic can be achieved.

Where the surface required is to be granolithic, then the aggregates should be clean granite, whinstone or limestone chipping, gauged with sand and cement and the minimum amount of water necessary to produce a workable mix to suit the method of laying.

Grit surfacing materials may also be specified, such as carborundum, which should be sprinkled on the surface of the screed and lightly trowelled in.

Separate Construction

Laying the topping after the base slab has hardened cannot be described as monolithic, and is generally called separate construction.

In this instance the screed must be increased to 40 mm thick and laid in bays not greater than 15 m² in a chequerboard pattern. Joints in the screed should coincide with the structural joints formed in the base slab, or the screed will crack. The base slab finish should be left straight off the tamp, as this provides a good key for the topping; if it is left until later, accumulated mortar and plaster droppings may have to be thoroughly cleaned off the surface before any screeds are laid.

Where the base slab is still 'green', preparation of the surface can be achieved by wire brushing, but if it is left until later the surface of the slab must be hacked and roughened to remove the laitance and then brushed over with a thin layer of grout. Unless a satisfactory measure of adhesion is obtained between the screed and the slab, there will be a danger of hollow screeds and subsequent cracking.

Where there is any doubt of obtaining a satisfactory key, a bonding agent of PVA can be used in accordance with the manufacturer's instructions, but bonding agents must never be regarded as an alternative to properly cleaned sub-floors.

Underlay Screeds

Screeds provided as an underlay for further finishes will not be as strong as those provided as wearing surfaces, and the mix will consist of well graded sand and Portland cement, with the water content as low as possible without restricting the workability of the mix. Rich mixes will result in greater shrinkage problems, but in reducing the cement content it is important to ensure that the dry materials are thoroughly mixed before water is added.

Conduits crossing the sub-floor must be securely fixed, and a band of chicken wire should be laid as reinforcement to the screed at this point. Where two pipes cross within the thickness of the screed, it may be necessary to form a chase in the floor to receive the lower pipe, but this should only be done after consultation with the structural engineer.

Levels for floor screeds are established by bedding timber laths in sand and cement to form working screeds; the topping should be spread over the floor between the laths and then levelled with the straight-edge bearing on the laths. The screed must be compacted by hand tamping or with a suitable roller before levelling off the surface and trowelling in. Trowelling is important to produce a firm surface to the screed, and a skilfully used power float having three or four adjustable blades is an excellent means of finishing large areas. A floor surface broken up with ducts and chases, however, can seriously reduce the usefulness of power floating.

Floating Screeds

It may be necessary to isolate the floor screed from the sub-floor so that differential movement can take place without damaging the surface, and this can be done by laying building paper over the base before the screed is applied.

It will be necessary to isolate the screed for sound insulation, and for heat insulation where heating elements are enclosed within the screed. Glass-fibre quilt is laid on the sub-base and returned up the wall to the full depth of the screed, and chicken wire may be included as a light reinforcement to the screed.

The quilting must be lapped over at each joint, and care must be taken when laying the screed to see that barrows, etc, are not allowed to run over the insulation. Where heating elements are included in the floor screed, it will be advisable to see they are not interfered with by any chicken-wire reinforcement.

Curing

Adequate precautions must be taken to ensure that the finished screed is protected from subsequent construction traffic, and that curing is allowed to take place under controlled conditions.

Cracks are more likely to result from intermittent wetting and drying than from controlled moisture, and the Clerk of Works should insist that screeds are covered with wet sacking, damp sand, or protected with building paper for at least 7 days to allow curing to take place.

The surface of the screed can be treated with one of the proprietary curing compounds, which are considered to be effective and economical.

Slow curing of the screeds is necessary to avoid shrinkage cracks, and it would be shortsighted for precautions to be taken in using the correct mix proportions and methods of application to form the screed if this were not followed by suitable curing procedures.

Magnesium Oxychloride

Composition floor is a loose term applied to magnesium oxychloride floor finishes, perhaps because the constituents of the mix were not always readily understood.

This type of floor finish is often specified for warehouses and factories where granolithic surfaces would be acceptable except for the dangers of dusting. Magnesium oxychloride is dust-free, but it is unsuitable where there is water present, and a damp-proof membrane should be used in the sub-floor where this type of surfacing is used.

The ingredients of the mix consist of calcined magnacite and fillers such as wood flour, powdered asbestos, limestone, etc, gauged with magnesium chloride. The fillers vary according to whether the floor is required for industrial or domestic use, and samples should be obtained before the work begins. Magnesium chloride is available as a solution or in flake form to be dissolved in water, and all materials should be delivered to site in separate containers and stored no longer than 14 days. Precautions must be taken to avoid magnesium oxychloride coming into contact with walls and floors in the building, and metalwork in contact with it should be treated with bitumen paint beforehand. Where the screed is laid on a concrete base, the latter should be tamped to provide a key and must be cleaned off before work proceeds. On timber floor bases galvanised wire mesh should be nailed to the boards with galvanised clout nails, and several rows of nails should be only partly driven home to provide additional key.

The materials are mixed to a stiff consistency and spread over the area of the floor between laths to act as screeds, and levelled off with a straight-edge. The surface should be trowelled when the screed has hardened sufficiently; mechanical trowelling is beneficial in producing a more compact surface, especially where single-coat applications are concerned.

Single-coat applications on concrete should be 10–15 mm thick, and two-coat work up to 40 mm, but on timber floor bases the thickness for single coats should be 15–20 mm and for two coats 10–25 mm. Initial setting times are from 3–6 hours with the final set occurring in 7–15 hours. On two-coat work the base coat is formed by using rough fillers, and finishing off with a similar mix as used for single-coat work.

After the screed has set, a solution of magnesium chloride is applied to the floor to seal the surface, which is cleaned off with dry steel wool or an abrasive machine. The floor should then be washed with warm water and, when dried, should be treated with wax or linseed oil and turpentine. The normal precautions should be followed to protect the finished work while

construction work is proceeding. Magnesium oxychloride screeds should be
laid by specialist contractors, and completed while finishing works are
proceeding in particular sectors of the building.

Floor Tiling

There is often confusion on site regarding floor tiling owing to the fact that
some tiles are called 'quarries', and this can best be overcome by recognising that there are two types of tile available. Quarry tiles are manufactured from clay ground to a plastic condition and pressed before being
fired at high temperature in tile kilns. Floor tiles are manufactured from
ordinary clay with ceramic materials added, ground to a powder and pressed
in a semi-dry state before being fired in the kiln.

Quarries are generally thicker than floor tiles and the tolerances are much
greater. Some are ground to a dust rather than reduced to a plastic state
before pressing.

Tiles must always be soaked in clean water to reduce the suction and
then allowed to drain before being used.

The specification may require the screed below the tiles to be isolated
from the main structure, and this can be done by providing a uniform
layer of damp building sand no more than 20 mm thick, or using a
separating layer of bitumen felt or polythene sheeting.

Any falls required in the floor must be formed in the sub-base, and
levels should be accurate enough to accommodate any variations within
the tile screed. In some instances the tiler will lay his own screed over the
sub-floor, in the form of a semi-dry mix firmly compacted and prepared
to receive the tiling, which will be bedded in a sand and cement slurry or a
ceramic tile-fixing compound.

The width of joints in the tiling may be varied to meet the requirements,
but should be no less than 3 mm wide to enable grouting to be carried out
properly. Neat cement should not be used for grouting the joints, as it will
only shrink and leave cracks all over the surface of the floor. When grouting
up has been completed, the whole floor should be cleaned off with fine sand;
it is not advisable to use sawdust for this purpose, as it will become embedded in the joints and produce a porous surface.

Movement joints must be formed where there are joints in the structure,
and they may also be required around bases and adjacent to walls. Movement joints must be not less than 6 mm wide, and continue the full depth
through thickness of tile and screed.

Waterproof compounds added to the base concrete will affect the bonding of the tile screed to the surface of the slab, but where there is any danger of rising damp, a proper damp-proof membrane must be provided in the sub-floor; otherwise rising soluble salts may affect the adhesion of the tiles or at least create efflorescence on the surface of the floor.

Plastic Floor Tiles

Thermoplastic and vinyl floor tiles account for a very large proportion of floor finishes today, especially in domestic and industrial buildings.

Thermoplastic tiles are manufactured from polyvinyl chloride, asbestos, and asphalt, which makes them suitable for ground floor finishes where no damp-proof membrane has been installed. Vinyl tiles are much more flexible than thermoplastic tiles, as a greater quantity of PVC resin is included in their manufacture. They also come in a wider range of lighter shades.

These tiles can be laid on either concrete or timber floors, but in the latter instance an underlay of hardboard, plywood, or bitumen felt should be provided to isolate any movement of the boarding and to avoid rippling of the tile surface. Concrete floors receiving PVC tile finishes may be finished in a monolithic manner, as described elsewhere. Alternatively a sand and cement screed may be laid with a well compacted semi-dry mix and finished with either float or trowel.

Large floor areas should be divided into bays with ebonite or plastic strips wherever any change in type of floor finish occurs, or where movement joints are formed in the structural slab.

The levels of the screeding must be reasonably accurate to receive the tiles, as variations will be clearly visible on the finished surface. Local depressions in the screed can be overcome by using a proprietary levelling compound, which can be finished to a feather edge. Tiles must not be laid on damp screeds, and the Clerk of Works should make this point clear when pressure may be put upon the flooring contractor to proceed. Where necessary, the Clerk of Works should have access to hygrometers that can be placed on the areas in question and read over periods of not less than four hours, but preferably overnight. Where the readings show a value of 75 per cent or less, it can be assumed that the screed is suitable for work to proceed. Moisture meter readings can also be taken, but where there is any light reinforcement in the screed, the probes must be kept from contact with it, or false readings will ensue.

Where priming of the screed is specified, this should be allowed to dry before the tiling proceeds, as the adhesives may be affected. Adhesives on this type of tiling will be bitumen-rubber emulsions, but these must not be regarded as damp-proof membranes. They should be spread with a notched trowel so that an even layer is formed over the area to be tiled.

Before any tiling is started, the Clerk of Works should agree the method of setting out, to avoid narrow strips of tile being inserted adjacent to walls and offsets. It may be better to set out each room separately, but this will mean altering the bonding at doorways to fit any tiling to corridors, and such an alteration may not be acceptable to the architect. It is a definite advantage to programme the floor tiling as one of the last operations before completion of the building.

Adhesive left on the surface of the tile should be cleaned off before it can set, or spirit will be needed to remove it and that can soften the tile. If too much adhesive is used, it will seep through the jointing of the tiles as they are subjected to traffic, causing them to be smeared badly. Where the adhesive has been left too long before placing the tiles, they will squeak as they are walked on, but this problem usually rectifies itself when heat comes on in the building.

Sheet Covering

Floor coverings have been traditionally available in sheet form for many year, and linoleum in particular has proved its suitability and wearing qualities where correctly laid. This material is very quiet underfoot, and in consequence is used extensively in offices, schools, hospitals and similar establishments. It is also used as a surfacing material to bench tops, counters, and desks.

Linoleum is manufactured from cork, wood flour, linseed oil and resins, with pigments added to provide colouring, and is rolled in a standard width of 1·83 m by 3·2 mm thick, although it can be obtained 2·0 mm and 4·5 mm thick where required. It is also cut into tile sizes with hessian or felt backing, and these are often used to produce patterned floors, and occasionally wall murals. Before fixing, lino should be cut approximately to size and laid flat to allow it to spread, otherwise it will spread after laying, and that can be difficult to rectify.

The adhesives for linoleum are spirit-based and should be used in accordance with the instructions of the manufacturer. Gum spirits, or by-products of the paper industry such as sulphite lye or lignin pastes, may be used, or resin-alcohol, which is manufactured as a grey or brown adhesive to be spread over the floor surface with a serrated edge trowel. After being laid, the linoleum should be rolled both ways with a 68 kg roller to ensure complete adhesion and to remove air pockets.

PVC sheeting or vinyl sheeting is used where tiles may not be desirable, either for hygienic reasons in hospitals, or perhaps for aesthetic reasons elsewhere. PVC can be obtained either with plain backing or with felt, while vinyl sheeting is available with PVC foam backing to provide a more resilient material.

Bitumen-rubber emulsions and resin-rubber emulsions are used as adhesives for bonding these materials, and where the adhesives are applied to both the sheeting and the base, the manufacturer's instructions must be carefully followed regarding the time which must elapse for the solvents to evaporate before bonding the material.

Plastic sheeting can also be welded at the joints, special tools being available for this purpose, and as the sheeting can be returned up the wall to provide a cove skirting, it is useful in areas where a certain amount of water may gather from shower trays, etc.

Rubber flooring is manufactured from synthetic rubber, and is quiet under foot, has good wearing qualities and can be used both internally and externally. Invariably rubber flooring has an indented pattern which provides a non-slip surface. It is cut into larger tiles than those generally produced in linoleum and plastic. Rubber solutions are used as adhesives, and are generally applied to both the base and the sheeting to ensure a good bond; it is important to make sure there is no air trapped under the sheeting.

The floor surface must be clean and dry before any sheet materials are laid, and the screed must be level and free from any damaged areas. Where it is necessary to level slight depressions, the Clerk of Works should check that this is not done with gypsum plaster, a practice that has been used in the past.

Most faults probably occur through using the wrong type of adhesive, or allowing the adhesive to be incorrectly used.

Sheet flooring is also used to cover stairways, but difficulties arise where the sheeting is returned around the nosing to the step. This is largely overcome today by fitting special nosings in plastic, metal, and rubber, some of which must be fitted before laying the sheeting.

Cork Flooring

This type of covering is produced in various grades of density, but cork tiles are generally laid in a similar manner to plastic and linoleum, except that cork tiles should be secured with headless pins to the base and be well rolled after laying to ensure good adhesion. Gum spirits are a suitable adhesive, but the manufacturer's instructions must be carefully followed to avoid failures. Any dampness present in the floor will cause lifting of the cork. After the tiles have been laid, it is usual to use a light sanding machine to remove any lippings and produce an even surface over the floor, which should be cleaned thoroughly and then waxed and polished. Sometimes a polyurethene finish is specified, but this produces a much harder surface again than the cork and is easily marked. Cork is also available in sheet form, and is used extensively in sports halls and gymnasiums, where it can be applied over existing floors, provided these are free from dampness and have a smooth level surface.

Carpets

The increase in the use of carpet tiles has no doubt accounted to some extent for the use of this finish in general contract work. Synthetic fibres have also contributed towards this increase, as cleaning is easy and worn tiles are simply replaced. Where carpet is laid either in rolls or as tiles, the Clerk of Works must ensure that the construction trades are not likely to be returning to those areas. Floors must be cleaned and made good where necessary beforehand. It is important to see that the carpet is stretched properly and that no ridges occur, as excessive wear will occur at those points. A range of metal fittings to act as carpet edging grippers is available, as are timber strips with nail grips incorporated for use on timber floors.

Terrazzo Floors

This type of finish is usually carried out by specialists, since cracks are likely to develop in the floor surface if the job is not properly done. The sub-floor must be level and free from mortar droppings so that a good bond can be obtained, and the terrazzo layer should preferably lay his own screed. An isolating membrane should be laid over precast floors, and chicken wire included in the screed; and where movement joints occur they must be continued through the depth of screed and terrazzo surfacing. The recommended maximum for *in situ* terrazzo floors is 1 m², and this should be divided with narrow strips of brass, plastic or ebonite.

The recommended thickness of finish and screed is 50 mm, but the terrazzo thickness will be controlled by the size of the marble aggregate, which should not be less than 3 mm. The aggregate must be clean and free from dust, and the shape should be angular. The finish should be laid while the screed is still green, or at least not later than 48 hours after the screed is laid, and full compaction of the terrazzo is essential to a satisfactory finish. Excessive trowelling is not advisable as this will bring a heavy cement layer to the surface, and when the final trowelling is applied the surface should contain a regular distribution of aggregate and very little cement.

Depending upon the hardness of the surface, grinding should take place after four days, using a coarse abrasive and plenty of water to expose the aggregates. This work is normally carried out with a machine today, and grinding should continue until a smooth surface is achieved. The floor should then be washed down with clean water and covered with a neat cement grout to fill all the surface voids; it is left for a further three days before receiving a final polish with a fine abrasive.

Terrazzo floors must be cured to avoid cracking, which will disfigure the surface and be difficult to repair.

Hardwood Floor Finishes

Damp-proof membranes should be included in the sub-floor wherever special timber floor finishes are to be installed, and the building should be completely enclosed. Where it is possible, the heating should be turned on and maintained, and no construction work should be allowed to follow completion of the floors.

Changes in moisture content are likely to affect the floor finish, and materials should be stored in those areas where they are to be used so that the correct equilibrium may be achieved. The recommended moisture content for flooring is approximately 12 per cent, although buildings with a high degree of central heating should have less than this.

Timber block floors are normally laid on a sand and cement screed and bedded in hot or cold bitumen adhesives, although for many years blocks were laid in hot pitch, which often made it unnecessary for damp-proof membranes to be supplied. Wood blocks may interlock with special tongue and groove or have dowelled joints. They can be laid in a variety of patterns but the 'herring-bone' is probably the most familiar. The variation in the wearing qualities of wood blocks can be seen in many existing floors, where certain blocks have worn badly, leaving depressions over the floor areas.

Movement is almost inevitable with timber floors and cork expansion strips are generally formed around the perimeter and where movement is likely to occur elsewhere.

The variation in block thickness will produce a certain amount of lipping, but this can be removed by sanding with the heavy sanding machine, using very coarse to finer grades of paper. The finished surface of the floor will be treated with several coats of wax polish and buffed off between each coat, or with several coats of polyurethene varnish.

Parquet floors are decorative finishes which can be formed by glueing or pinning hardwood strips to a timber sub-floor. The strips may also be obtained in preformed panels, to be secretly nailed down. The sub-floor must be level and have an even surface, or the finished floor will be uneven after sanding has taken place and the wax finish has been applied.

Hardwood strip floors use boards not more than 100 mm wide and 25 or 32 mm thick: they are tongued and grooved to the ends as well as to the edges to produce a continuous floor without cutting back to form joints over the joists. Where the ends are T & G this is referred to as 'matched ends'. The strips are secured to the joists by secret nailing through the tongue, and nails must be punched to allow the next board to fit over the tongue.

The boards are in random lengths to prevent joints occurring together and this should be checked by the Clerk of Works.

The density of hardwoods makes it unnecessary to specify quarter-sawn rather than flat-sawn, as with softwoods, but quarter-sawn oak may be specified because of its decorative effect. Quarter-sawn timber is less liable than flat-sawn to distortion across the width of the boards, which does provide more stability to this type of flooring. A gap can be left around the perimeter of the floor, which can be obscured with the skirting, to accommodate any further movement. After the boards have been laid, they will be sanded off and finished with either a wax polish or a polyurethane varnish, as described for wood blocks.

CHAPTER TWENTY-SEVEN

Plumbing Installations

Mains Supply

The supply of mains water to public or private development is the responsibility of the local water board which lays the pipes up to the site boundaries. Even after the pipes have been laid, the authority may withhold water supplies until it is satisfied the regulations have been met concerning waste or storage of water.

The authority must be supplied with information at the planning stage of what services it is intended should be installed within the development, including all fire-fighting methods, to enable it to determine the routing and size of pipes for the mains water supply.

Water pressure variation from district to district may affect the fittings and supplies within the building. The water board will install a stop-valve between its supply pipes and the owner's main service pipe to give it control over the supplies.

Water mains are laid with pipes of various materials – cast or spun iron pipes, steel, copper, or PVC – depending upon the supply required. Protection will be necessary for the mains, either because of corrosive elements in the ground or in the water supply itself, or where the use of different metals may set up electrolytic action. Steel and iron pipes will generally be treated both internally and externally with a bituminous compound often referred to as Dr Angus Smith's solution.

Where possible the water mains should be laid in a combined trench with electric, gas and telephone services, with the distances specified between each of the services being carefully observed.

Where ducts have not been provided for road crossings, it may be better to thrust-bore below the road level to lay service mains rather than cut up the road surface.

The supply pipe from the mains must be fitted with a stop-valve and drain-off where it enters the building, and before rising to supply the main storage tanks at higher level. The supply pipe is referred to as the rising main, and all drinking supplies will be drawn direct from this pipe to the drinking points.

Cold-water Installations

The installations may be specified in copper or plastic but the pipes will be connected to standard fittings on the appliances, as a wide range of fittings are available in both types of materials. Plastic pipes can be obtained in PVC, ABS, and polythene, although on most contracts where plastic pipes are specified, rigid PVC will be used. It is not recommended that PVC pipes should be bent, and fittings are available for bends, although by applying heat to the pipe and using a plumber's spring it is possible to bend them. Solvent welding is probably the best way of jointing PVC pipes.

Repairs to PVC pipes with solvent welding create a problem because of the delay of several hours before the supply can be used, but a compression fitting incorporating rubber inserts is available for quick repairs. Polythene tubes can be jointed by applying heat with a special tool.

Copper pipes can be obtained in several gauges, and the Clerk of Works should give special attention to which type is specified, as this will affect the fixing procedures.

Pipes are supplied in 6 m lengths and jointed with compression fittings or capillary fittings; the latter are obtainable in two types, one where there is a ring of solder in each end of the fitting, and the other (known as 'end feed' fittings) where the solder is applied.

The Clerk of Works should make periodic checks upon the methods of jointing copper pipes to see that the ends are clean cut, and sharp edges removed and cleaned with wire-wool. Where this is not done, burrs can be left in the end of the pipes, causing obstruction to the flow and depositing small particles of metal in cisterns, boilers and even pumps, where these have been included in the system.

The rising main should be fitted to an internal wall wherever possible because of frost which could affect the supply, and where it is considered necessary, lagging should be carried out to the pipework.

It should not be overlooked that where ceilings are insulated, little heat will reach the roof space and pipework will require lagging there.

All pipes must be clipped according to the specification or to manufacturers' instructions, distances varying according to the size of pipes. While adequate clips are necessary to support the pipes, care must be taken not to distort the alignment or cause stressing to the pipework. Where fittings are provided to tanks and cylinders, the connections to fittings must not be considered as a reason to omit clips, which should always be provided adjacent to bends in the pipework.

The walls of the copper tube are parallel to provide an even bore – otherwise the head of water might be reduced through friction – and it is important for all bends to be carried out correctly. On the smaller gauge pipes a bending machine or a spring must be used, but even then, when work is not carried out properly, the bend can be deformed, reducing the size of the bore. Crimping will also occur, affecting the thickness in the wall of the pipe; such work should not be acceptable to the Clerk of Works and pipework of this standard should be replaced.

Care must be taken when thin-wall copper tube is used for plumbing installations, because it must not be bent, as light gauge copper pipes can be. Fittings must always be used with thin-wall tubing for any change of direction. Although it is possible to bend thin-wall tube, the ultimate stressing of the pipe walls is unacceptable.

All pipework should be installed in such a manner as to produce a neat appearance to the finished work, with pipes either level or falling slightly towards the fittings as required. Where crossing of pipes is unavoidable, a pattern should be established to overcome any unsightly appearance. It is always useful to agree a 'mock-up' of pipework before installation begins, for it will assist the men involved and avoid unnecessary alterations.

Storage Tanks

Storage tanks will vary in size according to the requirements of the installation, and the size can determine the materials from which the tanks are made.

Large storage tanks may be constructed from prefabricated steel panels, but the domestic type could be galvanised metal, fibre-glass, asbestos cement, or high density polythene.

Metal tanks should be treated internally to resist any reaction to the metal from the water supplies, an application of non-toxic bituminous paint being one method of treatment.

To prevent any pollution of the water supplies a loose-fitting lid should be provided for the storage tank, and where there may be danger from frost, adequate lagging should be fitted. Any supports or bearers used to carry the tank must be carefully calculated to make sure they will support the loading, and for the same reason erection procedure must be inspected. The supports may be merely timber bearers for smaller tanks, but larger tanks will probably require designed steel framing. Plastic tanks should be provided with a platform to support the base and prevent the tank becoming deformed over a period of time.

While it may be fairly easy to assess the water supplies for domestic purposes, it is a much more complicated process to do this for large establishments such as hospitals or hotels. Water supplies are calculated on a formula by which a certain number of gallons are necessary for each person per day; in a hotel this might be 45 litres per day for each resident, and in a normal dwelling house it might be 114 litres. Storage tanks for dwelling houses should contain no less than 114 litres, and if they also act as feed tanks to the hot water supply, this figure should be increased to not less than 224 litres. These requirements are changing, however, owing to the installation of combined cylinders and storage tanks, and water boards may be prepared to consider alternative designs.

High-rise buildings will have storage tanks at roof level and additional tanks at ground-floor level, the former supplying a gravity feed to several upper floors and the latter providing a pumped feed to the remainder. If there is insufficient pressure on the mains, it may be necessary to incorporate a pump into the installation to supply the tanks at roof level.

Ball-valves, Overflows and Stop-valves

All tanks and cisterns receiving a direct supply of mains water must be fitted with a float-operating ball-valve, set in such a way that the valve will close when the water in the tank has reached the waterline. Several types of ball-valve are available, but large storage tanks will most likely be fitted with the equilibrium type, which is quite suitable for either low or high pressure supplies. Other types include the Croydon ball-valve, which operates through a vertical piston that seals the entry to a horizontal inlet pipe; or the Portsmouth, which has a horizontal piston and inlet pipe. Modern WC cisterns are fitted with plastic ball-valves and siphon assembly produced from Building Research Station designs.

Overflow pipes must not be less than 20 mm in diameter, and should always be greater than the diameter of the supply pipe. They should be positioned 25 mm lower than the supply pipe and at the opposite side of the tank. Overflows must not be less than 25 mm above the full-water mark shown on the tank. Although it is expected that overflow pipes are only likely to have intermittent use, they must be correctly installed, with a slight fall to the outside; they can then give clear warning of any water wastage, besides danger to the building from flooding. It is intended that the overflow pipe will dispose of any build-up within the tank from a faulty valve, but blockages can occur through many causes, not least that of the pipe freezing up in winter.

Stop-valves are required wherever it may be necessary to isolate any part of the installation, and the first one to be installed is that to the rising main. Other stop-valves will be necessary where sections of the installation supply other parts of the building, as well as on supply pipes to such appliances as storage tanks. WC cisterns, sinks and ranges of lavatory basins will require stop-valves to isolate them in case of repairs.

Stop-valves may be the screw-down type similar to ordinary taps or the full-way or gate-valve type operated by a crutch fitting on the spindle. They may also be operated with a wheel fitting, or by means of a key fitted into the top of the spindle.

The purpose of the stop-valve is to cut off the water supplies, but invariably this still leaves a certain amount of water in the branch pipes. As this water constitutes a hazard from frost or an obstruction to repair work, consideration should be given in the design stage to the installation of sufficient drain-off cocks, but the Clerk of Works must take note also.

It is well to remember that some water authorities will not accept gate-valves on main pressure supplies.

The term stop-valve is likely to be misleading in certain instances, so it is probably better to describe it as an 'isolating valve' which is really its purpose in the installation.

Water Taps

These may be manufactured from brass, gunmetal, or plastics in a variety of designs ranging from the ordinary bib tap to foot-operated spray taps. Combined hot and cold water taps operated by the elbows are used extensively in hospitals and similar establishments, while other types, which operate with a capstan head, are used in laboratories. The domestic type is used for kitchen sink units, and baths where a shower fitting is also incorporated.

Taps are generally connected to the supply pipes by screw fittings which in turn are fitted to the pipe by solvent welding or by solder where compression fittings are not used.

In fixing the taps to the appliance it is advisable to ensure they are securely held, as taps are subject to a great deal of leverage, particularly sink and bath taps. Taps for baths made of plastic, a flexible material to begin with, should be connected through the frame supporting the bath wherever possible.

All taps must be clearly identified to distinguish between hot and cold, and where combined taps are used, it will be left to the user to balance the temperature of the water required. Controlled temperatures can be achieved by installing a mixer valve, which can be manually or thermostatically operated, and these are very useful where sick or young people are concerned.

Taps can be positioned some way from the discharge point, as with shower fittings, although the nozzle enables the flow of water to be controlled from a jet to a fine spray. Standard taps have diameters of 13 mm, 19 mm, and 25 mm, although they are also available down to 6 mm and up to 50 mm. Where high pressure water is available, 13 mm taps are adequate, but low pressure supplies need something larger. Self-closing valves are used nowadays for drinking fountains in place of the tap control.

A special type of valve used for flushing WC pans works automatically when activated to supply a predetermined quantity of water. These valves are not always acceptable by water authorities for direct connection to the mains supply, and would need to be fed from a supply cistern controlled by a ball-valve.

Sanitary Appliances

Sanitary ware is generally fixed after plasterwork, or when wall and floor tiling has been completed, but consideration must be given to the fixing positions of the appliances beforehand. It may be necessary for brackets to be built in to support sinks, etc, for fixing blocks to be provided, or even for holes to be cut through walls for service and overflow pipes.

Heights of urinal bowls, washbasins and sinks can vary within the same building, and where a sanitary ware schedule is provided, the Clerk of Works should note the heights given.

The practice of propping the feet of cast-iron baths with timber pads to gain height for the bath waste should be discouraged, for these feet can be obtained in two different sizes and the manufacturer will be pleased to supply information.

The supporting frame for acrylic baths should be levelled and also secured to the wall to prevent undue movement of the bath at a later stage.

WC pans should be bedded in putty to the floor and screwed down with brass screws to prevent movement that may lead to leaks at both flush-pipe and soil connections (which should have flexible joints). WC pans are supplied either as washdown or siphonic types, and where the outlet is an 'S' trap, the position of the drain must be carefully established. Flush-pipes may be jointed to the pan with a rubber cone or a neoprene ring, while the soil connection can be made with a neoprene ring, or plastic sleeve to provide a flexible joint. Alternatively a lead-caulked joint may be used where the pan is fitted to a cast-iron stack.

Cisterns manufactured from plastics are in general use, with both siphon and ball-valve also in plastic, but care must still be taken to check whether a high or low pressure ball-valve is being supplied. The material in some forms of plastic cistern is quite flexible, requiring the lid to be fitted carefully to ensure the strength of the unit. High level cisterns must be fitted to ensure the flush-pipe is not less than 1·5 m to provide sufficient head of water, and automatic flushing cisterns must be fitted for urinals to discharge through spreaders or sparge pipes.

Where ranges of lavatory basins are fitted, a gap of 75 mm should be allowed between each basin to enable cleaning to be done, but where required, the gaps can be sealed with a closure strip. Brackets used for supporting lavatory basins must be securely fitted, and those used with plasterboard partitions should be provided with legs, since the wall fixing can hardly withstand the leverage upon washbasins. Framing can be provided behind the plasterboard to stud partitions, but timber inserts should be also provided in Paramount partitions before these are fixed in position. There is always a tendency for the brackets to flex slightly where fitted to plasterboard and this is best overcome by securing a backboard to the timber inserts. The basin must be properly bedded with putty where the leading edge of the bracket fits into the recess on the basin. Slop sinks should be fitted either on built-in brackets or with leg type brackets, and care should be taken to ensure sufficient clearance between the sink and the taps, to enable the metal grid to be fully opened back to the wall surface.

The heights for shower fittings are particularly important, as these will differ according to those who are likely to be using them most regularly: for example, in showers for females the fitting will be arranged to operate at shoulder height.

Urinal bowls should be fitted to correct heights, and some water authorities require an additional water supply tank besides a bib-tap supply. Slab urinals are manufactured so that the slabs form a complete unit, but some distortion does occur in the firing, and it is necessary for the operative to make allowances when bedding and jointing the slabs. If leaks are to be avoided, especially in installations on upper floors, the slabs must be laid on a waterproof membrane, and bedded and jointed strictly in accordance with manufacturer's recommendations regarding falls.

Sometimes membranes are omitted, but then there is great danger of leaks on ceilings below, difficult to stop at this late stage.

Trap Fittings

Traps can be defined as sections of pipework designed to retain a measured quantity of water to restrict the passage of air. Where the air pressure becomes too great, the water will be displaced and the seal broken.

All connections to soil and waste systems must be trapped to restrict gases escaping from the sewer or drain into the open air or into the building.

Traps are designed for connection to the main pipework either horizontally or vertically, and are referred to as 'P' traps or 'S' traps. On single-stack systems traps should be used with a minimum water seal of 75 mm, while those on a two-pipe system can be efficient with a water seal of 38 mm. Traps fitted to drinking fountains, washbasins, sinks and baths will be 32 to 50 mm in diameter, while those fitted to WCs will be 100 mm in diameter.

Cast-iron, earthenware and plastics are used for the manufacture of trapped fittings to external drainage, and traps fitted to appliances connected to the internal drainage system are generally made from brass, copper, lead or plastics.

Internal Drainage

The Clerk of Works must make himself familiar with the main drain runs shown on the drawings, so as to be in a position to recognise major problems before the work is too far advanced.

Where the pipes are fitted into ducts, both the position and the tolerances to which the contractor should be working must be clearly defined, rather than allowing the practice of 'first come, first served' to operate, creating problems for the person who might be last, as well as increasing the maintenance problem.

All pipe runs must be carefully aligned to avoid final lengths being fixed at an angle to meet roof openings or connect with underground drains. Failure to achieve reasonable alignment is a common fault on sites, resulting in the spigots not being seated properly into the sockets of the pipes, and other services having to be rerouted. By using a chalk line to mark out the pipe runs, it is easy to avoid these problems from the beginning.

The type and spacing of the specified fixing brackets or clips should be carefully checked, not only because they are there to retain the pipes but also for the support they provide.

There is sufficient thermal movement with plastic materials to move the pipe where it passes through the roof, so that precautions should be taken at this point, especially where built-up roofing has been specified.

All jointing must be checked when the work begins, as bad practices are liable to increase rather than decrease, and where rubber-ring type joints are used, careless fitting can result in an inefficient system. Pipes in an enclosed duct must be tested separately before the duct is sealed, and the Clerk of Works must see that all sections are tested completely before the building is handed over.

A particular point to watch is the bend at the foot of the vertical stack, which should have as large a radius as possible, not only because it is the most vulnerable point for blockages but because sharp bends may create back pressures. Where there is a problem with detergents, the bend can contribute by creating a build-up of foam which may find its way into the lower appliances.

The two-pipe system may be used on very large contracts, where it is the most suitable answer to the requirements. It consists of one pipe to accommodate the waste discharge and a second pipe to receive the soil drainage. Both pipes are connected to a third pipe, which is providing air to the system to overcome the problems of siphonage and back pressure.

Confusion sometimes occurs in distinguishing the difference between one-pipe systems and single-stack systems, and the Clerk of Works must be perfectly clear on this point. The one-pipe system uses the vertical stack to drain soil and waste, and a second pipe to act as a vent pipe, and on a traditional layout all the traps are vented to this pipe. On a modified one-pipe system the vent pipe is connected at strategic points to vent the system and guard against siphonage problems. The single-stack system also uses the vertical stack to drain soil and waste but does not use a separate pipe to vent the system, relying entirely upon certain basic rules being followed to overcome any siphonage problems.

The drawings and specifications should provide the Clerk of Works with all the information he requires for the particular installation he is supervising, but where the single-stack system is used, he should also be aware of the following basic rules.

The WC connections to the stack should be formed with an angle bend of 104 degrees, and no connection should be made from bath or lavatory basin within 200 mm below the centre-line of the WC connection. Waste connections can be made above the WC connection, of course, but as the minimum recommended fall for waste pipes connected to a single-stack system is only 1¼ degrees, there is generally a problem with the bath waste.

P-type traps should be used on the single-stack system wherever possible. The water seal on pipes of 50 mm and below must not be less than 75 mm, while pipes above this diameter should have a minimum seal of 50 mm. The single-stack system is used a great deal on housing, both low-rise and high-rise development, but where a number of appliances are likely to be connected on the same floor, such as may be the case with schools and offices, the one-pipe system is more often the answer.

Siphonage

This is a problem which occurs when a pipe is discharged at full bore, taking all the air with it and causing pressure above the water seal, which then breaks as the vacuum is filled from the outer air.

There are three recognised pressure changes affecting the water seal in soil and waste traps:

(a) Induced siphonage, caused when the main flow of water sucks all the air from a branch connection as it passes. A WC discharging from an upper floor might cause this reaction to a lavatory basin or bath waste.

(b) Self-siphonage, caused by the flow in a branch being sufficient to draw the whole weight of the discharge with it and so breaking the water seal.

(c) Back pressure, caused by the flow of water being suddenly slowed down, such as may occur at a sharp bend; the weight of water following compresses the air in the stack and forces it along any adjacent branch, discharging the water from the trap up into the appliance.

Water flowing back into the trap will seal it again, but if the pressure has been combined with soil waste, the result can be most unpleasant.

The object in using single-stack systems is to remove the need for a vent pipe and avoid a siphonage by preventing full bore discharge; and with careful design any back pressure or induced siphonage can be offset.

Access and Rodding Eyes

It is quite common today to omit rodding eyes and access points from drainage systems as an economical measure. On many other contracts these are provided, but they are unusable because of the way they have been installed. Some access points are turned at such an angle to the wall that it is almost impossible to get even the most flexible rods into the pipe. Others can be completely built into the wall – often on high-rise buildings where the drainage stacks are installed before internal walls and partitions are erected.

The purpose of rodding eyes and access points is to facilitate maintenance of the system, and, in consequence, they should be checked for accessibility during construction.

Provision for Rainwater

Once the roof has been completed to a stage where it begins to shed water, gutters and rainwater pipes must be fitted to prevent that water being directed into the building or down the façade. Water entering the building will slow progress and increase the subsequent 'drying-out period', while water cascading down the face of the building will cause efflorescence to the finished building.

Gutters to flat roofs must be checked thoroughly, as future leaks, difficult to overcome, will result from any careless work. Where asphalt or bitumen felt is used as the roof finish, care should be taken at the outlets and adequate fall should be ensured for the gutter. Eaves gutters should be fixed with gutter brackets spaced as recommended by the manufacturer, and sufficient fall allowed for the water to drain towards the outlets without exposing too much gap between the gutter and the overhanging roof finish for the wind to drive in the rain.

The gutter should be completely assembled, including outlets and stop-ends, with the rainwater pipe fitted from gutter to rainwater gulley. The Clerk of Works should not accept the practice of leaving rainwater pipes partly finished, with water discharging to the work lower down, even if it is necessary to provide temporary measures to overcome the problem.

Valley gutters may be provided in lead, copper, bitumen felt, or tiles. These are generally laid upon a valley boarding, with a layer of felt between metals or tiles. The Clerk of Works should check the system of laying the gutters where this may be repetitive work, as faults may not develop until an extensive amount of work has been completed.

On industrial buildings prefabricated gutters manufactured from asbestos cement, galvanised pressed steel, or cast iron may be used and they may be either half-round or box-section.

Plastic rainwater goods are used extensively on housing projects. The neoprene or foam plastic gaskets fitted to the joint sometimes break down with the abrasive action of sediment as the plastic gutter is affected with thermal movement.

CHAPTER TWENTY-EIGHT

Painting

Inspection

Painting to internal surfaces may be for decorative effect as much as for any other reason, but the application of paint should be regarded by the Clerk of Works as a barrier against corrosion and decay. He should be able to appreciate whether the correct type of paint has been specified for this purpose, and then see the paint is applied in the manner recommended by the manufacturer. Although there is probably very little difference in the quality of paints manufactured by reputable concerns, there is a tremendous variation in the way these paints are applied.

The Clerk of Works should check the paint when it is delivered to site, satisfying himself that all the tins are still sealed, and the brand of paint is that quoted in the specification and the paint schedules. The contractor is often given several alternative brands of paint in the bills to enable him to select one and submit it to the architect for approval, and in other instances the paint may be a nominated supply. In the latter case the Clerk of Works would be well advised to contact the paint representative before the painting begins, so that he can clarify any points regarding application with which he may not be familiar.

Paints should not require the addition of thinners such as white spirit, etc, as they are mixed and ready for use when despatched from the factory. However, the heavier constituents tend to sink to the bottom of the tin during storage, and the paint must be thoroughly mixed when the tin is opened if the consistency and colour are not to vary.

Paint can be stored too long, and where the Clerk of Works has any reason to suspect this may be the case, he should either submit samples to the laboratory or contact the paint representative. Arrangements can often be made with the paint manufacturer for paint samples to be tested, especially where he may be a nominated supplier, as he too will be concerned with the condition of his product.

When the work is in progress, it will be necessary for the Clerk of Works to satisfy himself that the paint used is from the branded tins, and that the consistency is not interfered with for ease of application. Samples of paint should be taken at regular intervals, and always from the source where it is being applied, before submitting it to the laboratory for testing.

Where the Clerk of Works decides it is necessary to obtain samples of paint, he should arrange for the agent and the foreman painter to be present. The sample should then be taken direct from the painters' kettle and be placed in two small sample tins marked with the date and place where taken. One tin should be handed to the agent for his attention and the remaining sample submitted to the laboratory, with other information regarding the paint specification which will assist analysis.

Paint manufacturers are always willing to assist whenever queries arise with painting, and where the Clerk of Works has reason to question the thickness of film applied, he may remove a small sample of paint film from the surface and have it micro-filmed. This will not only show the thickness of each layer but emphasise the reduction in the layer where there are projections in the surface, such as knots in timber or screws, etc, in metal. The reduction is caused when the brush hits the projection and bounces over it, leaving a thinner layer at this point that may very well be a weakness later in the whole paintwork. Painters should be encouraged to use painters' kettles instead of applying the paint direct from manufacturers' cans. Apart from the evaporation of solvents which affect the consistency of the paint, dust and dirt may contaminate the contents of the can.

Manufacturers' cans should be opened and stirred thoroughly to mix the constituents of the paint before pouring sufficient into the painter's kettle for the work in hand. Cans should also be used up and disposed of in the order in which they are opened, as paint left over several days will develop a skin, part of which is inevitably incorporated in the paintwork.

Preparation

Successful paintwork depends upon good adhesion of the priming coat to the surface to be treated, as well as equally good adhesion of subsequent films of paint. If adhesion is poor, the paint film will break down, allowing decay or corrosion to develop unless urgent remedial work is implemented. Before receiving primers, the surface to be painted must be thoroughly cleaned and freed from plaster or cement splashes.

Steel should be shot-blasted or treated with a chemical solution, though this type of treatment is best carried out under factory conditions; site treatment invariably stops short at wire brushing to remove rust or mill scale. Steelwork should be primed before delivery, leaving site priming to touching up where required before painting.

All knots or other resinous sources in timber should be sealed before painting, and the moisture content of the timber checked before any primer is applied. Internal timbers are allowed 10 to 12 per cent moisture and external timbers 15 to 18 per cent. Where timbers have been treated with a preservative, it will be again necessary to check that the moisture content has been reduced to these levels before priming proceeds.

Priming

This is the first, and most often the worst, coat of paint applied to any surface, although its poor application is due more to ignorance than to any other reason.

Primers must be regarded as the foundation to any satisfactory paint system and should preferably be applied under workshop or factory conditions rather than on the site. Unfortunately even in factories there is a tendency to adjust the consistency of the primer, which results either in a thick application necessitating subsequent treatment or one so thin that it merely acts as a colouring medium to the surface to be treated.

It is of paramount importance that the correct type of primer is selected in the first instance, for it must be compatible with any subsequent undercoat or finishing coats, as the manufacturer of the last two may not be prepared to guarantee his products over other primers. The Clerk of Works should see that this matter is settled at the priming stage to prevent problems arising later.

Where there may be a danger to health through contamination in any form, lead-based paints are no longer recommended, but for weatherproofing, lead-based primers are difficult to improve upon. Primers may also be based on aluminium leaf with alkyd resins, or with linseed or tung oils, but these should not be confused with aluminium paints, which are unsuitable as primers.

Aluminium primers are normally used on hardwoods to seal oily surfaces before painting, but they can be used on softwoods also. Where only one surface area of timber is treated, any moisture penetrating the timber from untreated surfaces may cause blistering of the aluminium primer. Where the primer is left too long, the surface can produce an aluminium dusting which affects the adhesion of subsequent coats of paint.

Oleo-resins and alkyds have become established as priming paints. Their weathering qualities vary a great deal, but for internal surfaces or where the priming is not left exposed too long they provide a satisfactory finish.

Acrylic primers, being waterbound, cannot be expected to provide any weather resistance, but they are successful on internal surfaces.

Red lead has proved to be a satisfactory priming paint for iron and steel-work over a number of years, but its thickness tends to produce heavy brushmarks and 'lumpiness' which must be overcome where the surface of the steel is to be left exposed.

Galvanised iron or steel surfaces may be primed with calcium plumbate, which can be brushed out more easily than red lead, although care must be taken in applying this primer under wet conditions. Zinc chromates or phosphates have better drying qualities than red lead, and zinc chromate is a good primer for aluminium surfaces. Where conditions are not so severe and where damage to the paint film is unlikely, red oxide primers may be suitable, but some of these primers may be inclined to dry too quickly and become brittle as a result.

It is important to provide sufficient thickness when priming steelwork to give it adequate protection during the period elapsing between priming and final painting.

It is worth noting that of 355 samples of paint taken on site during a recent survey, it was found that 21 per cent of the primers were not up to the BSS.

Stopping and Filling

These are two separate operations, although generally regarded as the same; stopping applies to filling cracks and holes in the surface to be painted, while filling is making up irregularities in the surface.

Priming should be completed before stopping and filling, as the materials used for these last two operations might shrink and fall out if applied direct to untreated surfaces.

Linseed oil putty is often used as stopping, but this is unsuitable not only because it shrinks but because it often is still soft when painted, and a depression is left in the surface. Adding white lead to the putty produces a good stopping both for exterior and interior surfaces. The work should always be left proud of the surface and rubbed down with a fine sandpaper to provide a smooth and even finish.

Cellulose fillers mixed with water are suitable for internal use, and an exterior quality is available, but the Clerk of Works should check on this before work proceeds. Exterior stopping and filling must be waterproof or it will break down and allow weathering to attack the paint film.

Stopping and filling should not be accepted as a substitute for bad workmanship, especially with timber jointing, for movement of the timber and shrinkage of the stopping will only allow weathering to attack the joint, resulting in timber decay.

Undercoating

Factory priming often means that timber or steelwork remains exposed for long periods and the primer has deteriorated by the painting stage. The Clerk of Works has then to check whether touching up will be sufficient or whether repriming will be necessary.

Before the undercoat is applied, the surfaces must be sanded down and the resultant dust brushed off to provide a clean surface to receive the paint film.

Undercoats are required to provide thickness or 'body' to the paint system, as well as opacity or 'depth', and to give a colour tone which will match the finishing coat of paint. The specification may call for either one or two undercoats, and in the latter case it will be important to ensure that the first coat has thoroughly dried before the second layer of paint is applied. Rubbing down must also be carried out between coats, especially where a gloss coat will be the finishing application. Matt surfaces do not show blemishes to the same extent, although an uneven application of undercoat will still be noticeable.

Undercoating should be done in a different shade from the final coat so that progress can be inspected, and where two undercoats are applied, they should be varied slightly. Paint must not be applied to damp surfaces, and painting may have to be suspended during damp weather. The majority of paint failures are due to methods of application rather than faulty materials, and painting on damp surfaces must be high on the list.

Finishing Coats

The finishing coat is generally selected for colour, but it is also the wearing coat and must completely encase the area to be protected. Unless the application of paint is carried out properly, that is, by brushing in two directions before lightly laying off, it is possible that small areas may be left uncovered; and while this may not be obvious when the paint is fresh, it will leave weaknesses in the paint structure.

Finishing paints must be compatible with the undercoat, and should preferably be of the same brand; and because there is a variation in the basic constituents of paints today, different brands of paint should not be mixed together.

Oil-gloss paints have gradually been replaced by resin-based products, and where the painter using oil-gloss paint could adjust the balance of his materials to meet each situation, he cannot with resin-based paints, which are carefully blended and must not be interfered with or adulterated in any way. Synthetic resin-based paints have good wearing qualities and dry evenly if correctly applied, although they are more difficult to use in low temperatures.

Thinners should not be allowed except after discussions with the paint manufacturer to meet specific situations.

All finishing paints are gloss paints, but the degree of sheen varies to meet the taste of the designer. Generally full-gloss paints are used externally, but internal surfaces may be completed with a matt finish. Alternatives between these are egg-shell gloss and semi-gloss finishes, but these are more often specified for wall surfaces than timber or steel surfaces.

Before gloss finishes are applied, the surface of the undercoat must be hard and completely free from any moisture. Sanding down is essential to produce an even surface, and uneven distribution of the undercoat may well show through the gloss finish.

Special Paints

Where conditions are likely to produce mild condensation problems, the specification may call for anti-condensation paints to be used. These paints contain either cork or vermiculite as a filler capable of absorbing the initial moisture build-up, but it is essential that the paint surface has the opportunity to dry out again if the filler is to be effective. Anti-condensation paints act as insulators to the surface, reducing one of the factors in condensation; but obviously paints cannot provide a solution to condensation and other precautions will be necessary.

Flame-retardant and fire-retardant paints are also available. The former contain compounds which have a chemical reaction when subject to heat, reducing the rate at which flames can spread over the surface. The latter decompose and swell under fire conditions, creating an insulating layer over the surface and reducing the spread of the flames.

Where paint is required for surfaces subject to higher temperatures than usual, it is important to know the temperature range if advice is to be obtained from paint manufacturers. The most suitable paints are those made from silicone resins with either zinc or aluminium pigments included, but for ordinary radiators and pipes any good class resin-based paints are satisfactory.

Where resistance to alkalis or acids is required, chlorinated rubber paints may be used, and these paints are used a great deal for painting steelwork and concrete surfaces, especially in seaside areas.

In bakeries or other food-producing areas where some form of protection against bacteria is desirable, fungicidal paints may be specified, but good preparation of the surfaces will be necessary before applying the paint.

Bituminous paints may be regarded as black coatings for treatment of concrete surfaces before applying stone or marble claddings, though these paints can also be obtained in colours. They cannot be painted over with ordinary gloss paints at a later stage unless a sealer is applied first, as the bitumen would obviously bleed through the gloss paint.

Emulsion Paints

Distemper and water paints have been almost entirely replaced by emulsion paints for wall and ceiling finishes, although vinyl water paints and vinyl distempers provide cheaper forms of finish. Emulsion paints provide a tough washable surface in gloss or matt finishes; they are also very easy to apply and it is not always necessary to wait for the plasterwork to be completely dried out. There is some danger, however, where efflorescence is likely to occur on the surface behind the emulsion paint, as this will cause blistering and eventual breakdown of the paint film. Emulsion paints are manufactured from both polyvinyl acetate and acrylic resins, and can be used internally and externally, though in its liquid state the paint can be affected by frost. Acrylic emulsion paints are also used for priming and undercoats to timber surfaces, asbestos-cement sheeting, woodwool slabs, and insulation boards.

Varnishes

Polyurethane varnishes are used extensively today; they are manufactured either as single or two-pack systems, one containing the resin and the other a hardener. The single pack has a limited life once the can is opened, but the two-pack must be used immediately the base and hardener have been mixed.

Where the varnish is required for weathering on boarding, it is most important that all surfaces are sealed. If not, moisture will penetrate the timber and cause the varnish film to lift; there will be a creamy effect upon the surface as the light shines through the film, which will eventually split and break down into brittle flakes. Then it will be necessary to remove the whole of the film from the surface, preferably with a hand sanding machine, before applying a further coat of varnish.

Varnishes can be obtained in matt or high gloss finishes, and are manufactured also from alkyd resins as well as phenolic resin to produce a good hard surface. Where it is necessary to provide a surface which is resistant to abrasive action, such as may be required to timber flooring, then urethane or epoxy resins may be the most suitable either as single or two-pack preparations.

A good copal varnish properly applied is still a reliable way to achieve a clear finish to any timber surface, providing a sound base for subsequent coatings.

Apart from prestige work, most furnishings no longer are finished with french polish, but treated with either cellulose lacquers or polyurethane finishes.

Application

The Clerk of Works should check the specification for the methods which are approved for applying paint to various surfaces within the contract, as it is often assumed that brush painting only will be accepted, whereas the contractor may wish to use alternative methods. Brush application can ensure that the paint is forced into the surface of timber during priming, which is very desirable if the paint is to fulfil its purpose. Where the paint is brushed on to the surface with sufficient pressure and then lightly brushed off, an even coat can be achieved with a close textured surface. Where access to surface areas is restricted, brush application is the only method suitable, as it is also on narrow widths such as window sashes.

Roller application has many advantages in speed and quality of finish where reasonably large areas are concerned, such as walls and ceilings treated with emulsion paints. Where roller application of gloss paints is accepted, the finish can be improved by lightly brushing off the surface as it is completed – erasing the orange peel effect given by the roller as well as improving the sheen provided by gloss paint.

The large expanse of walls and ceilings which occur in cinemas and large halls can be painted more quickly and effectively by spray-gun methods. Some spray-gun finishes would not be possible by any other method, such as superimposing one colour upon another to create a marble appearance, or by blending and shading various colours into each other to produce skilful patterning. The paint is atomised by compressed air at the nozzle of the gun, and special thinners are necessary to maintain the consistency of the paint, though this must not be overdone.

An alternative method of spray painting referred to as 'airless' spray introduces compressed air into the paint container to force the paint through a high-pressure hose to the gun, which has an extremely fine orifice in the spray cap. The fog which accompanies ordinary spray painting is avoided, and the paint can be used without thinning, so providing a heavier film to the surface.

CHAPTER TWENTY-NINE

External Drainage

Drainage Systems

Approval of the local authority will be required for any drainage system to be laid in the area, and the system they approve will be dependent upon the one in existence, although certain areas now operating a combined system are gradually moving over to a separate system.

Under a combined system all soil and waste are drained into the same sewer as rainwater and surface water; the resulting effluent may then be treated in some way or discharged direct into the sea. In a separate system rainwater and surface water are collected into one drainage system and discharged into rivers or the sea, while soil and wastes are collected in a separate drainage system and directed to a sewage treatment works to be chemically treated before finally being discharged as pure water into either river or sea. The discharge of trade effluent into public sewers depends upon the nature of the effluent, and the applicant may be required to treat the effluent himself before he will be allowed to discharge it into the public sewer.

It is important for the Clerk of Works to bear in mind that the treatment of sewage can be seriously unbalanced by any excess of water discharged into the foul sewer. This can easily occur either through poorly constructed, foul manholes allowing subsoil waters to leak into them or surface water gaining access through poor finish to manhole covers. The problem can arise in other ways, as when contractors resort to pumping from the excavations direct into adjacent foul sewer manholes.

The main drainage system of the area is referred to as the public sewer, for which the local authority is entirely responsible. Owners of property are entitled to connect their own drainage to the public sewer, provided they conform with the regulations. The developer of an estate will be obliged to construct a sewer for the disposal of all soil and waste upon the estate, and this must be constructed in a manner acceptable to the local authority as that authority will probably be required to adopt the sewer at a later date.

Sewer Construction

The construction of sewers may relate to the work required in the development of an estate, or to establishing a main trunk sewer over difficult areas of the countryside. The former may quite capably be carried out by the general building contractor, but the latter is likely to be allocated to firms specialising in this type of engineering work, which may involve deep excavation and tunnelling, and long experience of the conditions likely to be met with.

Sewers are formed with spun concrete pipes, especially large diameter sewers, some of which may be reinforced to meet the initial loading upon them. A 150 mm surround of concrete is likely to be specified in a number of instances.

The pipe sizes may vary but can be obtained from 300 mm up to 1,250 mm, although pipes less than 300 mm are available as standard drainage pipes. The gradients on large sewers are very shallow, but they are calculated to carry all solids and liquids adequately, not only catering for immediate requirements but often taking into consideration future development.

The drawings for sectional layouts of sewers are produced to separate scales, the horizontal being 1 : 1,000 and the vertical 1 : 100, which can be slightly confusing in the beginning to the person reading the drawings.

Because of the depth to which they may be taken, manholes will be fully detailed on drawings and constructed in the form of a chamber, with head height of approximately 1,800 mm and a shaft extended to ground level for access.

Medium depth manholes may be constructed with concrete rings backed with concrete, but deep chambers will be constructed with engineering quality bricks in English bond in sand and cement. The channels and benching may be formed with half pipes or in mass concrete, although equally they could be formed in brickwork or glazed stoneware, but the benching will accommodate a suitable platform upon which personnel will be able to operate when carrying out maintenance work within the manhole.

On this class of work the Clerk of Works will be involved in measurement as well as inspection of work in progress.

Drainpipe Materials

Many of the changes that have occurred in the materials and methods used for the drainage of buildings over the past quarter of a century have arisen from the desire to achieve a more satisfactory system, but a proportion of them have been due to economic demands. Traditionally drains have been formed in glazed clay or earthenware pipes with spigot and socket joint sealed with tarred gaskin, sand and cement. While glazed pipes are still used extensively on a number of contracts, the jointing has been almost entirely replaced with rubber or plastic forms of jointing.

Pitch fibre pipes were probably the first serious challenge to traditional materials, as they were obtainable in greater lengths, and consequently more economic in the number of joints required; also, they were laid on a bed of sand (though this is no longer recommended practice), in contrast to the need of a concrete bed for glazed pipes.

Where settlement was likely to occur, glazed pipes were invariably replaced with cast-iron pipes sealed with lead joints, especially where the drains passed under the building. The introduction of rubber 'O' rings and plastic jointing collars, however, provided a flexible joint, making this type of drain acceptable to many authorities in place of cast iron.

The popularity of plastics has widened the choice of materials still further, with plastic drainpipes and even complete systems now in use.

Drainpipes are available in any of the following materials, and while some may be suitable for all drainage purposes, others will only be suitable under certain conditions:

Cast iron spigot and socket
Spun iron
Concrete
Vitreous enamelled salt-glazed fireclay
Salt-glazed clayware
Pitch-fibre (no longer recommended to be bedded in sand)
PVC plastic.

Drain Fittings

Wherever changes in pipe sizes occur or where the direction of pipe runs are affected, tapers or reducers, junctions and bends are available to fit cast iron, earthenware and plastic drains. Junctions must be set at a suitable angle when they are laid to avoid unnecessary use of bends, especially those referred to as acute bends. Bends are available in a number of types identified by parts of a circle – 90 degrees, 45 degrees, etc – or as $\frac{1}{4}$ bends, $\frac{1}{8}$ bends, as well as by the terms slow bends, fast bends and knuckle bends. Channels or half-pipes are used to continue the drain through the manholes and inspection chambers, and channel bends can be obtained either as half-pipe bends or as three-quarter bends for discharging over the channels.

Where the drain may have to be sealed against sewer gases, an interceptor may be specified; this is a trap to hold a water seal and includes a rodding eye sealed by a stopper.

Gullies are also trapped against escapes of sewer gases, and those joined to a separate system may have rainwater pipes connected into them by back or side inlets.

Since grease entering the drains will solidify and cause blockages, a special type of grease gulley has been designed with a metal tray to retain the grease and allow the water to escape. Grease gullies must be cleaned regularly, or grease will escape into the system. Special gullies are available where petrol is likely to be washed into the drains, to nullify its effect in a combined drainage system and prevent a possible explosion.

Inspection Chambers

Inspection chambers should be provided wherever there is a change of direction in the line of drain, or where a branch drain enters. They provide means of rodding and clearing the drain in the event of any blockage occurring.

Traditionally drains collect a number of appliances and connect them into the drain at one point, where an inspection chamber is formed. Modern practice uses fewer manholes by connecting individual appliances direct to the drain, with a rodding eye for cleaning purposes. On shallow drains the inspection chambers are constructed in brickwork or concrete rings, with a concrete base and benching, while the manhole cover is cast into a concrete slab placed on the top.

Drain-laying

In laying drains it is good practice to start at the low end of the drain, and lay the pipes from manhole to manhole, leaving junctions at appropriate positions to accommodate any future connections shown on the drawings.

All drain runs and manhole positions should be established before excavation begins by fixing pegs at appropriate levels above the pipe invert; this will highlight any problems which might be expected concerning line and level of the drainage system. The contractor will erect his profiles from the manhole pegs, and it is worth noting that these should be placed consistently to either right or left of the manholes wherever possible, to avoid any danger of the excavator operating to the wrong side of the profile when excavating the trench. It may not appear to be likely on short runs, but this problem has occurred more than once, especially on longer trench runs, and can be expensive on deep excavations. The Clerk of Works should always check the level given on the profile to ensure that the drain will be laid to the correct falls.

Profiles must be securely erected and the cross-member painted in a suitable colour to enable the boning rod or traveller to show up clearly against it.

The boning rod is a T-shaped rod and rail, with the rail painted black to show up against the profile and the rod varying in length to suit the depth of the excavation. The bottom of the rod is placed upon the base of the trench, the rail is sighted between the two profiles, and the level of the base is adjusted until the boning rod and profiles match. The 'traveller' is a boning rod, usually with a fairly long rod section, and a 'shoe' or short piece of timber fitted at the bottom; this is inserted into the invert of the pipe, which is then adjusted so that the reading of the rail and profiles again coincide.

The ability to read a boning rod will save the Clerk of Works much time otherwise used in setting up the level, and it is a ready means of spot-checking the drainage and general excavation work while it is proceeding.

The boning rod can be used to check the levels of pegs placed along the base of the trench to establish the depth for concrete or granular fill, whichever is specified, to support the pipes when completed. The pipes must be supported by packings when they are laid, to assist handling and jointing, but these packings must not be allowed to remain where plastic or pitch-fibre pipes are used, as settlement might damage the drain.

It was the practice to lay a rigid line of pipes for drainage, but modern practice favours the use of flexible joints to accommodate any settlement. This method also reduces the problems of laying, as the joints are usually a push-fit and, in consequence, the pipe-layer does not require the same working room as he does to make a sand and cement joint.

With a rigid system of drainage the pipes will be laid on a bed of concrete, and then haunched by bringing the concrete up to the level of the top of the pipe, or surrounded, by raising the concrete to the same height above the pipe as it is below.

With flexible pipes a granular fill is used to support the pipes, and it can be brought up in the same manner as the concrete to encase the pipes. Granular materials should be uniform in size with ease of compaction, the size varying in accordance with the ground conditions and size of pipes; but on normal house-type drainage, a mixture of sand gravel or broken stone passing through a 13 mm and retained on a 6 mm sieve would be suitable.

Where the base of the trench has been over-excavated or is of an unsuitable nature, it must be made up either with concrete or 'fill', but where the trench is close to the foundations of a building, the make-up must be in concrete to meet the Building Regulations. These require the trench to be filled with concrete level with the underside of the foundation where the edge of the trench is within 300 mm of the foundation. Where the distance is 300 mm or over, the concrete must be brought up to a level equal to that distance plus 50 mm: for example, where the trench may be 450 mm from the foundation and 700 mm deep, it would be necessary to fill the trench with 200 mm of concrete – $700-(450+50)=200$.

Backfilling must be carried out in layers, especially with the first few feet above the pipes, to avoid damage or displacement.

Testing Drainage
(As recommended in CP 301:1971)

All lengths of drain and all manholes and inspection chambers should be capable of withstanding the appropriate test.

Water or air tests should be applied after laying and before backfilling or placing concrete surround or bedding concrete, and will reveal cracked or porous pipes and faulty joints. Any leakage, including excessive sweating, which causes a drop in the test water level, will be visible, and the defective part of the work should be rectified. After backfilling, tests should be made and may reveal faults in the bedding or support of the pipe, inadequacies in design or accidental damage during, or subsequent to, backfilling, and show whether or not the finished work meets the specified requirements regarding watertightness.

Wherever possible, testing should be carried out from manhole to manhole. Short branch drains connected to a main drain between manholes should be tested as one system with the main drain. Long branches and manholes should be tested separately.

Water Test

Drains should generally be subjected to an internal pressure test.

The test should be carried out by inserting suitably strutted plugs in the low end of the drains and in connections, if necessary, and by filling the system with water. For small pipes, a knuckle bend may be temporarily jointed-in at the top and a sufficient length of vertical pipe jointed to it so as to provide the required test head. Alternatively, the required test head may be applied by means of a small bore pipe leading from a suitable container and connected to a plug. Precautions should be taken by strutting or otherwise to prevent any movement of the drain during testing.

Fall of the test water in the standpipe may, among other things, be due to one or more of the following causes :

(1) Absorption by pipes or joints.
(2) Sweating of pipes or joints.
(3) Leakage from defective pipes or joints or plugs.
(4) Trapped air.

Some pipes absorb more water or trap more air at the joints than others. Allowance should be made for this by adding water to maintain the test head for appropriate periods before the test is commenced.

The test before backfilling should be commenced as soon as practicable after laying but the drain should have been filled for approximately one hour, or such other period as may be agreed with the manufacturer, before test readings are taken.

A test pressure of 1·2 m head of water above the soffit of the drain should be applied at the high end but not more than 2·4 m at the low end. Steeply graded drains should be tested in stages where the above maximum head would be exceeded if the whole section were tested at once.

The loss of water over a period of 30 min should be measured by adding water from a measuring vessel at regular intervals of 10 min and noting the quantity required to maintain the original water level in the standpipe. The average quantity of water added for drains up to 300 mm nominal bore should not exceed 0·06 litre per hour per 100 linear metres per millimetre of nominal bore of the drain.

The specification for the work or the Testing Authority will usually require an additional test after completion of bedding or concrete surround, backfilling, compaction and reinstatement. Where a final water test is specified or required, it should be applied in accordance with the requirements of the specification or of the Testing Authority.

Air Test

It is often more convenient to test drains by means of internal air pressure. However, while an excessive drop in pressure when employing the air test may indicate a defective drain, the location of leakage may be difficult to detect and the leakage rate cannot be measured. Air pressure can be affected by temperature changes or by defects in the testing apparatus. Consequently, failure to pass this test is not conclusive and, when failure does occur, a water test should be made and the leakage rate determined before a decision as to acceptance or rejection is made.

The length of drain under test should be effectively plugged and the air pumped in by suitable means (e.g. a hand pump) until a pressure of 100 mm head of water is indicated in a U-tube connected to the system.

The air pressure should not fall to less than 75 mm head of water during a period of 5 min, without further pumping, after a period for requisite stabilisation. Drains which incorporate traps can be tested only to 50 mm head of water. The permissible loss is then 12·5 mm head of water in 5 min.

Infiltration Test

Tests after backfilling should include an infiltration test where the soffit of the drain, at the high part of the length under test, is more than 1·2 m below the water table.

All inlets to the system should be effectively closed. Visual inspection at manholes or inspection chambers will then reveal any flow, the cause of which should be investigated.

In small drains, points of infiltration may be located visually with a traversing light and mirrors, or by proceeding in sections with an inflated rubber plug or, when conditions justify it, with a television camera. The rate of infiltration is dependent upon so many factors that a guide to its permissible extent cannot be given and must depend on the judgement of the engineer.

Tests for Straightness and Obstruction

Tests for line, level and freedom from obstruction should be applied
wherever possible and may be carried out by means of a mirror at one end
of the drain and a lamp at the other end.

Inspection of Chambers and Manholes

If the ground water level is likely to be seasonably above the soffit of the
drain, chambers and manholes should be inspected for watertightness
against infiltration when the water table is at its highest.

Tests of Petrol Interceptors and Wet Wells

Petrol interceptors and pumping station wet wells should be tested for
watertightness by filling with water before backfilling of the excavations
is commenced. After a reasonable period has elapsed, the water level should
be made good by adding further water as required. This water level should
be maintained for 30 min without adding further water.

Records

Complete records should be kept of all tests carried out on drains, both
during construction and after being put into service.

CHAPTER THIRTY

External Works

Service Mains

Since most external works tend to make progress at that stage in the contract when the Clerk of Works finds most of his time taken up with internal finishings, he should make himself familiar with the external drawings and specifications at an earlier stage of the contract.

Water and gas mains may be laid during the progress of the structure, but testing and connecting up will not be completed until after the installation within the building has been tested and accepted by the authority.

Statutory authorities are entirely responsible for installing the mains, and, depending upon the point of entry to the site, the mains may follow a different route from each other. The advantages to be gained by co-ordinating the services so that they can be incorporated into one common trench has been recognised for many years, but attempts to achieve this on the site have met with little success.

Sometimes the services will be accommodated in the grassed area alongside footways, or even within the footpath, with the pattern of the paving arranged to provide easy access.

Where a common trench is used, both the gas and water mains should be laid first, as they require a deeper trench and a minimum cover of 900 mm to main runs and 750 mm cover to branch pipes as protection against frost and other damage. The pipes are spaced 75 mm apart, and valves will be required to both mains for the control of supplies. The water main will probably require facilities for washout points, and the gas main will require siphons for removing the condensation which occurs. Depending upon the size of the mains, concrete anchors may be necessary to resist hydraulic thrust at bends or dead-ends in the water mains, and brick chambers will be required for access to the valves.

The electric cable and ducts for the telephone mains can be laid after backfilling the section over the water and gas mains, as these only require 350 mm cover. They will be laid one on each side of the trench 75 mm away from the line of the other mains; an additional service will also be required in many instances for television.

Where the services are required to cross roads or pathways, a section of pipework can be installed earlier, or provision made by laying ducting below the formation. Where ducts are provided, it is important that they are properly marked on the drawings and on the site for those looking for them at a later date. Where ducts have not been provided, it will be necessary to consider whether it will be more economical to lay the pipes by cutting through the road formation to form a trench, or by thrust-boring from the back of the kerb position.

Boring or excavation is often carried out because the ducts cannot be traced, even when they have been provided.

Access Roads

The access roads may be excavated and blinded with hardcore temporarily at the start of the contract for the use of the contractor; such roads will obviously be well consolidated with site traffic but still require rolling to produce a true formation to receive the surface finishes.

The line of the roadways should be marked out by fixing pegs at the back of the kerb line, and the road excavated to the correct depth to receive a blinding of ash and then the hardcore. The type of hardcore to be used should be considered before the work is due to start, and approved hardcore must be clean and of a hard material. This will vary from district to district – slag, limestone, chalk, sandstone, whinstone, etc – but it must be well compacted by a mechanical roller to the specified thickness. The depth of hardcore will depend upon the amount of traffic using the road, but for ordinary access roads this will be 150–225 mm, while the width of roads may be 3·6–6·0 m.

Kerbs can be laid (1) forming a concrete base first, bedding the precast kerbs and channels in sand and cement, and backing up the kerb with concrete, or (2) by bedding the kerbs or channels direct on a semi-dry mix of concrete. Both methods provide equally satisfactory results, and are dependent upon the operator in each instance to provide a true line of kerbing.

When the base has been properly consolidated and rolled to formation, which may be to a camber or side fall, the surface will be laid with 50 mm or 38 mm of bitumen aggregate. The surface will then be rolled to the same formation as specified and prepared to receive a final wearing coat of 12 mm thick bitumen aggregate or cold asphalt. Final rolling of the surface must be accompanied by spraying with water to produce a dense finish to the bitumen or asphalt.

Concrete roads, if specified, will be laid in bays, and expansion joints will be provided either as the work is formed or cut later with special mechanical saws and filled with bitumen mastics. Mesh reinforcement will generally be used to reinforce the concrete, and care must be exercised in its positioning if it is to serve its correct purpose.

Gullies may be fixed before or after the kerb race has been laid, depending upon the type specified, but in any case it will be necessary to surround the gulley with concrete to bring it up above the gulley carrying the grid, which will of course be subjected to traffic loads. Correct distances and falls must be maintained between gullies to prevent water lying in the channels.

Paths and Pavings

Pedestrian routes may be surfaced with bituminous compounds or precast concrete flags, although certain self-binding gravels like Breedon gravel can be used.

Precast concrete edging or granite sets bedded on concrete can be used for edging the paths, or creosoted timber may be secured to timber pegs driven into the ground.

The foundation to gravel paths or bituminous compounds is made with clean hardcore blinded with ashes and rolled to produce a camber or sloping surface to receive the finishing layers. Care must be taken at this stage to provide sufficient falls in the paths without creating slopes which may be too steep, and gullies should be provided to remove any build-up of water. Surfacing paths with bituminous materials is carried out in a similar manner to roadworks, the first layer being of larger aggregate well rolled to form a foundation for the wearing coat, and creating a total thickness of finishing materials of 50 mm. Sometimes this surface is treated further with a coat of hot bitumen, and a fine layer of chippings spread over the paths to provide an additional wearing coat.

Hot rolled asphalt produces a harder and more even surface finish for footpaths, but unless grit is rolled into this surface, it can be very slippery and dangerous in certain conditions.

Breedon gravel and similar self-binding gravels should be well rolled and watered to produce the binding qualities necessary to create a satisfactory wearing surface for paving.

Precast concrete flags, hydraulically pressed, are used extensively for footpaths and can be bedded direct on to a bed of ashes or sand, although sometimes mortar is used for bedding.

Tight joints do not allow the grouting to penetrate, and wider joints are much more suitable if evenly distributed. The grout should be a weak sand and cement mix which will avoid the cracking produced by stronger mixes, and make subsequent maintenance simpler.

Wherever it is desired to overcome changes in level or to discourage pedestrians from walking in certain areas, cobble paving may be used. This is laid on a sub-base of concrete and bedded into a sand and cement mix, then grouted over, the grout brushed in with a semi-dry mix to avoid marking the texture of the cobbles.

Landscaping

This work can be divided into earth-shaping and then planting and seeding, and the Clerk of Works should be considering the requirements when work starts upon the site.

This is when the valuable topsoil is stripped from the surface and stored for re-use. On smaller sites there may be time to re-consider the positions for storage or reshaping of mounds, but on the large sites, where heavy and expensive machines are operating, there will be little time for such delay.

The Clerk of Works should have sufficient information at an early stage to be able to check the contours which are to be produced when earth-moving begins, and the areas where both topsoil and surplus excavated materials are to be stored. The contractor will require this information before he can proceed with the work, but if the Clerk of Works does not have it, he will be unable to carry out his task of supervision. Drawings will give the finished contours and the quantities and disposal of materials should be available from the bills.

The Clerk of Works should take particular note of the methods for stripping the topsoil, and ensure there is no subsoil included, which can very easily happen where there is a variation in the thickness of topsoil throughout the site. Valuable topsoil will also be lying over areas to be mounded and these should be stripped first. The heights of topsoil mounds should be restricted if the material is not to be unsuitable by the time it becomes necessary for re-use; these matters will be included in the specification and should be noted by the Clerk of Works.

In order that he can maintain a close check upon the levels for embankments and mounding the Clerk of Works should insist upon pegs being fixed for contours, enabling him to check them without having to resort constantly to the level.

Land drainage is essential, especially where mounds are created, and all broken land drains must be reinstated. Traditional materials may be used for land drainage, though perforated plastics and pitch-fibre can be installed with greater ease.

Once debris has been removed, the surface must be broken up and the layer of topsoil spread to the thickness quoted in the bills, which will depend on whether the area is to be grassed or planted with shrubs. Generally, grassed areas require 150 mm of topsoil spread over the area and shrubs need at least 300 mm. Specially dug pits filled with soil and humus will be necessary for tree planting, the depth of the pit depending upon the age of the tree. Mature trees can be planted, but special arrangements will be required for transporting and planting, as these trees are removed from their source with the root formation still intact within a block of earth. The depth and size of the pit to receive these trees will depend upon the size of the tree bole, and, once planted, stays and wires will be needed to restrain any movement until the tree becomes established.

All trees require firm staking, otherwise they will be damaged by winds and subjected to vandalism. Shrubs must be planted at the spacings detailed in the drawings and bills and in the correct order as shown in the planting schedules. The maintenance clause usually calls for the plants which fail during the liability period to be replaced, but this is no reason for the Clerk of Works to allow materials which do not meet with the specification to be planted.

Grassed areas must be completely free from builder's debris, and the top 150 mm should be free from stones and brought to a fine tilth ready for sowing. Levels must be carefully checked to ensure that there is natural drainage, and where grassed areas meet with pavings and manholes, they should be raised by 50 mm to enable mowing machines to operate without causing damage.

Small areas may be sown by hand, but machines will deal more efficiently with larger areas. Slopes which are manageable can be turfed or the banks reinforced with hemp or fibre matting before mechanical sowing. Grassed areas require cutting twice during the maintenance period, and the first cut should be made by rotary cutter when the grass is 150 mm high.

The seasons for planting and seeding are defined but can be either reduced or extended according to the weather conditions prevailing at the time. Seeding can be carried out between March and September and tree and shrub planting between September and March. These factors highlight the need for careful planning, for failing to complete an operation within the period means that no further work is possible for at least six months.

Preparation of the ground is of vital importance, and the Clerk of Works will find greatest difficulty in the first task of ensuring that the contractor removes all debris from the areas to be cultivated. Once an area has been prepared for landscaping protective measures must be provided to prevent builders' debris spoiling it. Plate 16 illustrates how vehicles from other parts of the site have shed part of their load, which has been allowed to accumulate on a finished area. This will create difficulties for the landscape contractor when he moves on to the site, and could result in additional costs for the client.

Part Four

CHAPTER THIRTY-ONE

Domestic Hot-water Supplies

Hot-water Systems

The term 'domestic hot-water' system does not necessarily mean it is
intended for use only for housing purposes, it merely makes a distinction
between hot-water supplies and central heating installations. The design
for a domestic hot-water system will be dictated by the particular requirements of the building: for example, hospitals and hotels will have far
greater demands for hot-water supplies than either housing or blocks of
flats, while office blocks, schools or factories will be dependent entirely
upon the layout and distribution of the toilet accommodation.

Hot water may be supplied either through 'direct' or 'indirect' systems,
and while both equally produce hot water, there are advantages to be
gained in choosing the correct system for the circumstances. In the 'direct'
system the water is heated by a boiler, and then it is circulated to a storage
cylinder, but as the hot water is drawn off from the cylinder, it is directly
replaced with cold water from the supply tank. Owing to the water
constantly being changed throughout the system, there is a danger of
corrosion in some soft-water districts, or of both the pipes and boiler
being furred up with lime deposits in hard-water areas. With the 'indirect'
system the water is heated within the boiler and then circulated through
the primary flow and return to a calorifier or storage cylinder. This is
designed so that the heated water in the primary circulators also heats
the water in the storage cylinder. Because the same water is continuously
circulating between the boiler and the calorifier, the 'indirect' system is

particularly suitable for use in districts where hard or corrosive soft water occurs.

Any water lost through expansion in the sealed system between the calorifier and the boiler is replaced from a separate cold-water feed tank connected direct to the boiler.

Since the water in the storage cylinder will expand when it gets hot, a vent or expansion pipe is taken from the top of the cylinder to discharge over the cold-water feed tank. A similar precaution is taken on the indirect system with the boiler and the expansion feed tank.

On a simple 'direct' system the hot water is distributed to the draw-off points from a connection to the expansion pipe just above the cylinder. In these circumstances the primary flow and return pipes should be kept as short as possible by siting the cylinder close above the boiler position; this will reduce the amount of resistance in the flow and return. A layer of hot water can be made quickly available by fitting the flow well up on the cylinder, and keeping the return pipe reasonably low will reduce the possibility of hot and cold water mixing. Where the distance from the secondary circulation to the draw-off point is too great to prevent cold water being drawn off, a secondary return will be introduced by returning the distribution pipe from the draw-off point and connecting it near the top of the cylinder, but below the level of the primary flow.

The secondary circulation depends upon the 'circulating pressure or head' created by the difference in density between the hot and cold water. This increases with the difference between the mean heights of the secondary flow and return. If this value is insufficient to promote circulation, a pump will be installed to provide the necessary 'head'.

The advantages of an 'indirect' system are that it enables a far wider range of boilers to be used, because it removes the problem of hard or corrosive water, and that it can be extended to include a radiator system.

Where the water is suitable and the system is only required for domestic hot water, it is likely that the direct system will be chosen. Where corrosive waters are present, cast-iron boilers can be given protection by treatment with the Bower-Barff process, which produces a magnetic iron oxide on the surface of the cast iron by heating it to a very high temperature and then subjecting it to a current of superheated steam.

Although it is recommended that the water temperatures in storage cylinders should not exceed 65°C, these temperatures are sufficient to drive off the gases from the bicarbonates of calcium or magnesium which are suspended in hard water, converting them into insoluble carbonates which are then deposited on the walls of the system. Deposits are greatest where the maximum heat occurs, in the boiler, and facilities should be provided for cleaning them off. Uneven deposits can create stresses in cast-iron boilers which may fracture them.

Distribution Pipes

While the design for hot-water distribution pipes will be affected by the layout of the building, the diameter of the pipes will be dictated by the number of draw-off points, the maximum demand of any one period, and the head available. The design will also ensure that the temperature of the water is not allowed to decrease too far on the return pipes.

The pipe from the cold-water feed tank will supply any water drawn off from the storage cylinder, and as this quantity depends upon the distribution of the hot-water pipes, the diameter of the feed pipe will vary. It should not be less than 22 mm, however, and where there is a danger of furring-up, the minimum should be 25 mm.

Secondary circulation pipes will be reduced in diameter as the system is extended, but these sizes will be shown on the hot-water layout drawings. The return pipes will generally be reduced slightly in diameter from those on the flow, but there may be exceptions to this rule. The primary circulation pipes on a direct system will be calculated to accommodate any furring-up which might occur, and while this problem does not apply to an indirect system, quick circulation is necessary in providing maximum heat to the calorifier for heating the water in the storage cylinder. Draw-off points should not be connected to the primary system at any time.

Facilities must be provided on vertical risers for air to be released wherever it may accumulate, and this can be achieved by a separate vent pipe, an automatic air vent, or by positioning taps at the highest point of the system.

The length of any hot-water distribution pipe from the hot-water storage unit must not exceed 12 m for tube up to 19 mm bore, 8 m for tube exceeding 19 mm but not exceeding 25 mm, and 3 m for tube exceeding 25 mm bore, without the provision of a secondary return.

Distribution pipes are defined by the water authorities as 'any pipe other than an overflow or flushpipe, conveying water from storage cisterns or from a hot water apparatus, cylinder or tank'. On high buildings distribution may be achieved by an 'up-feed' system consisting of vertical risers flow and return, from which distribution pipes may be taken to service each level.

Where there is a heavy draw-off on the lower floors of a high building, installing a hot-water head tank at the top of each riser will provide a reserve supply which can be drawn upon by upper floors when the demands are heavy below. A further method is the 'drop-system', in which the flow riser delivers hot water direct to a feed tank and all the taps are fed from a series of drops. This system requires the flow main to be run at roof level, which can provide further problems.

Independent Systems

An independent supply of hot water is referred to as a 'local' system, and implies that the heater is placed close to the supply point. Electricity and gas probably provide the most suitable heat sources for this type of hot-water supply, and electrical or gas units will produce either small or large quantities of hot water. They can be combined with a normal cylinder and feed tank, or act as completely integrated units supplying up to 2,275 litres capacity.

Small domestic systems may be required to operate from cast-iron or copper boilers built into combination ranges, or fitted as small independent boilers operating from gas or solid fuel.

Free standing boilers may be manufactured from cast iron or steel finished in vitreous enamel, or can be cast iron and enclosed in an enamelled metal box so that they are acceptable as installations in domestic kitchens or similar rooms.

CHAPTER THIRTY-TWO

Heating and Ventilation

Heating

The Clerk of Works is not expected to have an extensive knowledge of heating systems, but in order that he can interpret the drawings and inspect the work as it proceeds, he must have an understanding of the principles involved.

There are two basic differences in heating methods, although there are numerous systems of heating. The first and best known method is where the fuel is actually burned in the area where heating is required, and includes solid-fuel fires and stoves; gas-burning devices such as convector heaters, radiators, gas fires, etc; oil-burning units; and electrical appliances. The second method is much more complex, for heat is manufactured at one point by oil, gas, electricity or solid fuel, and sent through pipes and ducts by means of hot water, steam or hot air.

Hot-water Systems

By raising the temperature of the water so that it circulates by convection, hot water at one point can be moved elsewhere, and circulation can be assisted still further by a centrifugal pump in the system. The temperature of the water will normally be raised to just below boiling point (82·2°C) to produce a low pressure hot-water system which will provide heat to radiators, ceiling heating panels, or pipe coils embedded in the floor screeds.

By increasing the pressures at which the hot water is retained, the temperature can be raised well in excess of boiling point, enabling much larger areas to be heated. Pressure can be increased by maintaining a head of steam within the boiler, or by introducing compressed air from a cylinder or an engine into the boiler, and this prevents the water from boiling.

High pressure hot-water systems make use of pumped circulation, and are used on large industrial installations. They can be taken long distances if well lagged and the level of pipe runs is not critical. Since a high temperature is achieved, there are fewer problems regarding heat losses; and as the circulation is maintained by pumping, the mean temperature is consistent. This form of heating can be used for a large number of manufacturing processes, besides providing heat through unit heaters, pipe coils, panel heaters, etc, and the amount of heat can be adjusted within fine limits. Because the temperature available is high throughout, it enables smaller diameter pipes to be used; and by using calorifiers, hot water supplies can be provided where required.

Medium pressure hot-water systems operate at a much lower temperature and are pressured externally by cylinder. They are suitable for small factory installations, as they operate with almost the same pressure parts as a LPHW system but will run strip heating, unit heaters and radiant panels with equal success.

Domestic hot-water systems can be adapted to provide heating by utilising an indirect cylinder for hot-water supply and a small electrically driven pump on the heating circuit. This method enables the same quantity of hot water within the system to be circulated at a fairly high velocity through small bore pipes connected to radiators in a 'loop' arrangement. Smaller bore pipes and advances with the type of valve connected to the radiators are helping to improve this system of heating. The pump and the boiler operate by thermostatic controls, and the pipes can be exposed or hidden without detracting from the decorations within the dwellings.

Warm-air Heating

Warm air is distributed through a series of metal ducts which end in registers or grilles in the areas to be heated, and the system can be employed on small or large installations.

The air is usually drawn through a grille placed in an external wall and heated for a small installation by gas or electricity in special units, after which it circulates by fan or convection to rooms by the ducting and is controlled by the setting of the registers. The heater unit is generally placed in a central position in the building, which reduces the amount of ducting necessary. Where the unit is placed within a cupboard or store, it is essential that there is sufficient free circulation of air around it, that adequate grille area is provided to admit cold air to it, and that doors are fire-proofed on the internal face.

On large installations the principle is the same, though where the cold air is drawn through the grille on the external wall, it will be filtered through a series of glass-fibre mats to remove any particles of dirt. The air is then passed through a battery heated by hot water or steam to increase its temperature before it is distributed through a series of ducts by a centrifugal fan driven by electricity.

As the air cools, it is drawn into an extract duct network which carries the cooler air back to the intake point, where it is recycled through the heater battery together with the intake of cold air. Warm-air heating can be used in conjunction with ordinary hot-water radiators or convector systems.

Steam Heating

Steam operates under pressures, and is similar to hot water in that it can be used at low, medium and high pressures, all of which are naturally above boiling point. Temperatures below this operate as vapour or vacuum systems. Convectors, radiant panels and unit heaters are generally used on the lower pressures, which require larger pipes than systems with a high pressure.

The pressure at the boiler will probably be lowered by a reducing valve, as this helps to overcome any water being carried over into the system and creating 'water hammer'.

The steam will develop into a condensate as it passes through the system, and will be drained off through a steam trap which allows the condensate to escape but keeps back the steam. This condensate may be allowed to drain away, or it may be collected in a tank and pumped back to the boiler for reheating.

Steam heating may be used for factories and workshops, where the system can also be used for industrial purposes, and steam may be used as primary feed to calorifiers to provide hot water for various requirements.

Pipework

In general, pipework should follow the line of the walls, steelwork, etc, with a clearance of not less than 50 mm from either pipe or lagging.

Pipes should be laid to a slight gradient to ensure adequate venting and drainage, and supported in a manner which will allow free movement for expansion and contraction. Rising mains should be properly supported to restrain the loading, and must not be supported by means of the branch pipes.

Joints must not be located within the thickness of walls or partitions, and where pipes pass through walls, mild steel sleeves should be built in to project 6 mm from the finished surfaces. Open ends should be blanked off to avoid damage to or debris entering the pipes during the progress of the works.

Welded joints must be butt-welded, and all branches, bosses, or drain-off points must be inspected to ensure that the pipe is not projecting into the main run and that welding metal is not restricting the bore.

Made-up bends can be of more advantage than fittings, but sharp bends made with gussets should not be accepted. Where trapped air is likely to occur, square connections may be preferable to long sweep fittings. The highest point in the section should be vented, though this information will be shown on the drawings.

Fittings will be supplied with flange joints, and these should be made up with full face joint rings and securely bolted.

Pipe Supports and Anchors

Supports should be provided in such a manner that there will be no resistance to expansion or contraction, and they should be fitted as close as possible to joints or changes in the direction of pipe-runs. Each pipe support must take an equal share of the total loading and be truly aligned to ensure a straight line of pipework. Where pipes are suspended from high level brackets cast in the soffit of concrete slabs, they can end in pipe-rings or adjustable hangers, but are best fitted to angle iron or uni-struts.

Brackets used as anchors should be welded to the pipework, and where this cannot be achieved, cast iron seatings should be secured with wrought-iron stirrup bolts, with plenty of thread showing when they are tightened up.

Where an expansion loop or bellows is fitted into the pipework, the brackets should be secured on either side of the expansion so that the movement will operate according to the design.

Where the pipes are supported on rollers, this fact will be shown in the details for the type of brackets to be used, and they should be fixed in accordance with the drawing.

Spacing of brackets will depend upon the size of pipes, and where two pipes or more are fitted on a common bracket, the bracket spacing must accommodate the requirements of the smaller pipe rather than the larger.

Builders' Work

The Clerk of Works must study the drawing carefully, noting the line of pipe-runs and sizes, which may affect constructional work and must also be considered with regard to supporting brackets and holes through floors and walls. The layout of plant and apparatus in the boiler-house and plant rooms must be thoroughly checked for position and height of bases, and for any ducting which may be required within the floor thickness. Entry of services into boiler-houses can create difficulties if not catered for at the proper time, especially where there may be site problems with water levels and the boiler-house is below ground. If fuel is stored within the building, delivery arrangements will have to be considered.

Bases for the boilers and other equipment must be set out together to avoid errors, and plinths supporting steel-frame bases must be to the correct height to avoid unnecessary packings. Bases and plinths for pumps, tanks and calorifiers may be constructed in engineering brickwork with bullnose brickwork to arrises; the mortar should be in sand and cement and all joints and perpends solidly built up. Where the shapes for plinths make it necessary to use concrete, the position of all cut-outs and pockets must be checked and provision made for holding-down bolts. If the plinths and bases are to be finished with clay tiling to form part of the floor finish, it will be advisable to check their positions with regard to tile sizes, allowing for both internal and external angles.

Where gas or oil-fired boilers are used, their bases may be specified as concrete and finished with clay tiling, but for solid-fuel boilers it will be necessary to form heat-resisting bases that will also allow the withdrawal of ashes from below the fire-box. Engineering quality bricks will be used as edging to form a bullnose to all external angles, and the centre filled with fire-brick and sloping towards the rear of the boiler. In some instances the infilling may be carried out with heat-resistant concrete, using an aggregate similar to Fossalsil.

Pipe ducts and air ducts may be required in the construction work, and if the latter are constructed in brick or blockwork, it will be important that they are solidly built.

Vertical service ducts must be carefully aligned to prevent pipes having to be fixed out of alignment, and opening sizes and position will require checking as suspended floors are laid. Floor ducts are often designed very tight for size and the Clerk of Works should see that there is no reduction in the specified sizes. Changes of direction are also likely to provide problems to the pipe-fitters if the pipes are not correctly positioned on the correct centre-line.

Fixing points for supporting brackets may require inclusion in the structural work, and they should be checked during the erection of the formwork if they are specified in reinforced concrete structures. Anchor points may be required for pipe-work, and their positions should be checked, as well as their details, where they may be in concrete block form; other anchor points may be merely additional bracket positions.

Pipes may also be continued externally on trestles, and these will require careful setting out at an early stage if the bases to receive the trestles are to be ready. The bases will be similar to stanchion bases in that they will require pockets for holding-down bolts, and the levels must be accurate. Trestles may also be required to carry flue ducting to chimneys, and where these are constructed some time before the ducting is erected, the accuracy of the connections must be closely watched.

Ventilation

Natural ventilation may be achieved temporarily by opening doors and windows, but more permanent means must also be provided. Open-air grilles can be incorporated in the structure, but these are invariably blocked off by occupants who object to cold air during spells of inclement weather. Hit-and-miss ventilators can also be installed but again these may be closed.

Adequate ventilation, especially in workshops and factories where harmful fumes and dust may occur, can only in fact be provided either by mechanical means or in the form of a purpose-designed natural system. The Factories Act requires ventilation to be provided in certain types of factory, and this may be done by fitting large extraction fans in the roof to create circulation and air changes by withdrawing the dust and fumes.

More refined systems require the installation of metal ducting, with grilles opening over those areas where dust and fumes are present. Fume-laden air is withdrawn by an extract fan in a chamber at the end of the main duct, and fresh air is drawn in to replace it through grilles in the external wall or through intake ducts.

To overcome the resistance created within a ducted system it will be necessary to use either an axial flow or a centrifugal fan. Special types of fan suitable for intake or extract ventilation are available for fitting into external walls or window frames, but while they provide a solution in certain instances, the extent of their use is limited.

Ventilation Ducting

Supports and brackets that are to be built-in should be supplied to the contractor early in the contract and fitted to provide correct alignment in securing the ducting.

Ducting may be galvanised, with mild steel angle stiffeners, and where any cuts are made in the ducting for access doors or branches, the metal must be protected with zinc paint or a similar product. Other forms of ducting available are of aluminium, plastics or even hardboard.

After delivery to site, the ducting must be properly stored, together with other equipment, such as fans, motors, silencers, etc, and protected against damage until fitted into the building. Dampers and mid-feathers, if fitted, should be checked for finish and gauge, and access panels, when provided at dampers or other points, should have properly framed openings. Ducting should have flanged joints to facilitate dismantling for cleaning or repairs, and holes should be drilled around the flanges to receive 6–8 mm diameter sherardised bolts and nuts. The joints should be sealed with a jointing compound or approved neoprene or similar gaskets.

Diffusers and grilles will be fitted as shown on the drawings, and should be aligned and secured.

Where necessary, the ducting will be isolated from the structure to prevent vibration, and fans must also be carefully mounted and bolted down.

Insulation will be necessary to overcome the problems of condensation on the ventilation ducting, and this will be fitted to supply, recirculation and extract ducting. The insulation might be glass-fibre quilting sealed over with a plastic vapour seal compound. The insulation to external ducting may be cork slabs sealed after fixing with an aluminium waterproofing compound.

Air Conditioning

The Regulations require a certain number of air changes to be provided to factories and workplaces to remove toxic fumes and steam, etc, which might otherwise affect the occupants. Public buildings must also be provided with a proper ventilation system. Air conditioning is a system of treating the air to provide a controlled temperature and humidity, and this is done by warming the air where it is cold to begin with and vice versa. Humidity is controlled by exposing damp air to cold surfaces so that excess moisture will condense and be removable, or adding moisture to warm dry air by passing it through a fine spray.

With a fully air-conditioned system, the outside air is drawn into the building by an intake fan through a series of filters to remove the atmospheric dirt before passing it to the air-conditioning plant room containing heater batteries, air washers, and a refrigeration plant. The treated air is then directed through a duct system to the areas where it is needed, and the air already in circulation in those areas is returned by an extract ducted system to the plant room, together with a controlled amount of fresh air. Recirculating the air instead of continually introducing fresh air into the system helps reduce expense. Where toxic fumes are present in the atmosphere, it will not be possible to return air to the plant room unless it is treated first.

In essence the system works by drawing fresh air through a ventilator grille in the external wall; and after passing through filters to remove the atmospheric dirt, the air may also pass a heater to remove fog. Before reaching the intake fan, it will pass a fabric type filter, and then through air cooling coils and a washer consisting of sprayed water which creates a fine mist. The air then passes above a series of 'scrubber' plates over which a constant stream of water is running, and then on to eliminator plates which drain away the excess moisture and return it for re-use. In summer the cooling coils are supplied with chilled water and the water to the sprays is cooled by the refrigeration plant, while in winter the cooler is cut off and the water to the spray is warmed by a heat exchanger on the pump delivery side.

The whole system is controlled by instruments to ensure that heat changes will activate the equipment in the plant treatment room and so provide air at a fairly constant temperature all round.

CHAPTER THIRTY-THREE

Fire Precautions

Water Supplies

Fire hydrants will be required at strategic points, and must be clearly identified as well as being accessible. Too often they are partly buried under landscaping operations. Underground hydrants are normally provided with a brick chamber and sealed off with a cast-iron box cover with removable lid. The outlet is designed to receive a standpipe connection which is fitted with a breach-piece to enable two fire hoses to be connected. Water pressures vary, but sufficient water pressure is vital to a fire hydrant and a minimum head of 30 m is normally required.

Dry risers will be required for use on high buildings. These are large diameter pipes provided from ground floor level throughout the full height of the building. A double-inlet breach-piece is installed to the external face of the wall at ground floor level, and outlets provided at each floor level, again in accessible areas. This arrangement enables the fire brigade to connect up hydrants to the ground floor inlet, and to operate hoses at any particular floor level if necessary.

Wet risers become necessary where water pressures are insufficient, and the height at which this happens varies throughout the country; in some parts any building over 15 m high will be affected and in other areas buildings over 60 m high can be fitted with dry risers.

Wet risers are provided by connecting up to a pumped supply so that the pipes are always filled with water. In some cases it may be sufficient to use roof storage tanks to meet the requirements. Where pumped supplies are used, it will be necessary to have a duplicate pump available in case one should break down.

Foam inlets will be required wherever inflammable liquids are stored, as in oil stores and boiler-houses. The inlet must be clearly marked and readily accessible to the fire brigade.

Hose Reels

Modern hose reels are referred to as hydraulic hose reels, and consist of a metal reel which revolves around a hollow shaft connected direct to the rising main. The hose is a reinforced rubber tube of approximately 19 mm bore fitted with a stop-valve. The supply is usually a 50 mm water main with a 25 mm connection to the reel. Sometimes the isolating valve or stop-valve is manually operated, but more often it is automatic, providing a flow of water immediately the reel is rotated and enabling one person to operate the hose reel in case of emergency.

Hose reels are hinged so that they can be folded back into recesses within the walls, and then easily pulled out as the hose is drawn from the reel in the event of fire.

In factories and similar buildings they will be installed in positions such that they may provide suitable protection to at least 836 m² of floor area; and in buildings where there are several floors reels will be positioned at the ends of corridors to each landing so that they are capable of reaching all areas within each floor. Hose reels are usually 21-24 m long; they can be obtained as long as 36 m, but these are not considered suitable by many fire authorities.

Hose reels should be available for use when the finishing work is proceeding to the building, and this availability will give a measure of protection at a time when there are positive fire hazards that might affect completion of the contract. Hose reels are of little use if they are inoperative when required, and a check will be made by the fire officer before a certificate is issued on completion of the building.

Sprinkler Systems

Specialist engineering firms are nominated for the installation of sprinkler systems, as both equipment and workmanship must be of a standard to ensure reliability. Any failure might result in the building being completely gutted by fire. The Clerk of Works should appreciate exactly what is required from the installation and satisfy himself that the work is proceeding correctly.

Sprinkler systems are designed as either wet or dry systems, with water supplied from pressure tanks or mains supplies, although other stored sources may be used.

Dry systems are used where there is danger of frost affecting the water in a wet system; the pipes are charged with air pressure instead of water, so that when the valve on the sprinkler head opens, the air is released and the system automatically fills with water.

The sprinkler head is probably the most important part of the system, being a specially designed valve which opens at a predetermined temperature and releases a jet of water under pressure. A deflector in the head of the sprinkler causes the water to be sprayed over an area of 4·5 to 9·0 m² of ceiling and floor. There are two ways of controlling the valve on the sprinkler head: (1) by fusible solder which melts at a recommended temperature and releases the valve, and (2) by using a small glass bulb containing a liquid which expands under heat to burst the bulb, at the predetermined temperature and release the valve. Bulbs are manufactured to operate at different temperatures, identified by the colour of the liquid. Systems are designed so that the sprinklers will only operate in the area where a fire occurs, avoiding damage being caused throughout a building. Immediately the system is brought into operation in any area, an alarm will be released, and this should be tested at intervals once the system has been installed.

Where there is any possibility of damage to the sprinkler heads in any areas, they will be fitted with guards, and this point should be noted during the construction.

Steel or wrought-iron pipes will be used for the installation, and all jointing screwed and threaded. Pipes should be treated with one coat of corrosion-resistant primer before delivery, and the final coat should be colour-coded according to the standard recommendations for service pipes.

The system must be thoroughly tested upon completion.

The insurance company concerned with the building will have certain requirements in connection with the sprinkler system which must be observed.

Working drawings and a layout of the system as fixed must be supplied by the sprinkler engineers for the use of the client when the contract is completed.

CHAPTER THIRTY-FOUR

Lifts and Escalators

Types of Lift

Passenger-carrying lifts vary according to the buildings in which they are installed; in small blocks of offices or flats the lift may only cater for four to twelve persons, whereas in department stores, large office blocks and places of entertainment lifts carrying ten to twenty-six persons at any one time are needed, often in pairs or in banks of three or more.

Hospitals require lifts to be capable of carrying passengers and also hospital beds or stretchers, and some of them have entrances from either side of the shaft, although single entrances are normally recommended.

Goods lifts operate at slower speeds than passenger lifts as a general rule, and are capable of carrying loads of 0·5–5 tonnes.

Small service lifts are installed for delivering documents, etc, between offices at different floor levels, or from vaults in banking departments, and are also used for transporting food from kitchens to dining rooms in restaurants. These lifts are usually supplied in an assembled form ready to be installed in the lift shaft, and their motors are normally situated in the lower part of the installation rather than over the shaft, as with the larger lifts.

Builders' Work

Although in some high rise blocks it may be necessary to arrange for installation of the lift while construction work is continued to upper levels, in general the builder's work should be completed before the lift engineers begin theirs. The contractor is responsible for the construction of the shaft and lift pit, as well as the machine room, which is usually situated over the head of the shaft. Door openings must be provided at all landings it is intended the lift will service, and a datum level must be provided on each floor landing to establish the finished floor level.

The contractor will be expected to provide and install the lifting beam in the motor room, and he may be expected to build in brackets to secure the lift shaft guides or merely provide pockets for the brackets to be grouted in by the lift engineers. Pockets will also be required to accommodate boxes for call-buttons and indicators.

Steel joists may be used to carry the floor of the motor room, but probably this will be constructed in reinforced concrete. Holes required to accommodate cables and lifting gear must be accurately positioned.

The depth of the lift pit will be shown on the drawings, and this will be related to the speed and loading of the lift car. A clearance is required between the underside of the car and the bottom of the pit when the buffers are totally compressed. The lift pit must be dry, and, if necessary, some form of tanking provided, and the pit must be cleared of all water and debris before the lift engineers will be able to start work.

Scaffolding must also be provided for the use of the engineers, together with all the necessary safety precautions throughout the installation of the lift car and equipment.

Tolerances

Dimensions must not be less than those given on the drawings issued by the manufacturer. Tolerances in the lift shaft must be checked at regular intervals during the construction by suspending a plumb-bomb on piano wire over the centre of the lift pit. In a lift shaft 30 m high the tolerances should be no greater than 25 mm, otherwise the lift manufacturer may be entitled to additional payments for carrying out adjustments to the installation. The diagonals of the lift well must be carefully checked, for errors in them can create problems when installation begins, and cannot be easily remedied without seriously affecting the progress of the work.

Programme

This should be agreed early in the contract in order that the installation will fit in with the construction programme. Motor room and lift shaft must not only be complete but must also be waterproof before equipment can be installed.

It may be necessary on certain types of contract to make use of the lift during construction operations, and in that case the date of its installation will be laid down in the contractor's programme.

Deliveries of equipment will have to be considered because of the question of storage, which must be adequate to prevent any damage to the equipment. Steelwork intended for painting within the contract must be ready primed before delivery, and, of course, must be given protection if not fitted immediately.

The contractor will also be obliged to provide temporary power supply for the installation of the lift, and this must be available at the correct stage in the operations if work is not to be delayed.

Power and Lighting

Supplies to the lift must be isolated from the mains supply and be available in the motor room or any other area where lift equipment is housed. Lighting in the lift car must be on a separate circuit so as to remain on in the event of an emergency. It must be provided in the lift pit as well as at the top of the lift shaft.

Lifts are normally powered by single or two-speed a/c motors for speeds between 30 and 60 m/minute, and by d/c motors and generators used with variable voltage controls for speeds up to 120 m/minute. Where speeds of 120 m/minute and more are required, gearless equipment will no doubt be provided.

Although they are only operative for limited heights, hydraulic lifts are still available. They have a very smooth action and require little maintenance, but they move at slower speeds than electrically powered ones. They work from a hydraulic ram situated below the lift car, and the ram is operated by oil provided under pressure by an electric motor to a cylinder. Telescopic rams, which are available, do away with the necessity to provide a shaft within the lift pit to accommodate the length of the ram.

Inspection

When the lift has been completely installed, the equipment will be tested and a certificate issued by the manufacturer to that effect. Where it is intended to make use of the lift to continue the progress of the work, the contractor will be held responsible for the lift and its subsequent inspection before handover of the finished works. It will be necessary right from the beginning for the doors and interior of the lift car to be adequately protected, and while there is little doubt that the use of lifts on high buildings can help the progress of the work, it is advisable for the contractor to employ one man to operate the lift throughout this period to avoid vandalism and possible accidents.

Ventilation should be provided to both lift shaft and motor room to prevent smoke building up in these areas in the event of fire.

Escalators

Department stores and passenger terminals at airports and railways provide easy access from one level to another by installing escalators, whose maximum height should not be greater than 6 m and speed (for this height) not more than 30 m/minute.

The steps on escalators are connected to chains which operate in such a way as to transport passengers at an incline of 30–35° while the steps remain horizontal. The handrails move in the same direction as the steps and are positioned at a height between 840 mm and 1,040 mm above the nosing of the steps, with the balustrading either in solid panels or laminated glass.

Where the escalator intersects with ceiling levels, guards must be provided, unless there is a distance greater than 600 mm from the centre-line of the handrail to the intersection with the ceiling. Access to all machinery parts and equipment must be secured against unauthorised entry, although access must be available for maintenance. A separate circuit is required for balustrade lighting, and a permanent light must be provided over machinery spaces, together with a three-pin socket outlet.

Starting switches should be of the key-operated type, situated at each end of the escalator, and stop switches must be provided in conspicuous and accessible positions, but protected against accidental operation. Suitable notices should also be fitted at the approaches to the escalator at both top and bottom to warn passengers before they step on.

CHAPTER THIRTY-FIVE

Electric Power and Lighting

Main Supplies

The main intake cable supplying electricity will be laid within the boundaries of the consumer's premises by the local electricity board. The supply for buildings will be brought in at basement or ground floor level and connected to a main fused unit. On a large scale development or in an industrial building the supply cable will be taken direct to a sub-station before being distributed to other sections of the development.

Power supplies may be described as low, medium and high voltage, with a normal domestic installation requiring a low voltage single-phase supply, usually 240–250 volts. Medium voltage is necessary for schools, public buildings, etc, with a three-phase supply of 415 volts. The requirements for industrial use are often heavy and high voltage is necessary to meet the demand; the cable will supply 11,000 volts and be taken into a transformer chamber.

Domestic Supplies

The supply cable should be brought into stores, garage, or porch unit, where meters will be accessible for the inspectors who have to read them. The cable will be connected into the board's main fuse box before being connected to one of two types of consumer unit – a switch fuse control unit or a consumer's supply control unit.

The distribution from the control unit will provide lighting, power and cooker wiring circuits, the number of socket outlets being controlled by the regulations and rating.

Power supplies will be on a ring circuit, enabling additional points to be added quite easily, while the lighting circuit will be on a 'loop-in' method. The cooker unit circuit is usually separate, and fitted with a minimum 30 amp fuse or circuit-breaker. To protect the ring circuit from being overloaded, electrical appliances should be fitted with fused connections that will break down before the fuses in the circuit.

Large Installations

Distribution of electrical supplies from the main intake may be by ring main, rising main, or the radial method.

With the ring main, the cable is laid around the site in the form of a ring, and cables are taken from this ring to whatever distribution boards are required in buildings or groups of buildings. This method of installation enables sections of the supply to be cut off without affecting the whole of the service.

A rising main system is the usual method for supplying tall buildings: sub-mains cables are carried within vertical ducts to the full height of the building, and connections are made at separate floor levels to distribution panels.

Where groups of buildings are erected around a large site, the radial method of distribution may be used, with service cables radiating from the main intake to distribution panels in groups of buildings or single buildings. More than one cable may be necessary to supply lighting and power where machinery and heavy plant is operating.

A special room will be set aside for the mains supply on a large installation, with switchgear controls for the whole installation and sub-mains cables distributed to other buildings or sections of buildings.

The main intake panel may be made up by fixing separate components to a free standing metal frame, or standard factory-produced cubicle switchboards may be used.

The mains supply is connected into a sealed chamber and fuse box belonging to the electricity authority and tails are taken from this to the busbar chamber of the distribution panel and then through fused switches to sub-distribution boards.

Where the load is likely to exceed 100 kW, the authority will require a transformer chamber to be provided, with transformer equipment and switchgear, so that a supply of 11 kV can be brought in and reduced to meet the needs of the consumer.

Cables and Wiring

Cables laid underground should be bedded on a layer of sand and covered with hardburnt clay tiles for protection. Where it passes below road formations or under concrete slabs, the cable should travel through earthenware pipes, and where the cable is brought into switchgear or transformer rooms, a shallow pit or slow earthenware bend should be formed to enable it to be bent and drawn up for jointing to the intake. Armoured cables cannot be easily bent, the recommendations for the radius which can be achieved being fourteen times the diameter. Main cables laid underground should have a minimum cover of 600 mm.

Unless mineral-insulated cables are used, smaller cables will be threaded through metal or plastic conduits, but where no conduits are used, care must be taken with the installation to protect the cables against damage. Cables installed beneath boarded floors must be at least 50 mm below the top of the joist and supported with adequate clips to prevent sagging. Holes in metalwork must be bushed to prevent the abrasion of any cables passed through, and in areas where oil or water is likely to affect the cables, special materials must be considered.

Cables installed vertically must be secured throughout the whole length to avoid their unnecessary compression at the top. Unless they form part of the lift installation, cables must not be run within the lift shaft, and wherever they pass floors, ceilings or walls, the surrounding holes should be made good to prevent spread of flame in the event of fire. Floors in vertical ducts should be made good around cables by packing them with glass-fibre or asbestos rope. Joints in cables should be accessible unless they have been designed to be buried in floors or plasterwork.

Trunking

Where a number of cables must be taken in the same direction, it will be necessary to provide some form of trunking, which not only gives protection to the cables, but provides access to them at a later stage. Trunking may be fitted vertically to carry cables in vertical ducts within tall buildings, or suspended under floor slabs or from roof trusses to finish flush with ceiling finishes or remain within the ceiling space. It can also be fitted within the floor finish or in the form of skirting to the perimeter of the building or rooms. Most forms of trunking are manufactured as galvanised or treated metal trough with a detachable lid, and divided into compartments so that communication cables can also be incorporated into the system. Trunking installed in a grid pattern suspended over floor areas can be used to carry lighting circuits and receive fluorescent tubes at standard positions to provide lighting systems for offices or other similar layouts.

Trunking can also be fitted in a grid over factory floors to provide ready access for power supplies to machinery. In certain trunking systems copper bars run within the trunking, making it easy to make positive connections at any desired position over the shop floor.

Conduit Systems

Conduit systems consist of metal or plastic tubing with switch and junction boxes fitted during construction to enable the cables to be threaded through the conduits at a later stage in the contract. Rewiring may also be carried out subsequently, whenever it may become desirable; and as single core wiring is usually fitted where conduits are available, the wiring can be carried out speedily and safely. Conduits can be fitted in areas where it is not planned to provide wiring for some time, in situations where buildings are erected in phases and provision must be made for future extensions. Steel conduit can be obtained in light or heavy gauge metal, finished in black bituminous enamel or galvanised. Heavy gauge conduits are screw-jointed and can be bent in bending machines.

Plastic conduits can be obtained as round or oval sections in rigid or flexible plastic, and can be buried in plaster thicknesses without any danger of the rust stains often caused by metal conduits.

Examples of Documents

Runcorn Development Corporation   Chapel Street, Runcorn, Cheshire   Telephone: Runcorn 73477

Order

Order No.........................../.........................../.........................

Please quote in all correspondence

To ....

Site/Premises ....

Particulars ....

Description of Works

i   All provisional work will be ordered, and instructions concerning p.c. items issued as required, and adjusted on completion.

ii   The Site was/will be handed over at   a.m./p.m. on   19

iii   The completion period being   weeks from the effective date of this order the DATE FOR
COMPLETION will be   19

iv   Where work is ordered on a DAYWORKS basis, weekly sheets are to be submitted showing in detail the labour and materials expended, together with a clear reference to the Order No. or Instruction No. authorising such dayworks, and such sheets are to be fully priced out, and the execution of the work certified by the Clerk of Works.

v   Any invoice submitted in connection with this order should quote the reference shown above.

Signature ....

Date..   ....

NOTE: The Contractor is requested to inform the Chief   ENCLS:
Clerk of Works/Chief Resident Engineer

Mr. ....

of ....

Tel.., when the works are about to
commence.

Copy of a Typical Starting Order

RUNCORN DEVELOPMENT CORPORATION

DEPARTMENT OF ARCHITECTURE AND PLANNING
Chapel Street, Runcorn. Tel. 73477

TO: ....
....
....

ARCHITECT'S INSTRUCTION

Instn. No. ..../.........................../........................

Date: ....19....

Mr ....

Site/Premises:...

Particulars: ....
....

Further to my Order No...................../...................../......................, please give effect to the following instruction(s) in connection with the execution of your Contract/carry out the undernoted Variation(s) in your Contract.
Where this Instruction authorises the execution of DAYWORKS, weekly sheets are to be submitted showing in detail the number of hours worked in each trade, rates of wages paid, cost of materials used, percentages added, etc., and such sheets are to be fully priced out, and the execution of the work certified by the Clerk of Works.

....Chief Architect and Planning Officer

(i)   The above Variation(s) will be measured and valued and adjusted at the settlement of your final account.

(ii) The above work is to be carried out/on the agreed DAYWORK basis/in accordance with/the schedule of rates/lump sum quotation/submitted by you.

(iii) **No additional period of time will be allowed in respect of this Instruction/Variation.**
     An additional period of...........................weeks/days will be allowed in respect of this Instruction/Variation.

(iv) The date of COMPLETION/remains UNALTERED/is AMENDED to...19......

Example of Architect's Instruction Form (also used as a Variation Order)

RUNCORN DEVELOPMENT CORPORATION

Department of Architecture and Planning

SITE INSTRUCTIONS No... Date..........................

CONTRACT...

TO: Site Agent	OFFICE USE
....	
....	

Distribution:
White Copy — Contractor
Buff Copy — C.A.P.O.
Green Copy — Job Architect
Pink Copy — Site Copy

....................................Clerk of Works

Clerk of Works' Site Instruction Form

SITE INSTRUCTION REGISTER

Date	Site Instruction	Verbal	Written	A.I. No.	Remarks	Date Completed	Diary Reference

Record Form for Site Instructions

Runcorn Development Corporation Department of Architecture & Planning

Interim Valuation

Contract			Amount of Contract	£
Contractor			Builder's Direct Work	£
Date	Cert No		P.C. & Provisional Sums etc Inc. Profit & Attendance	£

BUILDERS DIRECT WORK	£	p	£	p
Preliminaries				
Site Clearance				
External Works				
Variations- Additions				
Omissions				
OTHER ITEMS (D/WORKS INS. ETC.)				
Materials on Site				
P.C. & PROVISIONAL SUMS ETC				
P.C. and Provisional Sums paid				
Ditto to pay				
Add Profit & Attendance				
FLUCTUATIONS Variation in Rate of Wages				
Variation in Cost of Materials				

Gross Current Valuation	£	
Less Retention (Limit £	£	
Net Current Valuation	£	
Previous Payments on Account	£	
BALANCE DUE	£	

Q.S.	
Section Head	

AMOUNT CERTIFIED   £

Example of Quantity Surveyor's Interim Valuation Certificate

SERIAL No. 5050

RUNCORN DEVELOPMENT CORPORATION

CONTRACT CERTIFICATE

Date ....19.....

Instalment No. ....

Contract ....

....

I hereby certify that the sum of...

....

is due to ....

of ....

as interim/final payment in respect of the above Contract.

£

....

CHIEF ARCHITECT AND PLANNING OFFICER

Particulars

Contract sum	£	Current valuation	£
Authorised additions	£	*less* retention	£
	£		£
Authorised deductions	£	*less* previously certified	£
Total	£		
		Amount now due	£

Expenditure Code	£

Initialled by ....

F28   GM68452

Example of Architect's Certificate of Payment to Client (Copy to Contractor)

RUNCORN DEVELOPMENT CORPORATION
Department of Architecture and Planning

CLERK OF WORKS REPORT No.................................

Week Ending...

Job No...

Contract Commenced..

Completion Date..

Contract

Main Contractor

LABOUR	No. of Men														Lost Time
	Main Contractor							Sub Contractors							
	M	T	W	T	F	S	S	M	T	W	T	F	S	S	
Foreman															
Excavators															
Concreters															
Bricklayers/Lab.															
Joiners/Lab.															
Plumbers															
Plasterers/Lab.															
Tilers															
Painters															
Electricians															
Heating Engineers															
Labourers (Gen.)															
Daily Temp. (Winter)								Site Instructions issued YES/NO							
Weather Daily								Site Instruction No.							

R – rain   F – fair· W – windy   Fr – frost   Copy Instructions attached YES/NO

Typical Example of Clerk of Works' Progress Report

Action taken by Office

Report on Progress

Visitors

Information Required

Signed .... C/W.

Reverse of Clerk of Works' Progress Report Sheet

RUNCORN DEVELOPMENT CORPORATION

FINAL DEFECTS CERTIFICATE   Date.....................................

CONTRACT...

Dwelling No...Road..

All items referred to on the Final Defects List have been inspected and are now satisfactorily completed.

.....................................C/W

OFFICE USE

Inspection of Final Defects Certificate

DRAWING REGISTER

Dates Received	Drawing Title	Drawing Number	Scale	File	Revisions

Example of a Drawing Register

UNIT CONSTRUCTION CO. LTD.

SPEKE BOULEVARD   LIVERPOOL 24

DAYWORK ACCOUNT

A/cREF.No.   DAYSHEET No.   279

Contract Ref. No._____ Contract_____

Account Chargeable to_____

For work instructed and authorised by_____ Dated_____ 19___

In accordance with { ‡Variation Order / ‡Site Instruction / ‡Order/Letter Ref. } No._____

Description of Work :_____

Carried out during Week Ending_____ 19___

LABOUR

NAME	TRADE	No.	Mon	Tues	Wed	Thur	Fri	Sat	Sun	Total Hrs	Hourly Rate	£

To Summary £

MATERIALS

ITEM	Quantity	Rate	£

To Summary £

TRANSPORT & PLANT

TYPE	No.	Mon	Tues	Wed	Thur	Fri	Sat	Sun	Total Hrs	Hire Rate	£

To Summary £

SUB-CONTRACTORS ACCOUNTS

COMPANY	Invoice No.	£

To Summary £

SUMMARY

		£
LABOUR		
Add	%	
MATERIALS		
Add	%	
PLANT		
Add	%	
SUB-CONTRACTORS'		
Add	%	
TOTAL / To Collection £		

Certified only as a true and accurate record of time and materials.

Signed_____ for Client

Date_____ 19___

Signed_____ Surveyor
for UNIT Construction Company Limited

Date_____ 19___

FORM UCC/QS6 (Rev. April 60)

Contractor's Daywork Sheet

Index

*Consult the contents list at the beginning of the book
for a detailed breakdown of chapter subject*